INTERACTION

Merrill's International Speech Series

Under the Editorship of

John Black
The Ohio State University

Paul Moore
University of Florida

INTERACTION

An Introduction to Speech Communication

Fred L. Casmir
Pepperdine University

Charles E. Merrill Publishing Company
A Bell & Howell Company
Columbus, Ohio

FLS

Published by
Charles E. Merrill Publishing Company
A Bell & Howell Company
Columbus, Ohio 43216

Library of Congress Catalog Card Number: 73-87529

ISBN: 0-675-08874-7

1 2 3 4 5 6 7—77 76 75 74

Printed in the United States of America

CONTENTS

PREFACE

At the present time there is no comprehensive theory of human communication. Obviously, the absence of such a theory does not prevent you and me from communicating. In one way or another all human beings around us are interacting—communicating with each other.

In order to achieve his purposes man has learned to combine oral and nonoral features in communicating with himself and with others. While theoretical concepts and the observation of current trends continue, providing us with valuable insights, it is equally important in the daily business of living, developing, and reaching for the future to apply these principles and bring them together in relatively simple, but relevant ways. Only applied knowledge of communication fulfills man's requirements and helps him develop that better world all of us desire. The book you are about to read is one attempt to make theoretical concepts meaningful in our daily attempts to live, work, and interact with one another.

As I planned and wrote the book thousands of personal and very real communication situations, which form a good part of my own experience, found their way into the summaries I tried to provide. There was really one major purpose in the entire project: to help those who read the book make their purposeful, planned communication more effective.

To be meaningful, any educational undertaking must go beyond theoretical studies, or the observation and critique of existing entities. Of necessity, education finds meaning in the future. Communication scholars stress the fact that meaning has to be found in the receiver of any message. If this book is to fulfill its purpose it must assist you in developing your communicative abilities, while improving your understanding of the vital concepts we have learned through empirical studies. In that way any learning which takes place will be of importance beyond the classroom situation in which you now find yourself. It is easy, however, to channel your own creative abilities and thought processes too much. For that reason this book was written in a way which will provide you with challenges, maybe even opportunities for thought. Hopefully you and your instructor will be able to use it as a launching pad for moving beyond the opinions and reactions of just one man. There should be enough questions raised, enough areas touched on, and enough sources provided to enable you to pursue any subject in which you are vitally interested.

This book was written in the belief that neither man's present nor his future can make much sense if he does not understand some of his past. It was also written in the belief that no *one* approach to human communication can provide enough insight into man's quest for understanding and greater happiness.

The chapters of this book move from a survey of past and present approaches to the study of human communication, and a critical evaluation of the place and purpose of communication in human affairs, to specific areas of communicative interaction between human beings, such as intrapersonal, interpersonal, and small group communication, as well as a study of public speaking. We are involved most frequently in interpersonal and small group communication. However, public speaking—speech communication with large groups—is vital in the affairs of entire nations, or at least significant segments of society.

Much of this book is descriptive rather than prescriptive, and hopefully it will provide assistance in your attempt to develop a personal approach or style as you communicate with others. The preparation of more formal messages can benefit from a study of the many factors which have been considered by public address scholars throughout the centuries. The specific steps and suggestions included in this book represent a summary of concepts which generations of public speakers have found to be helpful in their attempts to communicate with large groups.

Man cannot NOT communicate, but he certainly can communicate ineffectively, negatively, destructively, or in a manner which is not fully satisfying. This book is intended to assist you in making your purposeful communication more effective.

Fred L. Casmir
Malibu, California

HUMAN COMMUNICATION: SOME DEFINITIONS

Identifying parameters, defining terms, and searching for common ground for the study of human communication is the purpose of this chapter. There are certain terms in any society which are widely used because they have an aura of great importance or because they appear to express very important ideas. *Communication* is such a word in contemporary America. Interoffice communication, dyadic communication, verbal and nonverbal communication are all terms representative of the importance we assign to the concept of communication. Such "god-terms" often take on meanings far beyond what we would normally expect. They are accepted almost at face value because of their sound or because they seem to have a very authoritative "feel" about them. An example is the use of the term "psychological" in conversation. No one may really know what it means, but a statement such as, "Well, you know, his problem is really psychological," is frequently accepted with a sage nodding of heads merely because it sounds impressive.

These god-terms often become status symbols as parts of professional jargons. They may be intended to exclude some individuals as much as they are intended to include others. In addition, they may become terms which are used to impress people who are uncertain of their meaning or the use which can be made of the terms.

At other times such terms may serve positive functions such as bringing about cooperation or quick agreement.

WHAT DO WE MEAN BY COMMUNICATION?

It is wise to ask those who use such god-terms what they mean by them. For that reason, it is important to indicate how the term communication will be used in this book. Any conscious, purposeful attempt by man to influence, control, direct, change, or make use of his environment is communicative behavior. Thus communicative behavior is intended to bring about some change either in degree or direction in man's environment. The emphasis in this book will be on verbal, oral communication, relating all major concepts to this specific area of human communication.

The term "control" is probably one of the most bothersome of the synonyms used in the preceding paragraph, and for that reason the overall purpose of human communication must be considered in more detail. Control in a free society seems to imply coercion, or forcing people to do things against their will, and for that reason more consideration must be given to what place communication has as a means of controlling our environment.

Since the concept of a free society and freedom will be frequently referred to in the following pages, it may be well to define a free society.

In a free society institutions and organizations exist for the purpose of supporting and encouraging the role and place of the individual. A free society not only makes possible but also encourages and attaches high value to the participation of individuals in decision making, the expression of ideas, and cooperative work. A free society accepts, possibly even encourages, disagreements, diversity of views, and individuality. It makes possible a variety of coexistent, different life styles and expressions with a minimum of public ridicule and oppression.

THE HUMAN NEED TO COMMUNICATE

Perhaps the best way to illustrate our need to communicate is by giving some examples involving human beings who have been deprived of their normal communicative abilities.

Brain damage can cause people to become aphasics. Depending on the type of aphasia from which they suffer, they will be unable to connect word symbols with objects, or they will be unable to form words which their brain correctly identifies as standing for the object they see. In either case, aphasics provide one of the most drastic examples of the human need to communicate. Their urge will become so strong at times that the frustration of being unable to produce the right words will cause them, although unable to speak coherently at other times, to curse forcefully, coherently, and very distinctly.

Men have lost the use of their hands and taught themselves to express ideas by painting or typing with their feet. Some have even learned to use a paint brush held in their mouths to fulfill the powerful urge to express themselves. If a man cannot speak he will invent sign languages. If he is kept by distance from seeing or personally contacting another human being he will invent whistle languages, fire languages, drum languages, or modern electronic marvels that carry his voice to those with whom he wants to communicate.

Man will create plays with stages on which to produce them, television to carry his messages to millions, and films to reach even more millions over a long period of time. Man will develop new art forms to allow him to express ideas and feelings in many different ways. Some of them are a conscious attempt to deprecate an art form developed by some other generation or individual. Tie down his arms, legs, head, and every other movable part of his body and man will still grunt or communicate his reactions through his eyes. The simple fact is that man has to communicate, man cannot *not* communicate.

Another aspect of communication must also be considered. The presence of objects, trees, animals, sounds, colors, temperatures, all kinds of factors in our environment communicate much to man. An important distinction needs to be made. Communication depends fundamentally on two factors: a *message* and a *receiver*. In other words, there must be something meaningful in our environment which causes us to react to it. The verbal message "Stop" could be such a stimulus. A temperature rise from 75° to 110° could provide another kind of message. A flashing light at a railroad crossing represents another type of message. The subtle perfume of the girl passing by carries a message. Messages consist of stimuli which cause reactions or responses within the human nervous system, leading to some sort of interpretation of those stimuli. The concept of the receiver also requires further explanation. For our purposes we will think of a receiver as more than a recording device. One could, for instance, put a sound-sensitive recorder in the middle of a forest which would turn itself on at the sound of every animal cry or falling tree. In the case of a human receiver an important and very different function is described by the term *interpreter*. The reason objects communicate ideas, create feelings, produce warnings, and do many other things for man is that out of the storehouse of his knowledge and experience man interprets everything with which he consciously comes in contact. Music may not be merely music; it may turn into "our song." A diamond is not merely a rock; it is discovered to be "rare" and thus "valuable." Certain colors are "cool," others "warm," others "appropriate." Obviously, meaning is not contained in what man observes, but the meaning it communicates to him is the result of his interpretations. Interpretations result from a vast network of learned concepts or experiences, as well as desires, drives, hopes, aspirations, loves, or hatreds based on them. Many of these factors are a result of the influence the family, society, and culture exert on man. Others are the result of biological predispositions.

The other side of the coin must also be considered. Man in the presence of other men cannot help but communicate. That is, he will be like any other *object* within the environment of those looking at him and listening to him. Even the withdrawn visitor who attends a party but sits silently in one spot all night communicates with other humans. Depending upon the culture, the message sent by such an individual may be that he is interesting, afraid, or introverted. The simple crossing of legs, the wave of a hand, or a smirk do not need words to accompany them in order to carry a message. It can be said then that human beings in the presence of other human beings will always communicate, whether it is verbally or nonverbally, as long as the other human beings are both able and ready to observe and interpret. Even if only objects, animals, or physical sensations such as cold, heat, wetness, or saltiness are present, man will interpret and receive meaning from these stimuli based on his past experiences and present needs.

It is obvious by now, however, that meaning associated with communication does not only depend upon the receiver. It must also have some sort of relationship to the sender. The simplest way to define the kind of communication to be discussed is to use the word "purposeful." Purposeful communication is intentional, planned, intended to bring about certain results. Most of this planning activity takes place within the sender. If the receiver understands or responds in the desired way, we think of the communication as successful. Regardless of whether or not the sender achieves his preplanned purpose, communication has taken place if the receiver has perceived and interpreted the message.

The following illustration should be helpful. Two men working in a lumber yard are moving boards. While one man's back is turned, he gets hit on the head by a board which "slipped" out of the hands of the second man. Accident? Purposeful communication of hatred? Did the second man hit the first man, or was it merely the board that hit him? In either case, the first man certainly was made aware of what happened; the lump on his head indicates vividly that the board made an impression on him. There may be even some strong verbal response. Whether the act will be interpreted as stupidity, "carelessness," or attempted murder depends on a great many factors. These center around the purpose, the intention of the sender, and the interpretation of the receiver. This example also illustrates that such interpretations do not need to be factual or accurate. It may have been the intention of the second man to kill the first, but if the first man is convinced that it was merely an accident, the intentions of his potential murderer are of no real importance to him at the moment. Of course, after a second board hits the first man and additional input of information is provided by the observation of the second man holding and swinging the board at his head, the first man may decide that his original evaluation of the situation was not entirely adequate.

All social animals have some form of communication. We know, for instance, that bees through an intricate system of movements inform other bees of the location of flowers which promise a good harvest. However, there are certain concepts which make human communication unique. Not only is it clear that human communication depends upon and uses more complex and different neurological systems, but also there are more readily observable factors which must be considered.

Some people have pointed out that probably the most human type of communication occurs when man communicates with himself. Meditation, thought, introspection, call it whatever you wish, but man's response to his own spirit, soul, or thoughts makes him a unique being. Not all of man's communication is directed to the "outside," some of it serves as an opportunity to think things out, to reach meaningful conclusions, to understand oneself, to recapture a pleasant moment, to make plans, to create something mentally. Some of this communication can be therapeutic and serves as a kind of safety valve. A man walking down the hall after an unsatisfactory meeting with his boss, mumbling under his breath and telling the "old fathead" off, is probably working off some tensions which might otherwise become self-destructive. Other therapeutic types of communication are represented by the nondirective approach of some psychiatrists, who let their patients "talk things out." Hopefully, having brought out ideas into the open, patients can deal with problems which were hidden and repressed until that moment. Role playing or group therapy sessions often are used for therapeutic purposes, but they obviously require more participants, and thus do not actually represent the kind of introspective communication discussed earlier.

Man's imagination is such that he can think of things and develop physical reactions to them even if these things do not exist. The power of self-suggestion can be effective both in a negative and a positive way. A man may doubt that anyone can die of voodoo until the witch doctor informs him of the fact that he is the target of the pins being stuck into a voodoo doll. Man can think about the future, plan for the future, and get ready for the future. These are all abilities which cannot be found in the other animals.

Whether an individual is making plans for the future, responding in a psychiatrist's office, making a speech at an alumni banquet, or calling his best friend on the telephone, he or she is always attempting to fulfill the ultimate human role: Becoming a being who feels the need to play a part in the control of his world, of himself, and of other people in order to achieve a specific purpose.

COMMUNICATION IN A FREE SOCIETY

The example of the two men in the lumber yard opens the door for some important considerations of communications in a democratic society. Under the definitions provided previously, using a board to kill another man is obviously one means of communicating intense feelings of dislike. It is also purposeful communication, and what's more, it can be very effective if the board hits the target. One of the most fundamental decisions man has to make about communication thus becomes whether his capacity to handle problems or challenges through abstract symbols, such as language, is somehow related to the concepts of freedom and cultural advancement. The question would seem to be whether human societies can be just as free, and human beings can function just as well, if reasoned discourse is replaced by physical, possibly violent, acts.

Of major concern in this book is the use of purposeful verbal communication. However, campus riots at certain American universities serve as reminders that to some people physical confrontation was an acceptable alternative to reasoned discourse, or was a means of accomplishing ends which could not otherwise be achieved.

One of the questions any student of human communication must answer for himself is based on a law of physics. In the physical world, and it would appear also in the area of human activity and experience, pressure creates counterpressure. Whether one reads Plato, Mill, or Burke certain concepts are repeated in the experience of all those who have studied human societies. Human communication can consist of a series of violent actions and reactions, or it can consist of a series of reasoned verbal actions and reactions, or a combination of the two.

It is self-evident that no coerced human being can be a free human being. However, it is equally clear that from Selma to Washington, Martin Luther King led march after march and engaged in physical acts because he thought it necessary to use other than verbal means of communicating his demand to white members of society to "let my people go." The American Revolution, and indeed every other revolution in man's history bears witness to the fact that man believes verbal communication does not accomplish all that needs to be accomplished. To many, reasoned discourse is too slow, and yet any society, although highly efficient, where reasoned discourse is frowned upon or suppressed, can never be a free society. Any attempt to gather information, relate concepts to each other, structure them into meaningful arguments, and present them effectively to carefully considered audiences takes time, especially if such reasoned discourse requires reasoned response.

It has often been pointed out that free speech and free societies have grown up side by side since the days of the city-states of Greece. It is also true that human freedom has always been a fragile thing. At times people sacrificed it for security, even at the cost of greater control by the state over their lives. At other times man allowed his frustrations to become so great that he destroyed others and himself in an attempt to solve his problems. The French Revolution, which became an endless bloodbath, sapping the strength of the entire effort, is one example. At other times calls for violent action became the means by which those who did not excel in reasoned discourse could wrest power from those unwilling or incapable of engaging in physical violence.

No doubt reasoned discourse without action is just as bad as action without reasoned discourse. However, as we study human communication we cannot overlook the fact that man has never remained free when his freedom of expression was denied him. It might be equally important to consider the fact that no human society which saw freedom of expression as an end in itself has ever survived. In other words, societies which interpreted freedom as absolute license seem consistently to have destroyed the very base for organized human interaction. The questions and problems touched upon in this segment have been debated for hundreds of years, illustrating a vital chapter in man's continuing quest for an understanding of his own role and place in this world.

Some of the most ardent advocates of free speech in contemporary America raised their cry for freedom only when they were underdogs. Any student of human history knows that one of the most consistent factors about man is his inconsistency. Thus, denying others freedom of speech after achieving it for oneself may simply be a *typically human* act, if one considers the fact that many humans believe their causes are the best, most honorable, and most just.

Marriage counselors point out that when husbands and wives refuse to communicate with each other, when they use the most devastating weapon of man against man, that of ignoring the other individual, or making him a "nonperson," no hope for reconciliation exists. As long as we talk to each other we still are responding, receiving, interpreting. The same basic concept appears to hold true in struggles within nations or between nations. When communication is broken off severe trouble often follows.

Of course, those who refuse to communicate with others will seldom be that blunt about stating their intentions. In a free society we can use many reasons for refusing to communicate which appear acceptable to the majority of people. Freedom to communicate also implies the right or freedom not to communicate. Obviously, it is not easy to judge the intentions or the reasons behind a refusal to communicate, or a call for more reasoned communication, or a call for violent action because communication is judged to have failed.

There is no way of solving the problems mentioned here easily and completely. Many books go into great detail concerning these complex questions. But no man can remain free unless he has carefully considered his own role in a free society, and his own reactions to the concept of free speech.

CATEGORIES AND MODELS OF COMMUNICATION

Communication scholars have attempted to develop a model or a system of categorizing communication in the hope of gaining a certain sense of control over the subject matter they are studying.

There are two basic classifications of communication. One is descriptive: If we say there are five branches of the Armed Forces in the United States— Army, Navy, Marines, Coast Guard, and Air Force—we are using a descriptive set of categories by listing existing, observable entities. At times, however, categories can become prescriptive. In this case the categories indicate factors which someone would like to see exist. For instance, the description of Boy Scouts as "loyal," "honest," or whatever else, doesn't mean we have a description of all Boy Scouts. Rather this represents an attempt to set down prescriptive categories and inform others of what a "good" Boy Scout should be.

Sometimes people try to confuse us, and make it sound as if their prescriptions for the world as they would like for it to be are descriptions of the "real" world. If they add impressive titles, statements about their own expertise, or use other god-terms of our society, such as "science," or "scientific," we may be sufficiently impressed to accept their prescriptions. That is, we will accept them until we run into a contradictory set of categories or concepts developed by another expert who appears to be as eminent. At the same time, to communicate with each other we need a framework of agreed upon definitions, a common set of concepts or terms, some language system, and possibly some graphic representations, called models, to clarify our ideas.

Human communication models are inadequate and can serve only as starting points for discussion and further thought. Human communication, as shown in the following chapters, includes so many varied aspects that it is impossible to bring them together in a simple model which could be readily comprehended, interpreted, or used. More significantly, communication scholars are intent on pointing out that communication is a *process*. It is a kind of living, moving, constantly changing activity which remains never the same from fraction of second to fraction of second because of all the factors in the total environment contributing to the communication situation.

All of us have attempted, for the sake of studying certain aspects of communication, to *freeze* this process into some model. An example from the medical field may help explain the problems faced in the construction of models. In order to determine the presence of cancer, surgeons will often examine what is called a "frozen section"—tissue removed from the suspect area and frozen. Undoubtedly, this frozen section is part of the original total human process, the total human being. It is in many ways representative of the cancerous growth being studied. Yet obviously the section is not all of the human being, it is not all of the cancer, and it is no longer part of the living process which has continued even after the tissue was removed from the body. As a matter of fact, if the same tissue had been removed somewhat later or earlier, it would have been different—minutely, undetectably different—because of the fact that all matter changes constantly.

So, the communication scholar looks at his own frozen section, his communication model, constantly reminding himself that it is only representative of some limited aspects of communication. He also reminds himself that all of his models up to this point, whether they consist of straight lines, bent lines, curved lines, helixes or what have you, are still linear models, while communication is a process which interconnects, interweaves, bisects, relates, merges, and does a lot of other things which no linear model can ever show. If you have seen slow-motion film of a bullet traveling through a smoke-filled chamber to make visible its path, you get a slight indication of what we mean by process. The distortion of the bullet because of the atmosphere through which it travels, the distortion upon impact, the disturbance of air and smoke molecules, the creation of heat through friction, and many other facts thus made visible in motion, are perhaps closest to showing graphically a process "in action."

Speech communication students have leaned heavily on models or concepts developed by scholars in psychology. Most of these models were linear, and the original communication models also used straight lines, later making use of curved lines or circles, and later yet helixes. Original concepts were based on the simple idea of stimulus–response models.

$$S \text{----------- } R$$

or   Sender --- Receiver   concepts.

More complex models later incorporated modifications in the S–R model made by psychology students. S——(O)——R Stimulus, Organism (or an interpreting fuction of the organism being stimulated), and Response. Basic communication models have usually been expanded to include SENDER——MESSAGE—— RECEIVER, and in an attempt to indicate the response features, or circularity of communication, *feedback* is usually included, as shown in figure 1.

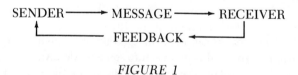

FIGURE 1

Taking into consideration the fact that communication occurs not in a vacuum, but within a given *context, situation* or *environment* forms the basis of extending these simple models even more (Figure 2).

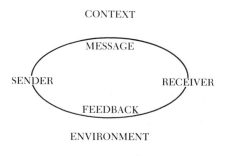

CONTEXT

FIGURE 2

A SOCIO-CULTURAL INTERACTION MODEL

It is well to remember that any model is an attempt at communication. Thus it represents as much an expression of the needs and orientations of the person developing the model as it does the "real" world, or reality as the author observes and interprets it. The orientation of this book is based on the concept that human communication is a result of need. Man is motivated by many factors, all of them are meaningful to him because they fulfill or at least contribute to the fulfillment of needs. Model construction can, for instance, fulfill needs for organization, codification, and the sharing of insights or beliefs. Communicative needs for control, security, enjoyment, and many other reasons have been briefly alluded to already, and will be discussed in much more detail as we consider these subjects in the following chapters.

The graphic-verbal model of figure 3 is complex and has many facets, but it fits the pattern of this book. It is an attempt to make you think, to consider other factors not mentioned explicitly, but intimated in our discussion of details. At the risk of becoming redundant, it is obvious that human communication involves so many facets that no one can hope to indicate them in any one model. You are encouraged, therefore, to consider other examples provided in the books mentioned in the reading list at the end of this chapter. Depending on need and specific circumstances, the present model can thus be expanded, modified, or abbreviated.

As you look at the model consider first of all the fact that, as is true of all human activities, communication is time-bound. It has to exist within a time framework. Historically man lives during a given period which has been influenced by all other time-bound historical events of the past and present, and in turn he is part of an ongoing process which continues into the future, as long as time exists. Time is also important from a neuro-physiological or psychological standpoint. All of us have a limited amount of time available, whatever our lifespan might be. As a result we have to be selective, and our needs and motivations take the form of a hierarchy. We choose, we discriminate, we select whatever appears most important or vital, at least for the moment. As a result many stimuli enter our field of cognition but are ignored or rejected because they do not fit our pattern of need or fulfillment. We are all conscious

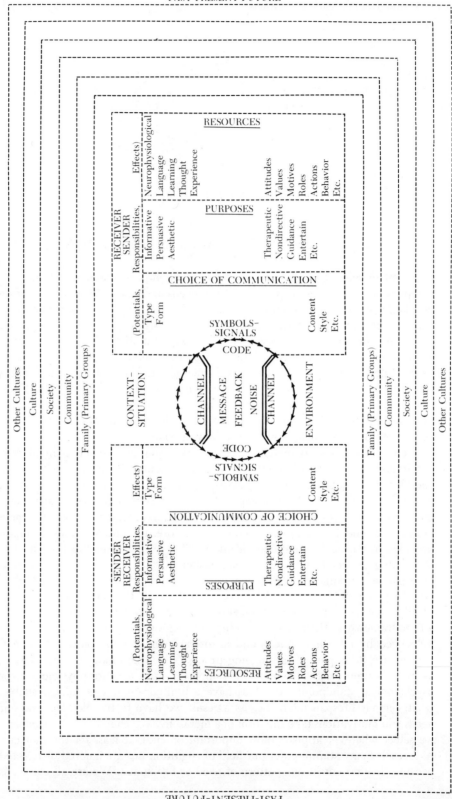

FIGURE 3

of time sequences, or the passing of time. Our entire physiological pattern of reaction either consciously or subconsciously includes time concepts, at least within any given culture, since time concepts are culture-bound. A frequently cited example is that of certain American Indians whose time concepts do not include the same relationship to the future and future events which are so vital in the thinking of white men brought up in the Western culture.

The entire model devolves from larger groupings or systems to the smallest system, the individual human being. Broken lines are used purposely. They are indicative of the fact that all parts are interrelated, and that they interact. This interdependence can be seen in the fact that an individual communicating with another is very much a "product" of the culture, society, and community, as well as the family within which he grew up. However, it must also be evident that families, communities, societies, and finally cultures are influenced, shaped, developed, or changed by the need of their individual human components. In other words, interaction occurs in both directions simultaneously, in a continuous process involving the overall system and subsystems created by human beings in their total process of socialization. New machines, new concepts, new tools, or ideas are developed by individuals. These individual inventions or developments are used by larger groups or systems in a culture to expand, change, or rejuvenate parts of the people's total cultural experience. Individuals have needs, and their fulfillment makes others aware of needs they had suppressed or could not hope to fulfill without the pioneer work of others.

Events influencing only small segments of a society thus become goals and needs for larger and larger segments. Think, for instance, of the technology which finally led to the production of television sets. The availability of sets produced a feeling of need for such sets among more and more people. Recreational needs and needs for entertainment and education increased with the availability of the sets to large numbers of people. As more subunits or subsystems of our culture had television sets with decreasing cost for their purchase, the products advertised, or the life style portrayed on television became part of their total experience. This in turn led to new needs for recognition, equality, sharing in the "good things in life," participation in decision making, habits of eating, drinking, smoking, dressing, and many other factors. In turn, programs on television began to change with the needs or interests of the audiences, since this medium exists and develops in direct relationships to the wants, needs, drives, or desires of those who watch it, or those who refuse to partake of its offerings.

Every individual is also shaped by inherited biological factors which are partly the result of prior social and cultural conditions involving nutrition, health care, and other similar factors. You and I are very much the products of the social and cultural framework within which we grew up. If we are born into a Polynesian or Asian culture, we are not the same human beings as if we are born into an American culture.

Socio-cultural factors help all of us evaluate the potentials, the responsibilities, and the possible effects to be expected from individuals within our culture. In the United States, concern with youth, material wealth, hard work, education, and a number of similar standards is the direct result of our cultural background and development. These concerns (among others) serve as criteria for determining or evaluating the role of the individual in communication. As surely as all parts of the system we have discussed so far are constantly interacting in the total process of human social development, so their influence is a constantly changing, modifying, varying process in communication. Man cannot not communicate on the basis of his social experience and culture. All of us respond to clues from our cultural environment which assist us in evaluating or at least checking our behavior against cultural norms.

At the same time all of us bring a storehouse of individual experience, knowledge, and neuro-physiological equipment to communication which makes us uniquely human, and uniquely individual. There is increasing biological evidence that human beings truly respond to communication situations or to stimuli as total systems, as total organisms. Stimuli of various types, in other words, cause reactions by all of the billions and billions of neurons in the human system. The eventual and particular response is the result of selection, or selective connection of specific factors within any human organism which produce the particular observable response out of many possible combinations.

Every human being has certain *resources*, and although incomplete, the list in our model indicates the wide variety of social, psychological, and biological factors which provide us with the basic equipment for communicating with other human beings. Again, broken lines between all of these categories indicate that you should not think of them as being rigid, but as being capable of modification or at least capable of being influenced by "outside" stimuli. Take just the area of personal experience. Obviously, an astronaut, *after* setting foot on the moon, will be a different person as far as his experience is concerned, from what he was while still on earth studying the possibility of a trip to the moon. The very existence and the cultural demand for the development of these resources requires that they will be used by man.

The use of resources leads to the consideration of individual determination of *purposes*. An individual can buy a painting for the purpose of investing his money, because he thinks it is beautiful, because he does not want some rival to own it, or for many other reasons. His purposes are determined by his needs, which in turn are the results of the resources with which his family, society, community, culture, and his own biological make-up have supplied him. Considering the biological aspects for a moment, it is readily apparent that an individual who cannot see or hear well, or one who is easily stimulated because of certain bio-chemical factors in his make-up, will have these factors influence the needs he feels and how hard he tries to fulfill them.

In communication, an individual may use his resources to guide another individual in decision making or learning, or he may use communication for the relaxation of tension in others or himself, for understanding of self, for enjoyment, or, among other reasons, for the purposes of influencing economic, political, or religious events. The list is truly as varied as are the needs man feels and the means of fulfilling them which he develops.

Resources and purposes lead to a need for *interacting* with other human beings, or, as we have thought of them, with other individual "systems" or organisms. All that has been said so far about one human being applies in varied ways to all other human beings. Communication becomes a means of *channeling* the resources and purposes of two or more individuals into a *symbolic interaction*, making use of *various oral and nonoral symbol systems*.

To accomplish his purposes man must decide which *form* or *type* of communication to use. Whether he writes a poem for the woman he loves, or develops flag signal-systems for ships at sea, whether he uses written or spoken communication, or whether he uses a florid or simple style again depends on the needs he has and how he perceives he can fulfill them in the specific situation with the specific individual or individuals with whom he wishes to communicate. This process of *selective perception, selective projection* of ideas, and *selective interpretation* of communicative content within the complex total situation we have discussed, considered in relationship with the complex nature of the individuals involved in communication, is only imperfectly represented by our model.

To make some sort of agreement or understanding possible, man develops codes, or languages, which consist of some mutually understandable symbols. They can be gestures, colors, sounds, or carved, written, molded symbols, and any other form of code on which two or more people can agree. He may even develop such a personalized code for intracommunication, for communicating with just one person, namely himself.

He chooses a connecting link or carrier between two or more individuals to which we refer as a *channel.* That channel could be an electric wire as used in a telephone conversation, or the airwaves as in visual, oral contact, or other similar connecting links between those sending and receiving a message. One important thing needs to be interjected here. So far we have spoken of communication as if it consisted of two discreet acts, sending and receiving. Nothing could be farther from the situation we experience when we communicate. Not only is each individual in the process constantly bombarded by stimuli from outside the specific limited communication channel, but he is also a receiver of *feedback* from the individual to whom he transmitted. Sending and receiving are part of a process constantly changing, constantly involving individuals engaged in communication. These communicative acts are, in other words, coactive components of communication.

At this point a message is being transmitted through the channel. One could also speak of messages if he considers the component parts, such as the words being spoken, and the nonverbal, bodily action messages being transmitted. One can even include the messages which result from the setting, the situation, and other outside factors. Since we are really not talking about a simple, straightline kind of transmission, a broken circle represents this interaction between all the factors mentioned here in the transmission of the message. It is difficult at best to illustrate graphically the evolution of the message and its sending and reception, but the circle is used to show that it is not a simple linear, cause–effect type of interaction. Again, the idea of a selective process both in the transmission of the message and its reception are vital. Depending on the needs of sender and receiver or, more adequately stated, participants in the communication process, the message will be shaped by those things they choose from the great number of available stimuli including the code, the channel, the setting, nonverbal cues, etc.

Other factors are present besides the actual verbal and nonverbal message, purposefully transmitted by the sender. These factors are referred to as *noise.* Commonly we think of such noise as interference. However, it could be thought of as modulation, adding some additional texture, color, form, or some additional information about the message, the sender, or the situation. While noise is probably most adequately described as interference, one should consider the possibility that to some people interference may become additional communicative content, depending on their own needs and attitudes. For instance, background construction sounds over a telephone conversation interfere with the transmission of the message, but they also provide the receiver with additional information about the nature of the call or the caller. It should be stressed that noise in this sense does not only refer to sounds which interfere, but to anything such as odors, color, temperature which has been nonpurposefully superimposed on or intermingled with the transmission of the message.

When any specific communication process comes to an end it is finished, a one-time occurrence, complete in itself. Its results, interpretations, or the use of information made available will have an influence on those who participated and received the messages transmitted. However, these results will be only indirectly related to the original process, having become subject to multiple interpretations and modifications by individuals or larger systems included in our model, such as the community, society, culture, or family. The influence of the original communication thus spreads and dissipates at the same time.

SUMMARY: FROM INTRACOMMUNICATION
TO MASS COMMUNICATION

One final area of concern needs to be mentioned in this introductory chapter. Obviously, purposes of communication vary. That is, *specific* purposes vary. If we can accept the fact that human communication is basically for purposes of controlling our world, keeping it safe, stable, in such a way that we can "handle it," we can also say that sometimes human communication has the purpose of keeping that world stable, meaningful, or under control through relaxation or aesthetic enjoyment. Poetry-readings, a theatrical presentation, a reader's theatre, a concert, or an art exhibit could fulfill that purpose. At other times we may wish to share information, an important factor in human communication making it unnecessary to gather all our information first-hand. Whether or not such information is used is left up to the receiver. Then again we may use communication for the purpose of persuading someone, for instance, to go out with us, to buy our wares, to let us win the law suit. In each case control was exerted, direction was given, or changes were brought about. However, in each case the intent and purpose of both the receiver and the sender have to be considered. Obviously *things* do not *mean*, people mean, because people interpret messages. Every man is a giant filtering system for all messages through many layers of experiences, emotions, and other factors. The fact that a sender intended merely to present information or that someone intended to persuade me, should be considered, even if my own response differs from the one the sender had expected.

We must be aware of the fact that human communication is presented in various shapes and forms, depending on human needs. Communication without need is difficult to imagine. The ways needs are met have already been mentioned to some extent. Paintings, music, the spoken word, all fulfill some need for communication, and so do thousands of other communicative acts in which we can and do engage daily. However, it should also be mentioned at this point that the beginning point of all communication is probably within man himself, internal communication or "intra"-communication within one human system. We meditate, we think, we feel, and we have an intricate neuro-physiological system of communication which forms the basis of all our actions. However, our main emphasis will be on man communicating with other men.

Matching the types of communication to our purposes is a uniquely human function. There is nothing inevitable about the choice of a thrown brick instead of the spoken word. Someone made a decision. It is of some concern to the student of human communication, however, that the final decision to communicate in just that way was predictable if one had only known enough about the sender, the message, the receiver, and the environment.

Beyond the types of communication mentioned above, man also has to choose among an arsenal of other factors. He has to make decisions if he wants to be involved in a dyadic communication situation, as represented by an interview, or if his purposes are better served by working with a small group of people who are in a position to make decisions and carry them out. On the other hand he may decide that he wants to make a formal public speech to a large assembly of individuals such as a political convention. That these methods of communication are not mutually exclusive can be illustrated by taking a closer look at a political convention. Small groups, or caucuses, dyadic communication for the purposes of "arm-twisting," public speaking, and even mass communication by means of television transmission of these activities to an entire nation or the entire world show the complexities of a total communication system.

Of course, sometimes the whole thing gets a little confused. For instance, how would you classify a billboard at a busy intersection of a major city, proclaiming to one specific girl: "MARY JANE I LOVE YOU. BILL." This illustrates the difficulty we have with all systems of classification. It is not easy to come up with simple, all-inclusive categories or definitions. Some of the specific approaches used by man throughout the ages in studying and categorizing human communication will be considered in more detail in the second chapter.

One final word. The term *man* has been chosen on purpose in discussing human communication. It prevents the stilted attempt at including both men and women in our study of human communication by the repetition of such phrases as "both he and she," or "male and female." Because this author recognizes that in contemporary America women, along with other groups, are striving for a clearer, more meaningful identity, this brief explanation was added. The use of the term man is meant at all times to indicate the totality of the human race, regardless of sex, color of skin, or any other categories man has devised to separate rather than unite us.

EXERCISES

1. Study a number of other communication models not mentioned in this chapter. Critically evaluate the contributions they make to your understanding of the

communication process in a one-page evaluation for each model. Consider both the strengths and weaknesses of each model. A number of models are discussed in detail, and graphic representations are presented in the Applbaum book listed in the bibliography at the end of this chapter. This should provide you with a starting point and necessary references for further study.

2. Make a three-minute oral presentation to your class, defining one or more terms relating to the study of human communication.

3. Study a speech or article attacking some part of our communication system in the United States, such as the press, radio or television, a specific political speech, a specific speaker, or a controversial book. Try to isolate the most important reasons given for the negative criticism, and evaluate these reasons in a 500-word essay.

4. Make a three-minute oral presentation in class summarizing the concept of free speech as it was developed by one of its major advocates in the Anglo-American culture or society.

5. Develop a list of the most common myths about communication existing in our society—what it is, what it will do, what it will not do. In a three-minute oral presentation state and illustrate these myths.

6. Develop a five-minute oral presentation making extensive use of visual materials illustrating how various artists throughout the ages expressed specific concepts representative of, or challenging to the values of their societies.

7. Defend or attack the concept of physical confrontation as part of persuasion, or a rhetorical device in contemporary America, in a 500-word essay.

BIBLIOGRAPHY

Applbaum, Ronald, et al. *Fundamental Concepts in Human Communication.* San Francisco: Canfield, 1973.

Cherry, Colin. *On Human Communication.* New York: John Wiley, 1961.

Cicero. *De Oratore,* trans. J. S. Watson. Carbondale: Southern Illinois University Press, 1970.

Johannesen, Richard L., ed. *Ethics and Persuasion.* New York: Random House, 1967.

Mortenson, C. David. *Communication: The Study of Human Interaction.* New York: McGraw Hill, 1972.

Nadeau, Ray E. *A Basic Rhetoric of Speech-Communication.* Reading: Addison, Wesley, 1969.

Quintilian. *Institutionis Oratoria,* trans. H. E. Butler. Cambridge: Harvard University Press.

Rogers, Carl. *Client-Centered Therapy.* Boston: Houghton Mifflin, 1951.

Smith, Raymond G. *Speech-Communication: Theory and Models.* New York: Harper and Row, 1970.

Thayer, Lee. *Communication and Communication Systems.* Homewood, Illinois: Richard D. Irwin, 1968.

2

FROM RHETORIC
TO COMMUNICATION

The Greek philosopher-rhetorician Aristotle, in his *Rhetoric*, was among the first to bring together many concepts he had learned from his teacher Plato, and others he had developed through personal observation of the public speaking with which he was familiar in ancient Greece. For hundreds of years, his ideas have been used, modified, attacked, rejected, and hailed as a basis for newer and sometimes more meaningful systems. According to Aristotle, rhetoric is the "faculty of discovering in the particular case what are the available means of persuasion." [1]

Basically, there are two ways to consider rhetoric: first, from the standpoint of teaching its use to speakers and writers, and second, from the standpoint of developing a theory or system for critically evaluating the use of the available means of persuasion by speakers and writers. There are many kinds of rhetoric. For example, Aristotle was mainly concerned with the spoken word and, to some extent, with the written word. However, many other materials, such as pictures, can be used to persuade, and standards for their effective use can be brought together into a rhetoric by defining who should use them where, when, how, and under what circumstances.

Many contemporary scholars are interested in continuing the age-old study of oral communication as an academic discipline in society. They point to the need for more empirical and statistically based investigations going beyond the ancient rhetorical approach which was usually based on highly personalized observations by students of speech. The present research in oral communication is not sufficiently developed to allow its complete separation from the older, basically Aristotelian point of view. However, philosophical, historical, and

1. *The Rhetoric of Aristotle*, trans. Lane Cooper (New York: Appleton-Century, 1932), p. 7.

empirical communication approaches can make vital contributions to improve our insights into effective human interaction. This chapter attempts to combine ideas from a number of approaches into one practical system of contemporary oral communication.

By redefining Aristotle's view of rhetoric and incorporating the contemporary view of the function of human communication, we will attempt to "discover available means of bringing about changes in human behavior and/or cognition through oral communication," or a *rhetoric of oral communication*. More than a theoretical discussion, later chapters attempt also to provide some specific tools and methods for use in a variety of oral communication situations. Rhetoric has at times been defined as the "handmaiden of politics." In the view of the author, it can be, or perhaps more accurately, must be, a handmaiden to many fields of human endeavor.

SPEECH: VERBAL-ORAL COMMUNICATION

> Speech involves both human cognitive and behavioral aspects in the production and verification of verbal language symbols and their transmission by means of sound waves, produced and modified by parts of the human organism. These language symbols may be either transmitted to a listener or listeners for the purpose of eliciting a response or used for the speaker's own cathartic, therapeutic or learning purposes.

This definition is a brief but meaningful summary to which you can refer as we discuss "speech" or "verbal-oral communication" throughout this book.

Speech or verbal-oral communication can be thought of as a vehicle for many forms of human interaction from dyadic to mass communication situations. As is true of many definitions, because they are brief abstractions of much more complex concepts, this one at first glance appears a bit difficult. Let's think it through together.

Some scholars include the vocalization of animals in their classification of speech, or define them to be similar to man's communication. However, as discussed earlier, the most fundamental neuro-physiological differences indicate that men and animals use totally different mechanisms in the brain for communication and speech. Therefore, this writer rejects any concept of speech or verbal-oral communication beyond human use.[2] Speech begins as thought, or neuro-physiological activity in the brain. After that we use various parts of our body, among them our lungs and larynx, to produce vibrations that can be heard by someone else.

While some organs involved in speaking help to produce the sound, others, called articulators or modifiers (lips, teeth, tongue, lower jaw, and soft palate), help to form sounds into specific words which are part of the language we speak. Purposeful oral communication, except when used for therapeutic purposes, is intended to be heard by someone. Usually we hope for some sort of response or change in the behavior of those to whom we are speaking.

---

2. See Mary A. Brazier, "Neurophysical Contributions to the Subject of Human Communications," in Frank E. X. Dance, *Human Communication Theory* (New York: Holt, Rinehart & Winston, 1967), p. 65.

The Verbal-Oral Message

> A verbal-oral message is purposeful arrangement of language symbols into a statement or interrelated series of statements to be presented orally before one or more listeners for the purpose of eliciting a predetermined response or series of responses.

This definition attempts to list factors which this author believes constitute a successful verbal-oral message. The most vital concepts in this definition center around the fact that a formal message requires *planned, purposeful arrangement* of ideas, and that its purpose is the *eliciting of a response* or responses from those who listen. This, in turn, implies that any sender must be aware of *who* these respondents are, *what* they are, and what they are *capable of doing*. One of the important features of any oral communication is that it makes possible continuing adjustments in the message as the sender delivers it. We discussed the receiver's interpretation of nonpurposeful, unplanned factors in the communication of any sender in chapter 1. It is furthermore implied in the preceding discussion that any theoretical system, or rhetoric, which does not stress the importance of all interacting parts relating to sender, message, receiver, and environment is insufficient.

DEVELOPMENT OF RHETORIC

Since the days of the Greeks and Romans, the needs of the times caused development of various schools of thought. Rhetoric, as far as the development of various rhetorical systems is concerned, has always depended on observation. These systems thus rely upon the quality and experience of the observers. A lack of experience and strong personal prejudices could result in a poor system, but excellent systems have been developed by highly qualified observers. In any case, rhetoric concerns itself with man's quest for truth, recognizing that his search for it is based on probabilities, on which we can and will disagree.

MAJOR RHETORICAL CONCEPTS

Aristotle's definition of rhetoric as the discovery of all available means of persuasion has already been cited. A discussion of persuasion traditionally centers around three major concepts, related specifically to public speaking situations. A fundamental facet of rhetoric is that man can be influenced and can in turn influence others, using reason.

Ethos

This is the persuasion which lies within an audience's view of the speaker. Aristotle wanted *ethical* persuasion to be the result of only the factors which the audience observed while a man was speaking. His appearance, his knowledge, and similar factors would tend to contribute to his effectiveness. Later writers, however, included those concepts which an audience had developed even before meeting a speaker for the first time. This approach is probably more realistic today when the mass media, and other means of publicity, tend to prepare us for a speaker and his message by reporting his qualifications or lack of them.

Pathos

In every audience there exist tendencies to accept or reject ideas. These may be the result of the audience's emotional involvement. The effective speaker will develop his speech in such a way as to respond to the already existing emotions, or he will attempt to stimulate the audience in such a way that it will produce emotional involvement. This is what the rhetorician means by pathetic persuasion.

Logos

Using logical persuasion meant to Aristotle that the speaker was appealing to the audience's reason. He produced understanding through the application of reasoned patterns of argument, especially the deductive process, making use of the rhetorical syllogism, or "enthymeme."

Obviously these three types of persuasion, logical, pathetic, and ethical, are interdependent. Ancient rhetoricians stressed the fact that if the outcome is to be a unified effort, all these aspects of persuasion should be considered as organically related. It matters little whether a speech fails because of the speaker, the attitude of the audience, the speech material or arrangement, or all three—it is still a failure.

Aristotle divided his study of rhetoric into three parts, dealing with the speaker, the speech, and the audience. Later rhetorical scholars added the fourth concept of occasion. Aristotle further divided speeches into three groups according to their intended purpose. *Deliberative speeches* were intended to exhort or dissuade and were concerned with the future or things to come, such as a speech calling for the end of a war already in progress. *Forensic speeches* had as their purposes accusation or defense, and dealt with things past or already done. They were basically "courtroom speeches." *Epideictic speeches* were given for praise or blame and concerned themselves with existing conditions, with possible reminiscences from the past. Honoring a company's leading employee exemplifies this type of speech.

As far as the speech itself was concerned Aristotle provided the following divisions: The *proem*, the purpose of which was to "make clear the end and object of the work," what today we would call an introduction; *narration*, and just enough of it to make the intent of the speech clear; *argument*, in an attempt to argue for or against the advisability of a case, for instance; *epilogue*, or a summary-conclusion, which should render the audience well-disposed to the speaker and his message. These divisions were modified by many rhetoricians. Cicero, for instance, divided a speech into exordium, narrative, proof, peroration.

To ancient rhetoricians there were two basic types of proof: *artistic*, or that which depends upon the speaker for its development, and *inartistic*, or that which already exists, such as a law or contract, ready for use by the speaker. Other basic contributions of early rhetoric to our construction of a system dealing with oral communication were the so-called five canons of rhetoric:

1. *Invention*. This term referred to the sources of ideas, or the basic discovery of any speech material.

2. *Arrangement*. The ancients called it disposition by which they meant an orderly arrangement and one which would be meaningful to listeners.

3. *Style*. This referred originally to the language chosen or the development of the "vehicle" for putting across ideas.

4. *Memory*. This concept referred to fixing material used in a speech in the speaker's mind.

5. *Delivery*. The ancient rhetoricians called it "pronunciation." The term referred to the controlled use of the body and voice suited to the subject matter and style.

An additional idea stated by Cato and made famous by Quintilian, is that a man in order to be a truly "good" speaker must also be a "good man" . . . speaking well. He has, in other words, certain moral responsibilities. The rhetorician's concern thus was overwhelmingly with: structure, reason, argument, persuasion, moral responsibilities, and the public speaker.

COMMUNICATION: A BRIEF BACKGROUND

Scholars of oral communication, especially those associated with speech, have become more and more exposed to the work by colleagues in such areas as psychology, anthropology, sociology, semantics, and cybernetics. Since the beginning of the twentieth century, a general "scientific," or even more broadly, "knowledge" explosion has taken place. One aspect of this explosion in the study of human communication is the insistence on the use of methods which enable scholars to go beyond the more impressionistic approaches of earlier rhetoricians. Two vital concepts are *prediction* and *control*. The use of statistical methods in the study of human behavior by psychologists and others indicate their potential value in the investigation of human communication. More than that, it is hoped that data gathered in this way would enable students to produce statistically valid findings which would provide a more meaningful and consistent basis for understanding, predicting, and controlling human communicative behavior.

Current Trends in the Study of Human Communication

Clevenger and Ellingsworth are only two of many authors who considered in some detail the relationship of oral communication to social action.[3] They substituted the words *change* and *change agent* for the concepts of persuasion and persuader, reflecting contemporary interest in the influence of information upon attitudes, actions, and the behavior of individuals. Such change can, of course, be either in direction or in amount. For example, it can change from left to right, or from less to more.

---

3. Huber W. Ellingsworth and Theodore Clevenger, Jr., *Speech and Social Action* (Englewood Cliffs: Prentice-Hall, 1967).

With the concept of change goes the idea of the effect we have upon others. Something about all of us tends to be communicated at any given time. Communication studies attempt to give this effect positive direction and control, make it useful for the communicator and the communicatee, or sender and receiver. More than that, these studies attempt to identify specifically the content of the communicated message. Much of this territory is either unexplored as yet, or it has not been unified from the varied areas of academic study which have considered it. An attempt is being made to discover what some have called "strategy." This is similar to the ancient rhetorician's arrangement. Stated simply, a good communicator develops his strategy for communication on as much detailed information about himself and his audience as he can gather.

Communication scholars have helped us consider the audience, the receiver or receivers, of our messages more carefully. If a receiver is not capable of understanding our message, or is physically incapable of even receiving it, then our attempts at communication will be hampered, completely thwarted, or changed in ways that are undesirable to the sender.

Communication also involves the sender's background, his abilities, his personality, as well as many other factors. Not only does the background of everyone in the audience cause a personal interpretation of the messages received, the background of the sender or speaker will also cause him to present his ideas in certain ways, as we discussed in some detail in the first chapter.

Both the sender and receiver, in other words, "interpret" the concepts being communicated on the basis of many factors in their background as well as certain factors in the situation during which they send and receive messages. For that reason another term is very important to certain communication scholars: *interaction*. It basically refers to those things that take place when the "uniquely programmed" individual A comes in contact with the "uniquely programmed" individual B or with a number of other individuals. One cannot merely take some sort of message like a neatly wrapped package and "send" it, or transport it to another individual in the hope that it will arrive on the other side exactly as it was sent. Therefore, the term *facilitate* will often be found in communication studies. Basically we think of making it easier for someone else to receive the message rather than being fully sure that it will arrive as sent.

Cybernetics

Literally hundreds of men and women, representing dozens of academic fields or areas from anthropology to social psychology, and from engineering to speech communication have contributed to our attempts towards a better understanding of human communication. One major influence in the development of nonrhetorical or non-Aristotelian systems has come from various areas of technology and engineering. Cybernetics is one area which has attempted to relate the use of communication control-feedback devices, like the thermostat attached to a heating system, to human communication. Norbert Wiener, a mathematician, has been consistently identified with these efforts.[4] The term cybernetics was

4. See Norbert Wiener, *The Human Use of Human Beings: Cybernetics and Society* (Boston: Houghton-Mifflin, 1954).

coined by Wiener from a Greek term meaning "steersman," or "governor." Wiener insists that there is no difference between a message passing through a machine and a human being as far as identifying and controlling the specific component parts of message transmission is concerned. Cyberneticists believe that organisms are basically constructible like any mechanical system. The major problem is that although control-feedback theories appear to work fairly well when it comes to information-sharing in human interactions, more complex human communications involving emotions, attempts to influence behavior, values, etc. are not as readily covered by cybernetic theory.

Information Theory

Developing out of cybernetics, and closely associated with technological areas of communication, such as telephone and television transmissions, is the work of Claude Shannon and Warren Weaver.[5] Their comparatively simple and neat mathematical formulations have been identified as *information theory.* Much of their work has assisted scholars of human communication in the development of a communication theory. While later developments caused some disappointments because the theoretical constructs developed by Shannon and Weaver were not as easily applicable to complex human communication, a number of scholars continue to work with these concepts and expect in the future a major breakthrough from their application.

The transmission of accurate, correct information is Shannon and Weaver's major concern. By eliminating the value judgments of human communication they worked with information as a physically measurable quantity. They applied the simple "yes-no" binary code system used by computers and human nerve cells in decision making. Information theory, therefore, does not really deal with meaning or knowledge concerning any area or subject. Shannon and Weaver pointed out that information is random and lacks predictability, something they called entropy. In closed, mechanical systems entropy tends to increase while organization decreases. Thus, the basic question information theory answers is: How many binary digits, or "bits" are required to leave a final alternative? In effect, using a binary system, each "bit" halves the previous information until only one choice is left. The most commonly used example is that of a set of playing cards. With 52 playing cards Shannon and Weaver apply their formula, and find that the logarithm to the base two of 52 ($\log_2 52$) is approximately 5.7 bits. In other words, in order to predict accurately a card which has been randomly drawn, approximately six questions (5.7) have to be asked, halving the available information with each one. For instance, the first question may be: "Is it a red or a black card?" In response to the answer: "Red," the questioner can now inquire: "Is it a heart?" Even if the answer is "No" he still knows to which suit it belongs. With four more such "bits" of information the correct card can be selected. Information theory deals significantly with the reduction of uncertainty. Out of these concepts Shannon and Weaver developed the formulation of "relative redundancy" or the degree of certainty in determining what the next event or factor is going to be. They also developed

5. Claude E. Shannon and Warren Weaver, *The Mathematical Theory of Communication* (Urbana: University of Illinois Press, 1949).

the concept of noise, discussed earlier, and applied their statistical computations to the determination of the amount of information any channel can carry without breaking down.

General Systems Theory

General systems theory emerged from the theoretical constructs developed in the areas mentioned above, especially in the application of cybernetic theories. It is an attempt to develop a rigorous holistic, rather than fragmented, atomistic view of science. Systems theory insists on looking at the world in terms of sets of integrated relations within a context of the whole. The experimental biologist L. Bertalanffy has done much to help develop the theoretical concepts forming the basis for general systems theory.[6]

In effect systems-oriented scholars deny the need of linear-causality, namely that one event must have preceded another. Basing their concepts on mathematical techniques which deal with continuous data, these scholars consider linear-causality to be only one subvariety of scientific thinking. Systems theorists advocate a shift to "systems thinking," requiring us to look at entities rather than parts. The example of two, straight, intersecting lines is used. Even if all the characteristics of the two lines are carefully considered, one will nevertheless not see the "whole" because angles have been created by the intersecting of the two lines. These angles would be measured in degrees while the lines might be measured in inches or centimeters. It is the organization and relationship of members of a system which are of importance. The theory is complex. It requires fundamental shifts in thought from former categorical concepts and concepts of causality which form the basis of much of our contemporary scientific investigation.

Applications of general systems theory to human communication are just now being made, or have been developed only within the last three to five years. Prominent among those who have written on the subject are Lee Thayer and, more recently, Brent D. Ruben, the latter providing an introduction to the subject. Sources are listed in the bibliography at the end of chapter.

Other Contributions

Alfred Korzybski will be mentioned here only briefly. He is the father of the science or study of the uses and misuses of language, called *general semantics*. Since many semantic principles will be applied or mentioned in later chapters, it will suffice here to mention that general semanticists have attempted to develop an area of scholarly emphasis which assists in the prediction and control of human communicative behavior through a study of meaning. The title of Korzybski's major work, *Science and Sanity*, gives an indication of the hope he had for his theory.[7] General semantics strives to provide man with means for improving his world and his relationships with other men, through the use, or controlled use, of language in a scientific age.

---

6. See L. Bertalanffy, *General Systems Theory* (New York: Braziller, 1968).

7. Alfred Korzybski, *Science and Sanity* (Lakeville, Conn.: International Non-Aristotelian Library Publishing Co., 1948).

Brief mention should also be made of one other, less rigorous approach to the study of language use in human communication. Bernard Berelson's name is frequently associated with *content analysis*.[8] The method consists of categorizing and comparing various component parts of human messages. Sentence structure, the use of specific terms or grammatical forms, like personal pronouns, are studied by way of frequency of usage. Various authors or speakers could thus be compared on the basis of these categories.

Value judgments are important parts of these studies, leading to conclusions based on concepts supposedly held by various societies, groups, or individuals as illustrated by the use of certain words. Categories are rather arbitrarily chosen and interpreted by those conducting the research, thus leaving them open to criticism from those who do not accept their categories, or the values they are supposed to represent. The inferential leaps from demonstrable terms to the "things" or "ideas" they supposedly stand for, or the implications which one could draw from their usage, often have been questioned. For example, can we establish any meaningful relationship between the number of times representatives of two different cultures use a certain term, such as the word "honor," and the overall value systems of the two cultures? More importantly, can we make any comparisons between the values held by each culture on the basis of numerical frequency of such terms? Obviously, the basis for such comparisons is very doubtful.

Communication scholars are influenced in their work and thinking by psychologists. This has been especially true of behaviorist psychology which has had a decided impact on communication studies in recent years. Out of the vast number of studies, theories, and approaches, one category or area will stand here for others. *Balance theories* have had a major influence and they will be brought together under that category or heading, though different scholars have used different terms to describe similar concepts.

Balance theories are based on the concept that human systems or organisms, human beings, strive for a balanced state. Imbalance is a threat, or it results in feelings of insecurity and uncertainty. Suppose a boy loves a certain girl very much. He likes the movies very much, she does not, as a matter of fact she refuses to go. Balance theories attempt to show how in such triangular relationships the individual must either change girl friends, preference for movies, or find a way of changing the girl's mind. Human beings thus strive to return to or approximate a state of balance. Communication, according to this theory, is the result, or at least a partial result when human beings attempt to restore equilibrium, or what psychologists call homeostasis. The most important individuals commonly connected with this concept will be discussed here briefly. Fritz Heider developed the concept and coined the word balance theory.[9] He studied the relationship of three entities: one individual relating to another individual, as well as to a third person or an object.

A somewhat different emphasis is represented by the work of Osgood and Tannenbaum who were primarily concerned with attitude change. They applied the term congruity to the state of balance discussed earlier.[10] In effect, our

---

8. See, for example B. Berelson, *Content Analysis in Communication Research* (New York: Free Press, 1952).

9. Fritz Heider, *The Psychology of Interpersonal Relations* (New York: Wiley, 1958).

10. C. E. Osgood and P. H. Tannenbaum, "The Principle of Congruity in the Prediction of Attitude Change," *Psychological Review* 62 (1955): 42–55.

responses to any existing situation will be either congruent, or in agreement, with our already existing frame of reference, or they will be incongruent with it. If we experience incongruity the resulting imbalance within our system will cause a striving towards renewed congruity. If you feel very strongly towards a political candidate, like him, and approve of him, and he makes a speech supporting some concept with which you personally disagree (maybe the continuation of a war, or greater financial assistance to foreign countries), incongruency results. The speech does not fit your earlier frame of reference. You will strive to fit the disturbing bit of input into the existing framework by ignoring the statement, claiming your "hero" did not make himself clear, or that he was forced to make the statement. All these attempts would make the message congruent with your earlier beliefs. Incongruent change, that is rejection of the political candidate and admission that your earlier evaluation of him was wrong, is much more difficult and probably results only when the perceived incongruencies are too difficult to reconcile with other beliefs or attitudes you hold very strongly. Strong ego-involvement combined with public statements concerning his beliefs make a person an unlikely target for those wishing to produce incongruent change in him.

One of the most frequently cited approaches is Leon Festinger's cognitive dissonance theory.[11] Cognitive dissonances occur when we discern inconsistencies between various attitudes we hold and our behavior, or possibly between different attitudes and different behaviors. Not only do we avoid such dissonances but we strive to restore consonance. Festinger recognizes that besides dissonance and consonance, there is also the possibility of some relationships being irrelevant to us, thus not causing us to see any relationships between the cognitive elements involved. It must be noted that at the same time, Festinger and other balance theorists make clear that human action is the result of a perceived dissonance, incongruency, or imbalance. As a matter of fact, action is produced by our desire to "get things back in line." We can do that by convincing ourselves of a certain fact, in spite of existing data, or information-input contrary to our belief system. For instance, an individual who is induced by a large sum of money to change his mind, Festinger points out, will experience less cognitive dissonance and will have to do less readjusting of his belief system than one who is induced to do so for a small amount of money. Such change is brought about by "finding new evidence," or we may selectively consider only evidence which agrees with our point of view. We can change our behavior, or modify it to decrease the feeling of dissonance, as we do when we switch from high nicotine to low nicotine cigarettes, instead of giving up the pleasure of smoking with its inherent health hazards. In all cases of perceived dissonance, what Osgood and Tannenbaum called congruent change seems easiest to achieve. That is, we follow the path of least resistance, and we are challenged most by those factors which indicate the greatest dissonance with our general attitude-belief system.

There have also been attempts to develop new, twentieth century rhetorics. Probably the best known scholar is Kenneth Burke.[12] In one sense Burke's work

---

11. Leon Festinger, *Theory of Cognitive Dissonance* (Stanford, Calif.: Stanford University Press, 1957).

12. See among others Kenneth Burke, *A Rhetoric of Motives* (New York: Braziller, 1950).

is neo-Aristotelian, because it is based on philosophical deliberations which in turn are based on observations of the rhetorical act in our society, rather than being based on the experimental evidence of today's empiricists. Burke does not resurrect, or attempt to restructure Aristotle's views, but instead uses a different philosophical or theoretical base for his rhetoric. Burke sees man as a symbol-using animal whose entire range of activity can be defined as rhetoric. Through a long period of study he developed what he called his "pentad," or a five-point approach to anything man may wish to consider. This is Burke's well-known "dramatistic approach" to rhetoric. The pentad consists of: scene, or the environmental aspects; act, the thing as it is represented in an idea; agent, or the cause of the thing; agency, the "how" of the act; and finally purpose, or the motivation of the agent. Basically Burke wants to view rhetoric as act, while analyzing the who, how, where, and why of that act.

Burke deals exclusively with abstraction, which he saw as "generalization" and as the specific ability of man to lift himself above the animals. He is equally concerned with the idea of the negative, disagreeing somewhat with the empiricist's view of the demonstrable. As Burke sees it, we can have a conception of "no" or "not," without having an image of it. For instance, "no house" or "not going" cannot be put into any empirically observable form. They are clear ideas, however, which we can think about as opposites to empirically observable entities such as "a house" or "she is going." Burke develops a careful system of motivation which he considers "shorthand terms" to pull us in definite directions. Identification becomes the central concept in that theory of motivation. He defines it as "consubstantiality," that is, people who are different in many ways have some aspects which make them substantially the same. In effect this is Burke's theory of persuasion. If we can become consubstantial with people or with ideas we will be persuaded. This brief summary can pull together only a few of the extensive contributions Burke has made in numerous books. However, they serve as an indication that both the rhetorical approach and the study of communicative theory continue into our day, and will probably do so for many years to come.

A THEORETICAL SUMMARY OF HUMAN COMMUNICATION

From the discussion in this chapter as well as in the first chapter, certain conclusions can be drawn which represent one attempt at providing a basis for a human communication theory. Human beings can be viewed as integrated, interdependent, interacting socio-cultural, neuro-physical systems. The ultimate purpose of their development is individually perceived adjustment to the total environment, resulting in a state of optimum, individual balance or homeostasis. When this optimum balance between the individual system and the environment has been achieved we consider it to be in a state of self-actualization, that is, the total human organism perceives its self-image to be in homeostasis with its environment. To assist in the achievement of this state of balance, human beings create implements, codes, organizations, institutions, values, and other devices which are used or discarded in agreement with their perceived value in achieving balance.

Human communication is the primary means employed by man to respond to incoming or internal signals in response to tensions created, needs experienced, and the awareness of factors within the cognitive field of each individual system. This is especially the case as the human system perceives incongruencies, resulting in an attempt to bring them into balance with the existing framework in which the system operates or strives towards self-actualization. This includes any response to any external or internal stimulus which the human individual system perceives and to which it attaches meaning, making use of a variety of types of communication, including oral-verbal, and nonverbal means. Human communication is necessary for man as a means of controlling, adjusting, and using his total environment as well as his own internal predispositions in his continuous striving for the state of being which he individually evaluates as most pleasing, his own individual state of homeostasis.

However, it must also be realized that human beings are very different from machines. They are open, biological systems in constant exchange, or import and export, with their environment. What we call human growth or development is thus not simply the result of linear-causality, or simple cause-effect relationships conceivably established or injected into the human system at birth. Human beings can import factors from the surrounding environment which counteract the deterioration common to closed systems, which results from what we call entropy. This import of negentropy, or negative entropy, results in continuous change, flux, or a total process of human growth and development, making it highly unlikely that homeostasis becomes a point of absolute balance, but rather a dynamic state as man continues to attempt to balance out new input and output demanded by the environment in which he lives.

ANOTHER FORCE?

At the present time there is no single theory, or combination of theories based on physical, biological, psychological, or sociological concepts which fully identifies, describes, analyzes, and synthesizes all of man's cognitive and behavioral processes. Certainly, there is no single theory or combination of theories which satisfies all scholars.

It is considered unscientific to introduce concepts of spirit, soul, and God into this kind of discussion. However, the simple fact is that no scientific procedure up to the present time has been able to disprove or prove the existence of any of the entities represented by these words. Rejection of any or all of these concepts, up to the present time, has had to be the result of personal preference, prejudice, or conditioning. It is a fact that no scholar, using the scientific methods developed by man, can lay claim to either scholarship or acceptable use of the scientific method if he rejects or willingly ignores any possible variable. That is true even if that variable, in his mind, may be associated with nonscientific, superstitious human traditions. It is, furthermore, a fact that every culture in man's history has in some fashion recognized and developed the concepts of a spiritual force outside of man, yet working in man. Not all of man's meditative, creative, and self-regulating or change-producing activity can presently be explained by the types of theories we have mentioned. It would be irresponsible to ignore the possibility of another influence on man's cognition and behavior. Certainly we need to acknowledge the fact that not only theologians, but also other scholars and scientists have claimed the influence of spiritual forces in their lives.

Admittedly, this is probably the most complex and most difficult to demonstrate factor. Such difficulties, however, have not kept us from theorizing or postulating in the case of man's cognitive processes which so far have never been studied directly either. Even those who have not introduced spiritual concepts into their studies, have acknowledged the existence of certain "integrating" factors, or some unknown factors postulated to explain interrelationships which otherwise did not fit their theories. This author accepts as basic, at least at this point in man's development, not the theological but scientifically obvious factor, namely that man's cognition and behavior adds up to more than we can explain either through the interpretation of others' or man's own insights. Our observations of man depend on our physical abilities and the instruments we develop, and are thus the result of training, physical and mental capacity, and opportunity. Therefore, it would seem reasonable to include a spiritual dimension as one possible variable in dealing with the yet unexplained factors in man's existence. Man's individual nature has been attested to by most theorists, even after they have established certain norms and made possible certain predictions. Man under stress, man in moments of serious trial or extreme joy, or in situations where he claims to experience spiritually based reactions, may provide us with the opportunities to break away from norms which freeze us into predetermined patterns, and possibly predetermined responses in studying human beings. As is true in cognitive processes, there are those who claim that the spiritual realm or power can be demonstrated by observable behavior. The true scholar, the true scientist, will take that variable into consideration.

Perhaps the most dehumanizing, yet understandable aspect of scientific endeavors (if one remembers how vital it is to man to feel certain, to keep his world under control) centers around our attempts to discover only commonalities, common predictable norms which allow us to control, supervise, and regulate man's behavior. It is not argued here that man "is greater than all of his parts," but it is most emphatically argued that some parts at this point defy scientific analysis. This fact may not prove that they do not exist, only that our measuring instruments may be faulty, or inadequate. Science and the inductive process are tentative and based on probabilities, yet in this one area we seem to have permitted this tentative nature of science to be ignored.

Human Language Development: A Case in Point

No area relating to human communication better illustrates the contention that nonbiological, spiritual influences outside of man or the existence of a Creator may play a part in his total development than the study of language development. For many decades a bio-evolutionary view, integrated into various learning and reinforcement theories, has prevailed in our attempts to understand and explain the development of symbolic language in humans. We have been successful in describing certain behavior and giving explanations dealing with certain readily identifiable learning processes, as in the modification of articulation, or the relationship of hearing to speech. We have not been able to provide one unified, and generally acceptable theory relating to the very earliest processes in Man, as he learns his symbolic language.

Here is what we do know. Animals have simple language systems, but even the most highly developed primates cannot be considered to use anything close to the symbolic languages man has developed. In all cases animals use signal-systems or -languages. Yet human language serves a universal function for man who has developed more than three thousand different symbol languages, with no clear proof that this ability has evolved from the language system of lower animals.

We are a stimulus-receiving organism with a brain which transforms what we receive through our biological system through our senses into ideas, and the effectiveness of this system depends on the development and use of symbols. We also know that human beings do not learn to speak merely because they have or feel a need to communicate. There is no evidence that a two-year-old child identifies this need which he then tries to satisfy with the development of a language. Nor is there any proof that his parents are in most cases sufficiently capable of providing him with the motivation for learning a language as a means of fulfilling his unspecified need. Similarly, the theory that we learn our languages through babbling has been a dead-end. There is no proof that we "accidentally" babble speech sounds or words, which then are reinforced by others in our environment until we attach meaning to them and use them consistently. Children learn only the melodic patterns of their language in this way, and not the complex linguistic patterns which make up language to such an important extent. There is also insufficient evidence that any language learning based on the selective reinforcement of the smallest sound units in our languages, phonemes or morphemes which are combined into words, can be considered an acceptable theory. Behavioral psychologists like B. F. Skinner have postulated that idea, but have not been able to defend it against extensive attacks by generative grammarians who base their theories on an innate human ability to recognize and use grammatical rules. It simply cannot be demonstrated that in this way a child learns to speak and use complex symbol languages in the short period between ages one and two. Sounds reinforced by his parents frequently have no value for the child's later speech or language usage, and the child himself has to produce meaningful speech sounds accurately from the start if effective reinforcement is to take place. Considering the number of sounds, words, and word combinations a child would have to learn through hearing and reinforcement, it has been shown that we would need considerably more time for this elaborate process than we have at our disposal during an entire lifetime. The truth is, however, that we learn what we need for language development within months, rather than hundreds or thousands of years.

Vocal development during the first two years of the child's life can be easily identified and demonstrated. By the time a child is two and one-half years old, after starting at about two months of age, he can produce all vowels and all but two of the consonants in American English which he will need for adult speech. He also learns intonation or melody patterns from his parents in his earliest babbling stages. The child learns in this way a communication system for relieving discomfort, expressing emotion, and a coordinated system involving breathing, vocalizing, articulating, and hearing, which equips him for the use of his symbolic language. He learns and develops biologically a communication sound system, a support system, but not a system of meaning or grammatical structures.

What we do not know. As Perkins puts it, man seems to be born ready to crack his society's language code.[13] Whether or not they can be easily understood, it is clear that even his very first words have meaning. In addition, within two years the child will have identified and will begin to apply the grammatical rules of his language, thus providing him with a semantic, syntactic, and grammatical framework. By age one and one-half he will put together simple sentences, applying his language's syntactical rules, and within twenty-four months after that he will have learned to decipher all the rules of grammar, an unbelievably complex task.

In addition he will learn to expand his vocabulary from 200 words at age 2, to about 2,500 words at age 6. By ages 5–7 he will have learned to use all of the three dozen or so sound phonemes of his language, if he speaks American English. His ability to learn the rules of phonology and morphology which we apply in the building of words, as well as the rules of syntax which we use in the development and structure of phrases and sentences, and then to apply them to vast numbers of different situations, remains the secret of human language development. *How we learn, acquire, or are provided with these rules we do not know.* Most parents do not fully comprehend the rules themselves, many misuse or abuse them in daily usage, and if they understood them fully, they would lack the ability to teach them to the average one- or

---

13. You are encouraged to read chapter 4, *Development of Speech*, in the excellent book by William H. Perkins, *Speech Pathology: An applied behavioral science* (Saint Louis: C. V. Mosby, 1971), which was used extensively in preparing this section. Perkins does not argue the specific case made by the author in this chapter, but he does provide one of the most concise and complete summaries of existing findings relating to human speech development.

two-year-old child. In spite of these problems the child understands and uses the rules.

There is a universal readiness to learn languages by about age two. Even mentally retarded children will have that readiness, although they will not fully develop the ability to use language after that, as their brains do not continue to mature normally. We know that maturation of the brain goes hand in hand with the development of language, but only in a "capacity" relationship, not as a major factor in explaining the semantic, syntactic, and phonological or morphological discovery of underlying rules of language and their use. At all levels of his development the child can differentiate ideas and expressions once he is ready to learn his language. The differentiation process continues until he has identified all the complex rules of grammar which allow him to adapt the structure of sentences, as well as meaning and sound in ways providing a wide range of expression of ideas, feelings, emotions, and thoughts through the use of symbols. Thus man learns in more and more adequate and economical ways (not by learning individual instances, but by learning generally applicable rules) to make symbolically meaningful the information input provided by his world.

We can easily determine the biological structures and factors involved in the production of speech sounds, our ability to hear, or our senses. Muscles, bones, and cartilages have been identified, as well as other neuro-physiological factors. We can even show how the sounds of speech and the melody of speech can be learned and reinforced or corrected in the overall learning process of the child. We are *not* able at this point to understand fully, nor have we made any meaningful progress in many years toward understanding, what makes man ready to speak and learn his language and enables him to handle efficiently the symbolic structures he needs to balance, control, and interpret his world from the very first attempts. It is possible that we will eventually find answers to this puzzle of human language acquisition. It is even possible that we may find a simple bio-evolutionary answer. However, it is a fact at the present that we have no adequate evidence that language readiness is either the result of evolution or creation, and it is a fact that from a scientific standpoint the idea that man comes equipped with an evolved, biological language readiness is something we have to accept on faith rather than scientific evidence. The point is simple. As we study human beings, and as we specifically study human communication, scientific rigor requires that we consider all possible variables, or we can no longer claim to be scientific in our approach to any given problem. All scholars agree that there is something, something difficult to identify and certainly difficult to describe and measure, which gives man this unique ability to acquire symbolic language communication. But how did that something come about?

Lest we find only what we are looking for, preprogrammed by our own personal limitations or prejudices, it might be helpful to consider a statement by Werner von Braun:

> We in NASA were often asked what the real reason was for the amazing string of successes we had with our Apollo flights to the Moon. I think the only honest answer we could give was that we tried to never overlook anything. It is in the same sense of scientific honesty that I endorse the

presentation of alternate theories for the origin of the universe, life and man, in the science classroom. It would be an error to overlook the possibility that the universe was planned rather than happening by chance.[14]

It would also be an error to overlook the possibility that man's language readiness and development are the result of creation or planning rather than biological evolution or chance.

SUMMARY:
LOOKING BACK WHILE LOOKING AHEAD

Your own characteristics and those of your respondents will deeply influence your structuring of any message. While you may perceive certain things as "real," you will soon become aware of the fact that every idea you transmit, or send, will be tested against the view of "reality" which your receivers hold. If you are a religious person, the concept of a soul may be very "real" to you. To someone who does not believe in the existence of a soul the very term may become a source for disagreeing with the content of your message. Some of the connections between you and your audience will be very close while in other cases the very code, channel, type, or form of vehicle you are using may interpose itself between you and your listeners. At times this cannot be avoided, but at other times your own awareness of these factors will keep you from making mistakes. For instance, the decision to send an interoffice memo to a disgruntled employee may add to the existing problem, while talking to him might solve it.

What we have said throughout the first two chapters holds true at this point. With greater availability of information, better understanding, and a greater variety of use of available media should come more effective communication, depending on your own flexible use of what man has learned in the past and is now discovering. When the communication scholar tells us that all messages have internal structure he is probably challenging us with a modern version of Aristotle's ancient view that we can arrange ideas in a "logical" order, or that we should apply some form of arrangement to our message which persuades the audience. Yet it is also true that more recent studies have given us deeper insight into the relationships of the parts of any verbal message. They have helped us, for example, to understand that there is no such thing as a neutral fact because of the interpretation given to it by receivers and senders. With new insights have come new terms, and you should at least be familiar enough with them to realize how they can best serve you in improving your own oral communication, or evaluating that of others more adequately.

Another concept should be mentioned here. Throughout the preceding pages you may have noticed that the term persuasion has been used, and little mention has been made of informational speaking, speaking for the purpose of entertaining an audience, discussion, and other types of oral communication. Aristotle referred only to persuasion in his definition of rhetoric. It is safe to assume that he considered all other categories of oral communication were included in that term, because he saw the function of speaking and writing as influencing

---

14. Excerpts from a letter published in *Creation-Science Report* 1, No. 4 (September-October 1972).

the receiver of these messages. Communication scholars feel the same way about the terms change and change agent. It is possible to spend much time quibbling over whether or not all human speaking is done for the purpose of persuasion. This book will simply accept the fact that all human communication includes some degree of change or modification of behavior on the part of the speaker-sender and some change or modification of behavior on the part of the listener-receiver, or the environment. Since there is a useful purpose in distinguishing between certain types of communication in our society, terms such as persuasion, information, discussion, etc., will appear in this book with an explanation of the author's use.

The use of all available means of persuasion in public speaking, placing great emphasis on the role of the speaker, was the basic function of early rhetorics. Today, the rapidly developing field of communication theory, or communication research, is concerned with integrating the findings of scholars in many areas of human endeavor into one unified interactional communication theory. Both views make contributions to man's understanding of his communicative efforts. It will depend in the long run on your own philosophy, on your own purposes, because all systems developed by man must either serve him or be discarded. This author considers oral communication (for the purposes of a first speech course) as a new name for an old art which has given it some new purpose, some new insights and additional information through contact with the natural and social sciences.

It has been pointed out by Kenneth Burke that the premises with which we start give us a different world view.[15] The semanticist reminds us that any world view is of necessity an abstraction of whatever "reality" there may be. What the world is really like, what is "truth," may never be understood by man, but his search for both continues. As long as you can deal with an existing situation by using whatever ethical means are recognized by you, or are available to you for "persuasion-change," you are accomplishing what this book intends to help you accomplish.

EXERCISES

1. Develop your own definition of verbal-oral communication and present it in a two-minute speech to your class.

2. Develop your own definition of a verbal-oral message and present it in a two-minute speech to your class.

3. Give a three-minute oral report in class providing information concerning a major rhetorician not mentioned in your text.

4. Give a three-minute oral report dealing with one of the major specialists in communication not mentioned in the text.

5. Give a three-minute speech discussing one of the rhetorical terms mentioned in the text in more detail, using definitions supplied by different authors.

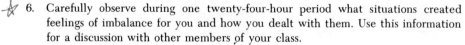 6. Carefully observe during one twenty-four-hour period what situations created feelings of imbalance for you and how you dealt with them. Use this information for a discussion with other members of your class.

---

15. See the discussion of this subject in Michael M. Osborn, "The Evolution of the Theory of Metaphor in Rhetoric," *Western Speech* 31 (Spring 1967): 129–30.

7. Consider a series of statements by political leaders, advertisers and others to see how they attempt to motivate you or bring about change in your behavior by creating imbalance. Write a three-page paper.

8. After considering statements by the political leader you respect most and the one you respect least, consider which statements by each individual are consonant, dissonant, or irrelevant to you. Use these data in a class discussion with fellow students whose opinions of these two leaders are opposite to yours.

BIBLIOGRAPHY

Allen, R. A. et al. *Speech in American Society.* Columbus: Charles E. Merrill, 1968.

Bailey, Dudley, ed. *Essays on Rhetoric.* New York: Oxford University Press, 1965.

Berlo, David K. *The Process of Communication.* New York: Holt, Rinehart, and Winston, 1967.

Borden, George A., et al. *Speech Behavior and Human Interaction.* Englewood Cliffs: Prentice Hall, 1969.

Borman, Ernest G., et al. *Interpersonal Communication in the Modern Organization.* Englewood Cliffs: Prentice Hall, 1969.

Broadbent, D. E. *Perception and Communication.* New York: Pergamon, 1958.

Brown, Charles T. and Charles Van Riper. *Speech and Man.* Englewood Cliffs: Prentice Hall, 1966.

Budd, Richard W. and Brent D. Ruben. *Approaches to Human Communication.* New York: Spartan, 1972. Especially chapter 7 on General Systems Theory.

Dance, Frank X., ed. *Human Communication Theory.* New York: Holt, Rinehart, and Winston, 1967.

Dibler, Robert J. and Larry L. Barker, eds. *Conceptual Frontiers in Speech-Communication.* New York: Speech Association of America, 1969.

Haiman, Franklyn S. *Freedom of Speech.* New York: Random House, 1968.

McCrosky, James C. *An Introduction to Rhetorical Communication.* Englewood Cliffs: Prentice Hall, 1968.

Redding, Charles W., and George A. Sanborn. *Business and Industrial Communication: A Source Book.* New York: Harper & Row, 1964.

Sanford, William Phillips and Williard Hayes Yeager. *Effective Business Speech.* New York: McGraw-Hill, 1960.

Schramm, Wilbur, ed. *The Science of Human Communication.* New York: Basic Books, 1963.

Sereno, K. K., and C. D. Mortenson, eds. *Foundations of Communication Theory.* New York: Harper & Row, 1970.

Thayer, Lee. "Communication and Organization Theory." In *Human Communication Theory,* ed. Frank E. X. Dance. New York: Holt, Rinehart, and Winston, 1967.

_____. *Communication and Communication Systems.* Homewood, Ill.: Irwin, 1968.

_____. "Communication Systems." *The Relevance of General Systems Theory,* ed. E. Lazlo. New York: Braziller, 1972.

3

THE SENDER-RECEIVER IN SPEECH COMMUNICATION

Man frequently uses communication to reduce uncertainty and to predict and control events in his world. Both social and biological motives determine our responses to the environment. As we saw in the previous chapters this is a complex interaction which makes it possible for man, through various internal and external communicative processes, to give positive meaning to his world as he strives for a feeling of balance.

INTRAPERSONAL COMMUNICATION

Much of our study deals with the social aspects of human communication. As a matter of fact, speech communication is primarily a means of social interaction. However, before we ever speak to anyone else, before anyone ever perceives and attaches meaning to any word symbols we transmit, we have communicated with ourselves. We have gone through a complex series of internal events within our own organism which precedes all externally observable speech behavior.

Not only do you and I have the ability to "talk" to ourselves, to meditate, to plan, and to evaluate, but there are also neuro-physiological processes which form the basis of our responses, our motivation, and our communication with other human beings or environmental factors. From the moment he is born to the moment that he dies (and possibly beyond), man communicates. Even his physical presence before he is born and after he dies represents a stimulus to other human beings who attach meaning to it.

Fundamentally, there are two aspects of human communication. One is the cognitive, internal, neuro-physiological, covert aspect. Only observable activity or behavior allows us to draw certain conclusions and develop theories about what happens inside of us. The other aspect is overt, readily identifiable, and definable behavior. Throughout this book the distinction between cognitive processes inside man and outward behavioral processes will be kept in mind.

Man as Stimulus and Man as Sender

It has already been explained that we cannot help but be stimuli, just as other objects or symbols with which other human beings come in contact as part of their environment. However, we should distinguish between this stimulus function which is largely unplanned, uncoordinated, and nonpurposeful, and the planned, purposeful, coordinated effort of man which we will call *sending*. In other words, we are distinguishing between intentional, purposive communication and nonintentional, nonpurposive communication. We need to understand the latter theoretically, we need to think about it, and be able to observe it, but our main concern remains an attempt to make purposive communication more meaningful and effective. Thus we return to an earlier statement in this chapter. Man *uses* communication to *reduce uncertainty*.

We are born facing an uncertain world and, outside of some biological and neurological predispositions, we have very little with which to handle our environment. That is especially true if we consider the fact that man's major difference from other animal life is his ability to communicate symbolically. Animals respond to signals and use signals. Signals require the presence of physical objects, and no abstraction process similar to the human use of symbols in communication exists among animals. Signal behavior, one could say, is "pointing behavior" which is also recognized by humans. A puddle of water is a signal that it has rained or someone left a sprinkler on, or someone spilled some water. Symbols, however, stand for other things, objects, ideas, or other symbols. Only man is capable of using symbols in the absence of the things they stand for. As a matter of fact, the symbol may stand for nothing except some image in our head. All of us "know" what a unicorn "looks like." Yet to the best of our knowledge there is no unicorn in existence now, and there probably never has been one. That fact did not keep imaginative people in the Middle Ages from grinding up "unicorn horns" as a supposedly potent aphrodisiac, nor did it keep others from buying this patent medicine made from nonexistent unicorn horns. Truly, the task faced by every human being in a world full of stimuli constantly bombarding his internal neuro-physiological system is vast.

The Cognitive Process

Over a period of years we gather experiences, information, or knowledge which serve us increasingly well in identifying, categorizing, interpreting, and using all of the stimuli in our environment which we judge to serve our purpose of controlling, balancing, and making our "world" more predictable. Little is known about the first processes of the new-born child. A sort of "imprinting" which provides the child with some early basis for recognizing the stimuli in his world has been postulated by some psychologists. Biologically we are all motivated or stimulated from the first, and no society can ever train these biological motives out of us. When I am hungry, I am hungry, and the signals and overall communicative activity in my system will be clearly directed toward solving that perceived state of tension, discomfort, or imbalance in my system. The biological factors are readily observed and measured. Their physical bases are much more easily identified than those processes involved in what we call thinking.

If we accept the original base of human communication to be the imprinting which takes place in a baby, we must still recognize the fact that man's perceptions throughout life are not merely the simple signal responses of animals or the kinds of biological motivations represented by our example of hunger. Our basic task is to sort meaningful stimuli out of the multitude of other stimuli surrounding us. But these stimuli do not come prepackaged with a neat label attached to them, providing the human being with clear identification of what they "mean."

We are "meaning-assigning" beings, not "meaning-receiving" beings. However, meaning depends on our ability to relate any kind of stimulus-input into our system to some factor or concept which we already know. Meaning is a process of relating and a process of taking the unknown and somehow measuring and understanding it by what we know. It is a process of taking any stimulus and either re-establishing meaning on the basis of our prior experience with it, or assigning it meaning because it relates to some prior experience to which we have already assigned meaning. The process is highly individualized and even arbitrary, and for that reason human beings are capable of "seeing" so many different things in the same object or symbol. Through our senses of hearing, seeing, touching, smelling, and tasting we receive the input, with our ears and eyes being the dominant receptors.

Not only our social interaction or communication depends on our perceptions of the world around us, but also our intrapersonal communication. We can be "tricked," as we say, by our senses. Books on psychology contain examples showing how *experience affects perception*. For example, we are accustomed to walking into rooms with four walls, a ceiling, and a floor, all of them in a specific arrangement to each other. Maybe you have visited one of those "crazy houses," where the usual kind of relationship of walls to ceiling and floor is changed. As a result you found yourself leaning forward to compensate for what looked like a slanting floor, or because the floor and ceiling were really slanting you perceived an individual at the other end of the room to be eight feet tall. We are used to seeing people in relationship to eight-foot ceilings, and when their heads suddenly appear to be touching the ceiling of a "normal" room, our previous experience tells us that they are giants. The intensity or length of another experience may cancel out the perceived relationship of such *optical illusions*. Husbands and wives who have lived with each other for many years will still see each other as being of "normal size." The point is: *we do not see everything there is to be seen in our environment, nor do we see everything accurately*. All of our perceptions are selective. Besides the factors we have mentioned, we need to recall our earlier discussion of the fact that physical or psychological conditions, such as emotional upsets, also influence our ability to perceive.

Having perceived something, we have somehow become attentive to it. It crosses the threshold of our attention. The input enters our system through our senses, and becomes what some psychologists refer to as a *percept*. That percept's future use depends on the interaction taking place in our brains, where ten billion or more nerve cells will determine what is done with it. Whatever the process—chemical, electrical, based on proteins, or whatever other explanation scholars have provided—the intricate, complex neurological system of man appears to consist of a network established by nerve contacts. The point of contact is called *synapse*. Here the input message may be stopped, re-routed, or passed along.

The message which has been allowed to reach the brain will be checked in some fashion, and meaning will be assigned to it. It appears that the percepts, which we have mentioned earlier, are arranged into concepts, and these concepts in turn are related to each other to form constructs. These are the factors, templates or models against which all new messages reaching the brain are compared in the process of assigning meaning to them.

Of course there are different results possible in this internal communication process. It may either *add information* to already existing information, or it may *reinforce* the existing pattern or model, or it may *modify* or possibly *replace* the existing model, the concepts or constructs mentioned earlier.

Language and Cognition

Considering the complexity of all information input it should be readily apparent that our ability to abstract, symbolize, and use words makes the entire process as effective as it is. This symbolic ability makes possible the storage and use of vast, possibly unlimited amounts of information. True, we cannot recall all the information, often because psychological factors inhibit us—we do not *want* to recall. Even the fact that some experiences are more intense, and others have been repeated frequently influences the ease with which we recall information. Nor do we necessarily recall all information accurately. Again our needs or desires cause us to recall information selectively, in agreement with what we want, rather than with the original input. So we tend to "forget" some details, and increase the importance of others, partially as a result of the ever continuing flow of incoming percepts and their modifying influence.

Human language plays an important role in all of the mental processes we have discussed so far. Words allow us to distinguish between objects, concepts, ideas, and symbols even though they are not present in some physical form. Man can connect these words and can think and reason, using his mind as a vast testing ground for thoughts and new ideas. The relationship of words or language to thought and the effective use of language in speech will be discussed in more detail in the next chapter.

Language symbols become means of making the fleeting neuro-physiological process more permanent and usable for later communication. We are not static systems, and our environment is not static either. Everything keeps changing, as long as we live. We are deeply imbedded in a stream of ongoing, forward-flowing communication which cannot be repeated or reversed.

Intrapersonal communication has been considered as if it consisted of bits, pieces, and chunks. In effect, like all communication it is a total process involving systems interacting simultaneously and constantly while man is conscious. The same is true in all other forms of human communication as we move from thought processes, to the processes of forming word cues, to the reception of these word cues by a receiver, and his feedback response providing new input data for the cognitive system. We appear to have a system of interlocking, continuous loops, through which symbols are checked against thought processes, the words actually produced against the original word-symbol model and against the original thought process. Similarly, reception by the other person or persons involved in communication is again checked against all the original steps.

The Self-Concept

It is important that we move beyond the neuro-physiological aspects of human communication. Any interaction with other human beings, any act of speech communication, in the long run depends on the image we have of ourselves. Insecure, frightened students in public speaking classes are known to all of us. On the other hand there are individuals who appear to have a great deal of self-assurance and confidence in any situation. When we ask such people to fill out self-evaluating inventories we usually discover that they see themselves in very different ways.

Part of an understanding of self depends on how well we communicate with ourselves, how much we are at ease with ourselves, how contemplative, thoughtful, and insightful we are. Overwhelmingly, however, our self-concept is shaped by our contact with the external world. The reactions we get from other human beings and our records of success and failure are vital. Self-concept, therefore, is only one more indication in our struggle for balance, for self-actualization, for keeping a world under control which can become frightening if we feel it is out of balance or we have lost control. There is a danger, however, that we consider self-concept in too limited a way, as if we functioned only in one unified manner or assumed only one role. This is, of course, not true. Not only do we play many roles in interacting with other human beings, but we tend to engage in some of them simultaneously. The roles of sender and receiver are representative of that idea. In electronics the term "transceiver" is used to describe a part which can both transmit and receive. Man, in speech communication, functions in a similar way.

Shakespeare observed that we are all actors playing many roles on the stage of life. Sometimes the roles are complimentary and sometimes they are antagonistic, depending less on the role per se than on our own attitudes. For instance, whether or not the role of a father wll become antagonistic to the role of a husband depends on personal adjustment to both parts. For the sake of understanding we tend to organize, structure, and categorize ideas. As one speech professor put it: "Depending on whether we are lumpers or splitters, we tend to see agreements between concepts or differences between them." That's the situation when we discuss your roles as speaker and as listener.

Personality: As We See Ourselves

Most audiences, most listener-receivers, think of you as they see and observe you. Personality to them depends to a large extent on their interpretation, resulting from inferences they draw from what they have observed, and from judgments they make, based on their own value systems. That is what most people consider to be the "real you." But you also strive for an internal consistency, what we have called homeostasis. Maybe this is the part of you people call character. Maslow called it man's striving to achieve self-actualization.[1] This is a set of values, standards, beliefs which convey the image you have of yourself. Hopefully, all aspects of you as speaker and listener will be in harmony, otherwise severe personality disturbances or conflicts may result.

You are an individual with your own ways of observing and judging things, and for this reason every communication situation is a sort of unique experience which can never be repeated because people and situations are changing constantly. You speak as a total person and that makes a difference. Give the same message, the same speech to several different speakers and it will be different each time it is delivered. Even if the speech is in manuscript form, individual styles of reading, emphasis, and the appearance of the reader would turn it into different messages. In effect, personality should depend on more than the judgment of others, and it usually does.

You are striving for *internal consistency* according to a pattern which only you might fully understand, or of which you might be more fully aware if you are well-adjusted and concerned about your role as a communicator in human society. If you can *respect yourself as well as others*, even though you may find it impossible to agree with their ideas, there is some indication that you are developing a meaningful self-concept. If, on the other hand, you find that you are cutting yourself off from others and their ideas, if you are constantly striving to get attention even at the risk of dominating and controlling other people, that image may be dangerously warped or nonexistent. *The ability to fail as well as to succeed*, and *the ability to work hard for success*—even in your oral messages—are but two indications of the kind of maturity which goes with a positive self-concept.

Stability, which makes it possible for you to continue a worthwhile effort and makes it possible for others to trust that you will carry on, is another vital factor. Tolerance for failure or delayed rewards is another indication that you have built more than a momentary situational concept of yourself.

Of course, there are underlying motives, which determine to a large extent how we evaluate our relationships to others. Our needs are basic: Our need to be accepted, our need to be understood, our need to belong or to be included, or our need to be loved. Seldom is it only one need which causes us to actively interact with other human beings, or to go to the trouble of communicating, even under difficult circumstances.

The mere mention of these terms indicates how vital it is for us in communicating with other human beings to try to understand the underlying motivational forces behind their actions. If one individual is willing to provide us membership in a group, that is inclusion, but not the respect or love that we want out of such an association, little common ground for interaction results. Such "pseudo-arrangements" have all the appearance of fulfilling our needs, but they often leave us more dissatisfied than if we had been ignored altogether. Self-image is significantly formed by an ability to understand one's needs, and

---

1. A. H. Maslow, *Toward a Psychology of Being* (Princeton: D. Van Nostrand, 1962).

a relationship to others is significantly influenced by an ability to let them know and understand what those needs are.

The ability to empathize, or to experience as much as possible the state of feeling and being of another individual, is described in this brief discussion, as is the ability to project our self-image to others. It appears that those who most completely understand themselves, and who have learned to accept while trying to improve that self, can most readily put themselves in another man's place.

The clearer our understanding is as to whether or not we seek information, whether we want to be reassured, or possibly convinced that we have made the right decision, or if we need inspiration to continue or to undertake a difficult task, whether we seek beauty or aesthetic satisfaction, the more meaningfully we can participate in any given communication situation. That is partly true because we will give our partners in the process clearer, less confusing clues to which they can respond. Out of this understanding of our own motives often comes a better comprehension and use of our individual human resources. Not all communication is based on information, or need for support of existing ideas, or the hope that someone will talk us into something we have wanted to do all along. We need to understand the fact that we are attracted to some people while that attraction is lacking in others.

Again, it is important that we are able to understand our internal motivations. Possibly the attraction is physical. Some people look good to us, others do not, some people dress in ways which attract us, others do not. Fragrances, colors, forms, all can be attractive to us because of our past experiences and cultural background, or even because of the direct physiological stimuli they represent. Other attraction is the result of status, power, or position. We may be attracted to people whose place in our society provides us with a feeling of sharing worthwhile, important, or valuable experiences. Security as a result of seeking out well-informed, competent people is frequently another attraction as we come in contact with many individuals and select those who help us fulfill our internal overall life plan.

While we strive for consistency, all of us know that our behavior is far from being consistent. We have a hard time being attentive when we are tired. We have a hard time being considerate when we are discouraged. We have a difficult time paying attention to someone else's priorities, even though we may love that person, when we are deeply preoccupied with a personal problem or challenge. Part of an understanding of self depends on an ability to accept one's varying moods caused by negative or positive experiences, by physiological needs, illness, fatigue, or myriad possible factors. In understanding these ever-changing bases for human behavior and recognizing their existence in us at any given moment, we can once more prevent significant damage to our self-image or to our communication with others.

Maslow indicated man's hierarchy of needs in a pyramidical fashion. There are first of all our most basic physiological needs, or our needs for *physical well-being.* When these are achieved, we become concerned with and work for the fulfillment of *safety* needs. That in turn allows us to move upward to another level, that of *belonging* and *love.* If we lose the existing base of any of the preceding fulfilled needs we may very well have to reverse our course, and seek fulfillment of more "basic" needs again. Otherwise we can move to the fulfillment of *esteem* needs, and finally to the highest level of *self-actualization*. Finally, we need to consider and realize our *individual limitations* caused by differences in physical or emotional preparation and ability. It may look easy when a highly trained runner circles the track, but without training he would find himself running out of breath and unable to complete the course. Our mental abilities may be good, fully adequate for our work and interest, but to duplicate the work of an Einstein takes special capacity and preparation. We may wish that we could paint a Mona Lisa or compose a Fifth Symphony, but merely wishing will bring us no closer to the accomplishments of artists whose temperament, abilities, and years of dedicated preparation enabled them to create these masterpieces.

Opportunity and special settings are needed to allow us to make use of our abilities and our preparation. A man may be fully suited to exploring a new continent, but that may be difficult to do at a moment in history when there are no more continents to explore. If he understands that fact, as well as having gained insight into his needs and the means at his disposal, he may rechannel his talents and live a very satisfied life. If not, he may fight himself and the world for whatever time he has. Habit also becomes a vital factor in these considerations of intrapersonal communication. Habits are our human way of generalizing behavior and many habits, such as automatically shifting while driving a stick-shift car, may even become vital to staying alive. Habits help us to do more than one thing at a time, or do something while thinking at the same time. However, they also tend to block new information, or stimuli to be perceived, or they can keep us from trying new and better ways. Being able to recognize one's habits, and judging their positive or negative contribution to what we must accomplish in communication is important, even in overcoming such annoying habits as using the expression, "You know," as a thought- or time-filler, or as a vocalized pause.

INTERPERSONAL COMMUNICATION: COMMUNICATING WITH OTHERS

During a lifetime we engage in many types of interaction besides intrapersonal communication. Speech communication with one or two individuals, with small groups, or with large audiences is the most frequent communicative activity of our lives, second only to the processes we discussed earlier in this chapter. The importance of interaction with other human beings is that in this way we gain much of our understanding, insight, or information concerning ourselves and the roles we play. We do not only see ourselves through introspection, we form many of the component parts of our self-concept through the perceived reactions of other human beings. Primary groups, such as the family, shape our self-image. A child who is told repeatedly that he is "stupid" by those who are his most important reference group, members of his family, will probably live a kind of "self-fulfilling prophecy." He may literally try to live up to his family's expectations.

It is clear by now that human beings and the stimuli that they provide for us represent an important part of the total cognitive storehouse of information which we use to understand and control our world. It is little wonder then that primary groups which we join voluntarily in later life are vital to us. They are chosen because they help us reinforce our self-image, provide us with opportunities for achievement and success, and protect us from negative reactions. They become great forces in shaping our lives, our learning, our perceptions. If a group cannot fulfill these functions for us it is a dissonant factor in our lives, and we either have to adjust our cognitive information storehouse, leave the organization, or change it.

By far the greater number of instances during which we communicate with other people will consist of conversations, discussions, dialogues involving only two people, or a small number of people in succession. Exchanges with fellow students as we walk across campus, and brief contacts with members of a family distributed all over the house before rushing off to work or school in the morning are examples of more casual interpersonal communication contacts. Often such contacts represent *pseudo-*, or *phatic communication*. No information is really given or expected when we call out to an individual as we walk past him, "How are you?" Asking an individual who has just fallen in front of us, "Did you hurt yourself?" when he is obviously bleeding, is not a statement asking for information as much as it is an attempt to open communication channels or to keep them open for other more important information input.

In effect these contacts are forms of *casual socialization* during which a minimum of information or persuasive data is exchanged. Such situations can lead to confusion. How often have mothers and fathers insisted that they "told" their children to do a certain thing that day, perhaps mow the lawn or clean the garage? Since that type of instruction was, however, carelessly related to some of the other pseudo-communication during the morning family rush, the receivers of the messages have at least fairly good reasons for claiming confusion about the intended messages. Since there is usually no great desire to do chores anyway, it is not difficult for the listener to categorize them with other, information-poor data received that morning, such as the statements, "Now be good," or "Pay attention to what the teacher says."

Interpersonal communication between a man and a woman in love may be relatively poor in informative content, but very rich in emotional, persuasive content. On the other hand, conferences with college instructors, or with work-supervisors may serve the specific purpose of gaining information. These few examples indicate how important it is for both the speaker and the listener, the receiver and the sender, to form some clear understanding of how to perceive their roles in a given communication situation. When we move from interpersonal communication to small or large group communication, difficulties arise in that the roles of the sender and receiver become more formalized, and there may be less distinct switching from sending to receiving and back. The factors typical of larger audiences, which will be discussed in another chapter, also tend to hide individual reactions and change the role of the individual as he becomes part of a larger group. A greater dichotomy, a more distinct separation between speaker and audience functions, is the result. In turn this often requires considerably greater effort to overcome the emotional and physical barriers which the group situation creates. Additionally, the greater variety of backgrounds or knowledge, as well as emotional states existing among larger numbers of people, can create problems for speaker-listener interaction.

The Sender-Receiver in a Free Society

In an authoritarian society the roles of speakers and listeners are usually clearly identified and delineated. Hitler scoffed at the idea of discussion, mainly because he was convinced that it was his God-given right to lead his people and *tell* them what to do. The leader speaks, the people listen and follow. There is very little thought given to a possible switching of roles, except when "representatives of the people" are permitted by their leaders to parrot statements of the controlling authorities. In dictatorships there is an endless repetition of the official party line by everyone who is permitted to speak publicly.

In a free society, on the other hand, a more meaningful form of communication can usually be found. The roles of sender and receiver are constantly changing and reversed which, at least in public disputes or communication situations, is not the case in dictatorships. At one moment a Congressman may be addressing a political rally, only minutes later he may be engaged in a heated discussion with one of his constituents. A professor may be lecturing to his class, and seconds later may be listening to a challenging question from his students. Thus, the basic attitudes of speakers and listeners are quite different in a free society. Every speaker realizes that he needs to stay in close contact with his audience, that he needs to be ready and well-informed to face any possible challenges to his ideas. Every listener realizes that he may be called on to participate actively as a sender or communicator. The total atmosphere is changed, and "real" communication involving both sender and receiver in a meaningful, responsive exchange is encouraged or made possible.

Since we are concerned primarily with the study of oral communication in a free society we will stress the individual playing roles of both sender and receiver. The following ideas are intended to help you be a better communicator who can adequately play any role required of him. Rather than taking the more arbitrary position that you are at times a speaker and at other times a listener, it will be our intention to consider you as functioning in a variety of ways, including the roles of sender and receiver simultaneously or in rapid succession. Furthermore, it is reasonable to expect that your own personality, your own character, your educational background, as well as any other support systems for your daily existence which you may have developed, will be the foundations for a characteristic reaction to any situation you will face. Thus, the situation and specific attempts to deal with any given situation are subordinated to the integrative factor of your personality.

Personality: How Others See Us

Speech communication is frequently like looking into a mirror and beholding a reflection of your face with the changes that result from imperfections in the glass. People listen to you, or they observe you as part of a given audience, and they draw conclusions from what they see or think they see. Genuine tiredness may be interpreted as discourtesy or an attempt to rattle your partner—be he sender or receiver—in the communication situation. Long hair may be a sign of rebellion rather than genuine preference on the basis of looks. All your physical activity—a stifled yawn, eagerly leaning toward the speaker or listener, tense movements or wiggling around in a chair—will be given some meaning. Whatever your particular role in a given speaking situation, you will look for clues leading to a better understanding of the message, the situation, and your partner or partners in that situation.

What do people look for in the communicator? Undoubtedly many factors must be considered, especially as cultural and social situations vary. However, there are certain concepts which are of major concern to anyone communicating with another human being.

We look for a pattern, for some sort of consistent behavior. That can become a bothersome thing. The preacher who finds himself closely scrutinized at an ice-cream social following an evening sermon may not be aware of it, but his parishioners may very well want to find out if he "really meant" what he said minutes earlier. A politician often finds himself in trouble after his election because his constituents are looking for a pattern of consistency in word and action which he may not be capable of producing. People look for a consistent pattern of sincerity, seriousness, humor or whatever they consider to be the outstanding personality feature in the person they have observed. Many "confession" magazines built their readership on the idea that people want to know if their favorite movie hero is the same in daily life as he appears to be on the screen.

We expect concern for people, concern for individuals. Much of what we call charisma is explained by the feelings of those on the receiving end of the communication. They feel wanted, they feel personally involved, they feel as if they know a man personally. Unknown musical performers, television or movie starlets, and unknown presidential candidates have become "super-stars" or meaningful contenders for office because thousands of people began to feel personally involved. For that reason any communicator commits unpardonable sins when he allows himself to become message- rather than receiver-centered, or when he appears to be more concerned with words than with ideas. The image any receiver wants from any sender includes the use of ideas which overcome triteness and hackneyed repetition because they are fresh, new, and appear to be directed to that specific individual or group in that specific situation.

Contact Points for Interaction

It is difficult to list all the factors which provide clues in any communication situation as we try to find some basis for speaker evaluation. However, the following key words summarize many identifiable concepts, and can be used to interpret your own role as seen through the eyes of your active partners in communication.

Significance: I really matter; "it" really matters; "they" really matter.

Humor: Laughing at oneself and laughing at situations which can be legitimately interpreted as being humorous without hurting anyone gives balance to communication.

The New: Challenges come from new ideas; new ideas indicate involvement and the ability to be creative.

The Familiar: If things get too new all of us feel threatened, insecure; we like the comfort of the tried and true.

Challenges: Man must reach out, he must find new ideas new ways of doing things, and he needs to be willing to put even life on the line for something that is very important to him.

The Specific: Vagueness disturbs us; we fear people who hide behind words and indefinite statements; we want to feel secure in the knowledge that you know what you are talking about; we want to know exactly what you want from us.

Variety: Monotony in all forms is deadly to man; change, if it does not cause him to come face to face with too many unfamiliar things, gives him a feeling of adventure and novelty; we like things to move and change if they neither change nor move too fast.

Conflict: Man needs disagreement to test ideas; he needs some competition as long as it is not threatening his very existence; he needs the feeling of accomplishment that comes from conflict resolution; he needs to know that you care enough about him, that you respect him enough to think of him as a worthy opponent whose knowledge and personal involvement represent a genuine reason for meaningful conflict.

All of these concepts also include the underlying desire on the part of anyone with whom you communicate for *specific direct contact.* The communicator who addresses himself to abstract concepts or to a straw man of his own creation, rather than his listeners, will soon realize that his image is severely lacking in positive factors.

The values of a given society may become the controlling concepts for which listeners watch in any communication. The following terms represent parts of a common value system which many contemporary Americans would like to see exemplified in those with whom they communicate. Combinations may vary depending on whether one is communicating with a younger or an older person, a small group or a large audience, male or female listeners, politically conservative or politically liberal audiences. But this list can be extended or developed on the basis of careful observation as you face new or different situations, cultures, and individuals.

Sincerity: He sounds like he means it.

Interest: He really cares.

Dedication: He'll give his all to a cause.

Skill: He handles himself like a pro.

Ability: He is a truly brilliant person.

Truth: He knows what he is talking about, minces no words, and lets the chips fall where they may.

Sensitivity: He cares about other people's feelings and ideas.

Alertness: He is aware of communication as a living, moving situation, adjusting himself to the needs of others as well as changing situations.

Association: He is seen with the right people, those with whom we agree, those we trust, those we respect, or with whom he should associate to prove his case.

Honesty: He can be trusted.

It should be clear by now that interaction with other people requires awareness of other people. It also requires a certain ability to adjust and change.

No one who deals with other people, or who wishes to engage with them in some mutually beneficial activities, can *force* his own prejudices, his own problems, or his own value standards on them. Interaction is truly a situation of understanding, compromise, and adjustment. It would be naive to assume that people will simply have to take you as you are and be done—they may simply decide that you are not worth the bother or concern. Idealistically receivers will permit you to be "yourself," whatever that means. Realistically you will have to make certain adjustments to overcome possible negative reactions or misunderstandings.

There is one almost fundamental factor for which many people look in any communications situation: *sincerity*. We expect others to really mean what they say, to be truly sincere, truly involved. Honesty, sincerity, and dedication, as already mentioned, are important attributes of any communicator in our society. These factors played a major role in the support many people gave to varied political personalities such as Barry Goldwater, Eugene McCarthy, Robert Kennedy, and James Buckley during the 1960s and 1970s.

There are times when we need to test an idea before fully embracing it. There are other times when we feel miserable and would rather stay home, but a speaking engagement requires attendance at a public meeting. At other times the requirements of a job may be very different from what an individual would like to do at that particular moment, but the job has to be done anyway. Sincere involvement in such cases may be hard, but we will fulfill our responsibilities anyway. A realistic evaluation of the communication situations we face is at least as important as idealism and honesty. Sincerity or dedication cannot merely be judged by appearance or a supposedly "firm" reply.

All the factors mentioned here should not overshadow the idea that you have to develop as an individual communicator. What is good for one speaker is not good for another. What worked in one situation does not work in another. What makes possible communication between two given people, does not necessarily make it possible between two other people. Do you have too much or too little of some personality feature? You should not merely be a copy of someone else who has functioned as a successful communicator because that in itself would violate some of the most important concepts of individual human communication in a free society.

SPEECH FRIGHT

There are some specific aspects in the sender-receiver relationship which are of a very practical nature, and will be discussed next. One major area of concern for many beginning public speakers is speech fright. Various authors have called it by different terms, but all the words add up to the frightening experience of standing before an individual or before a group trying to communicate ideas. Some things we know about speech fright, others are not yet entirely clear. Some experienced actors and public speakers may be nearly overwhelmed by it in certain situations, others have never experienced more than slight nervousness. Some situations and some individuals frighten us, others do not. One basic rule seems to apply: When a great deal depends on the success of our communication or when possible social or physical punishment could result, and when we are uncertain about how well we will perform before a critical listener‘ or group of listeners, speech fright is likely to occur.

Definition

Fundamentally, speech fright is the result of a feeling of dissonance or deep disturbance in man, who needs a certain balance to function adequately. It is easily recognized by dry mouth, shaking knees, trembling hands, rapid breathing or rapid heartbeat, accompanied by blushing or blanching. The physical, observable reactions are commonly the result of psychological factors such as fear of people, fear of failure, the culturally determined desire "to do well," past experiences of failure, or other threatening concepts which we may have difficulty identifying at a conscious level.

There are indications that individuals who experience speech fright most consistently and most severely have three basic problems:

1. Lack of experience in appearing before audiences or making public statements
2. Lack of involvement; they tend to be shy, have less social life
3. Lack of expressive ability, especially in the area of oral expression; they tend to have less oral communication with others.

In effect, speech fright appears to be a strong psycho-physical conflict-reaction to a potentially threatening situation. On one hand the body physically prepares for flight or fight, on the other hand we have been culturally conditioned neither to run nor fight but to face the situation and make the best of it. The body is supplied with more adrenalin to face what it interprets as an emergency situation, yet we are forced by custom to stand in one small spot while we communicate with someone else. Our muscles are tensed for strong action while the situation demands that we control physical activity, resulting in a struggle of tensed muscles fighting for relaxation, causing visible trembling. The heart either rapidly pumps blood into the outer layers of the skin resulting in blushing, or withdraws it resulting in blanching and possibly fainting. Both responses are means of warding off dangers from possible wounds.

As a result there is a conflict between our subconscious physical reaction to a danger which really does not call for extreme physical emergency preparedness, and what we can rationally do about it. All these ideas were not presented because you do not know what happens when someone experiences speech fright, but because available information suggests that understanding the phenomenon is the first step in dealing with it.

The challenge is to gain control over these psycho-physical reactions. Knowledge of the problems involved and understanding of the vital processes causing them are the first steps. Second, there is a very real need to understand the positive functions of controlled nervousness. The additional supply of adrenalin, for instance, provides any communicator with energy which can be helpful in presenting a more powerful, meaningful message. Control is the key word. Many speakers are actually afraid when they do not experience some nervousness before a public speech, especially if it is an important occasion. They reason that their mental and emotional batteries are probably not "charged" enough for an effective presentation.

Ways to Overcome Speech Fright

What are some of the things you can do to overcome the negative aspects of fear which might lead to speech fright?

Many people become afraid because they no not feel adequately prepared. The obvious answer is *meaningful preparation.* Know your subject, and know more about the subject than you can possibly hope to present in the time available. Know your audience, your receiver, the situation, the environment. All that will give you a feeling of confidence. If you are scheduled to give a formal speech, don't memorize it, because even one forgotten word can trigger the physical reactions we have mentioned. One forgotten idea, from among a number of worthwhile concepts, may be a loss but it is not a tragedy. One forgotten word which interrupts your entire train of thought can become a disaster. *Start your preparation early.* Let your brain help you to gather information, sort out ideas and outline or structure them long before you actually sit down to compose a formal speech or have to face any other communication situations. The best way to assure panic during a speech is to prepare it a short time before it is to be delivered. Try to be in the best physical and mental condition possible. Poor health, lack of sleep, overconsumption of coffee, and many similar factors add to physical tensions and problems which will make it much easier for your body to become the controlling factor when your intellect should be.

Relax tensions, even if you have to go through some fairly vigorous physical activity before you get up to make a speech. Remember, you have an oversupply of adrenalin in your system, as well as muscles which are ready for action. Walk off your tensions, and avoid standing stock-still in one place clamping your hands to the speaker's stand for "control." You will only add to the problem. Instead, use up the added energy.

Focus on the importance of the subject, the friends you have in the audience, or both. Concentrate on what you want to accomplish and the positive factors which can assist you, rather than on the possible threatening parts of the situation.

Experience helps. The more similar experiences you can look back on, the more positively you will tend to look at other, or new communication situations. That is one of the reasons for practical experiences in speech classes, experiences which we expect will have a positive influence on later communication situations outside the classroom. The knowledge that "I have done this before" is helpful.

Never allow yourself to give up. Quitting once makes quitting twice even easier, and from then on it is anyone's guess if you will ever be able to communicate effectively with anyone. Remember that others have problems too, and try to look positively at your own abilities, and the positive factors which you are bringing to the communication situation, such as your knowledge, your involvement, your concern. It is not your purpose to be the greatest speaker or communicator of all times, but to be the best speaker or communicator *you* can be—if that also happens to be the best the world has ever heard, so much the better.

LISTENING

This chapter began by pointing out that we are considering a total process of communication of which both sending and receiving are interacting parts. However, for the sake of studying some specific aspects of receiving, listening will be considered here as a separate activity because of the problems which many individuals have with it. Attention is a vital factor in any listening we do, and that attention is in turn determined by what motivates us to listen in the first place.

Reasons for Listening

Listening may be for the purpose of:

1. Security or learning: In this case the listener will want great clarity and sufficient detail to understand the subject under consideration.
2. Encouraging the speaker: Every political speaker knows how vital it is to have his supporters sprinkled throughout the audience during a political rally. They may have heard his speech many times, but familiar, friendly faces, and responsive reactions will be of great assistance to the speaker. As far as listeners are concerned this type of response may be very meaningful to them also because they feel they are supporting "their man."
3. Fulfilling emotional or aesthetic needs: Certain dramatic performances, poetry readings, eulogies, etc. are intended to make the listener feel good, encourage him, make him happier, and he expects to hear words which will fill his needs of the moment. Often it is not even the intellectual content or wording but the sound of words which satisfies these needs, and at times even the feeling of being part of a group is sufficient.
4. Being polite, or fulfilling social obligations: In this case there will probably be very little active listening involved. People attend such occasions mainly to be seen and to see—like Easter Sunday church services, or charity affairs.
5. To get "one's money's worth": This is another rather negative response. Some people have season tickets for a lecture series and they are not about to miss a certain speech and thus lose money on the deal. The last two cases can, however, be turned into a more positive listening situation if the sender, the message, the situation, or a combination of these warrant a readjustment of purposes by the listener as he receives a message.

Basic Types of Listening

There are two basic approaches to listening.

1. Positive, supportive listening: This in effect constitutes one part of a positive, creative interaction between a sender and a receiver. It does not necessarily mean that they will agree with each other, but it does mean that they are aware of their interdependence, and the listener is willing to assume a responsible role. This type of listening can still lead to conflicting solutions.

2. Antagonistic, challenging listening: This type of listening, on the other hand, starts with the negative assumption that no agreement is possible, that in effect some kind of battle is about to be waged and that the result will have to be absolute victory by one side or the other. This type of listening looks for weaknesses in the message, not for the purpose of resolving differences and disagreements, but for the purpose of destroying a real or fancied opponent.

Much depends on the preparation for listening in both cases. In other words, most of us approach our listener's role with certain preconceived ideas in mind. We are not blank pages waiting to be filled by the sender-speaker. Our attitudes, our knowledge about the subject under discussion, and our emotions will determine, even prior to the actual occasion, the type of listening in which we will engage. Individual members of a group of professors attending a formal lecture by one of their colleagues could be listening with genuine interest because of the novelty of the approach discussed, or because they wish to use the material in an attack upon its author. On the other hand they may only have wanted a comfortable place to sit and figured this particular lecture would be dull enough to allow them to take a little nap. In each case, prior knowledge of the subject and personal attitudes resulted in a specific type of listening or nonlistening. This example illustrates that many more complex factors than physical presence and the ability to hear the speaker determine our listening. However, lack of knowledge or antagonistic attitudes on the part of the person to whom we are listening may change us from positive, supportive listeners, depending on how dedicated we are to the role we feel we must or should play. Many belligerent or defensive speakers have turned cooperative audiences into hostile groups. On the other hand, antagonistic, challenging listeners may just as easily change their attitudes if they discover positive features in a sender or his message while he is speaking.

Hearing, Listening, Interpreting

It may be well on the basis of what we have discussed so far to consider the various acts or activities in which we engage, often included under the term listening.

Hearing: The physical ability to receive the message.

Listening: The emotional and intellectual determination of an individual to receive the words and total message presented to him.

Interpreting: The inferences drawn from the message and actions of the speaker as well as the situation, and the value judgments resulting from these observations and inferences. The key concept here is that we assign *meaning.*

Listening must include all three if a meaningful evaluation of the total process is to be made.

Effective Listening

Communication implies selectivity, choice, sometimes resulting in the slanting of information because no one can say or hear everything about anything. This idea applies to the sending as well as to the receiving of messages. One additional problem in listening is that we can think faster than we can speak, which frequently results in listeners' going off on tangents. As a result some people have trouble recognizing which are their own ideas or tangents and which are the speaker's. Some of these negative possibilities can be counteracted if the sender remains constantly aware of the receiver, and if the "face in the crowd" indicates to him how adequately his message is being received.

As listeners we can be most effective if we

1. *Focus attention on the message.* External influences, the influence of personal problems, and many other factors will cause us to miss vital parts of a message.
2. *Get clues to intended meanings.* We may see one meaning in what is being said, while the sender intends another. That may be his fault, but frequently it is also the fault of the listener who is not paying attention to gestures or words which are used to underline ideas the speaker considers to be vital. Summaries and introductory remarks indicating the areas to be covered, as well as any other indication of structure, can provide clues to meaning in formal speeches.
3. *Delay judgment.* The sender needs a chance to complete his message before we draw our own conclusions. At times he may say certain things for effect which can lead to a wrong interpretation if we do not listen to *all* he has to say.

Additional concepts will improve overall communication if the listener uses them purposefully.

1. A listener may be interested in only one idea, but the relationships between all the ideas a sender presents need to be considered. Interpretations or use of one idea can become dangerous, if all relationships are not considered. Some children learn quickly how to strike a match, but they become frightened when they don't know how to put it out

without burning themselves. If listeners keep the overall purpose in mind
as they listen communication will improve. The title of a speech or
advance publicity may serve as other means of identifying a formal
speech's purpose more clearly.

2. It is also helpful if a listener considers the sender, the message, and
the occasion, as well as the receivers, while he listens. If there is only
one physician in a group of laymen he cannot expect the speaker to
reach him on his level of understanding concerning some medical problem. Adjustment to the audience and the situation in such a case may
become entirely the responsibility of that one listener.

3. Communication is improved if the definition or data presented by the
sender, representing one reasonable way of interpretation, are accepted.
The receiver of a message may prefer different concepts, but unless
the purpose of the exchange of ideas is quibbling over words because
he enjoys that sort of thing, a listener should accept the sender's statements for his defined purposes.

Communication is a process of interaction and as a result responsibility
for its effectiveness must be shared by all who participate in it. There is some
poetic justice in the fact that in our society we must assume many roles throughout life, and the biblical Golden Rule has added meaning to all who communicate
with their fellow man. There are certainly worse ways of starting our interaction
with others than by treating them as we would like to be treated ourselves.
In later chapters we will consider a number of other important clues with
which we are provided when we become part of a larger audience. However,
these concepts overlap with our discussions in this chapter. They are often
equally applicable in one-to-one communication, or in small group communication, not merely in public speaking situations.

The environment or setting is important to us as we try to identify our
role as sender-receiver. Martial music, loud shouts, drum rolls, flag waving,
bright colors, all these factors become part of our cognition and thus part of
the interpretation of the total situation and our response, or the response we
think others expect of us. Temperature, odors, or our physical closeness to others
in a crowd will cause us to approach or to withdraw, largely depending on
our cultural background. We may have received printed information or instruc-
tions prior to a given communication situation which will cause us to react
to the written as well as to the spoken communication. Our prior experience
with similar situations, possibly our expectations of either a positive or negative
nature, will cause us to respond in specific ways. A college student who has
found that on all previous occasions a conference with a professor turned out
to be a negative experience, will be well-programmed for his next encounter
with the teacher. These concepts will be studied in much more detail when
we consider language and nonverbal communication as well as formal audiences.

YOU AND YOU IN COMMUNICATION

We have considered the fact that you play both the roles of sender and of
receiver in oral communication. Your personality, your attitudes, your learning,
your emotions, your judgments determine how you function. If you can under-

stand what is expected of you by others and what your own personal desires for development and achievement demand, the integration of these concepts will help make you a more effective communicator and well-adjusted person. In a society which stresses communication, listening is often the forgotten part of a total process which usually requires that someone receive the message if communication is to take place. While it is easy to prescribe certain rules for effective listening, personal needs and desires are often the real barriers. "Know thyself," becomes once more a vital factor to the speaker-listener.

Understanding what happens physically and psychologically inside the communicator is vital. Control is a word which can be applied to all communication activities, and control results to a large extent from better understanding and knowledge of self and others, as well as understanding of the situations in which people communicate.

EXERCISES

1. Make a list of what you consider to be your positive personality traits which should help you in communicating with others.

2. Present a three-minute speech in which you briefly define two theories of personality.

3. In an informal group define as concisely as possible what to you is the most threatening communication situation—one in which you would expect to experience speech fright—and try to explain why.

4. Make a list of all the different communication situations in which you have been engaged during a 24-hour period. Describe and evaluate the roles you played in each situation.

5. Give a five-minute speech comparing the most important differences between the roles of sender and receiver in a free and in a controlled, authoritarian society. Cite specific examples.

6. Fill out a personality or similar self-evaluation inventory, which your instructor will supply. In a private conference discuss your answers and reactions.

BIBLIOGRAPHY

Baird, A. Craig, Franklin H. Knower, and Samuel L. Becker. *General Speech Communication.* New York: McGraw-Hill, 1971.

Barnlund, Dean C. *Interpersonal Communication.* Boston: Houghton Mifflin, 1968.

Dickens, Milton. *Speech: Dynamic Communication.* New York: Harcourt, Brace, and World, 1963.

Johnson, Wendell. *Your Most Enchanted Listener.* New York: Harper, 1956.

Maslow, Abraham H. *Toward a Psychology of Being.* Princeton: D. Van Nostrand, 1962.

Overstreet, Harry A. *The Mature Mind.* New York: Norton, 1949.

Ross, Raymond S. *Speech Communication: Fundamentals and Practice.* Englewood Cliffs: Prentice Hall, 1970.

Southwell, Eugene A., and Michael Merbaum. *Personality: Reading in Theory and Research.* Belmont: Wadsworth, 1964.

4

THE EFFECTIVE USE
OF LANGUAGE

Man is a symbol-using, symbol-creating being. In speech communication he uses extensively, though usually not exclusively, his primary and most highly developed language system consisting of verbal-oral messages. Therefore, we will consider the spoken word first. At the same time, it must be clear by now that man receives and sends all kinds of messages, making use of a variety of languages or symbol systems.

In formal speaking situations the importance of oral-verbal language becomes more evident, since it is the primary means used for interaction between listeners and speakers, senders and receivers. The physical and emotional settings which help to make up a formal, public speech are quite different from those found in small groups or in dyadic communication. As a result, public speeches will be considered in a separate segment of this book. It will suffice here to point out that there is usually no opportunity for a great deal of overt response from a public-speaking audience, especially not distinguishable, individual response. Applause, brief bursts of laughter, uncomfortable shuffling of feet, or movement in the seats may provide some clues for the public speaker, but there is comparatively little direct interaction between speaker and listener.

In addition, formal speeches, even in their most conversational form, consist of more structured, preplanned, longer, verbal messages than do interactions with individuals in small groups or one-to-one situations. As a result public speaking often provides special opportunities for focusing on the effective use of language. The most important clues an audience receives from a speaker tend to be his word messages. Frequently there is no opportunity to check the information or impressions received, at least not by immediately questioning the speaker concerning a difficult point. Even a delayed question-and-answer period cannot compensate for the personal, direct interaction of two people conversing.

However, once these handicaps have been recognized, it is equally important to point out that communication with large groups of people has very positive aspects. More people can be reached in a shorter length of time. Often our participation in group activity serves as a positive reinforcing factor causing greater involvement. None of this is meant to indicate that what we say and how we say it does not matter in interpersonal communication—it does! We are merely indicating a degree of difference. Since so much depends on the word message in a public speaking situation, we will at times focus on some of the more important factors relating to a speaker's attempt to communicate verbally and orally. We begin with a definition of language, and our considerations will clearly indicate that the principles apply to a variety of communication situations.

WHAT IS LANGUAGE?

There are many types of languages, ranging from drum signals or hand signals to those used by various people in speaking. However, all languages have two fundamental things in common:

1. Languages rely on the use of symbols.
2. Languages make use of a syntactical structure relating symbols to each other.

Basic Considerations

Semanticists, linguists, psychologists, anthropologists, and others have long been fascinated by the relationship of word symbols to the things or ideas they represent. In effect, they have been interested in how man attaches *meaning* to words. Many theories have been proposed, some of which suggest that man is not capable of thinking of a given object or concept unless he has a word for it. Some have suggested that the relationship between words and things or events is so strong that the absence of a certain word may result in the absence of the thing it stands for. For instance, certain Indian tribes do not have a word for "stuttering," and indeed seem to have no stutterers.

Without going into unnecessary detail on these theories, it is safe to say that man will develop a word for any object or idea to which he needs to refer. It seems equally true that if man is made aware of the existence of an object or an idea and is given a word for it, he can recognize its existence much more easily and will feel that he can control or handle that object or idea more adequately, at least on an intellectual level. If you do not know what a wetbath spirometer is you may feel very insecure in a conversation where that term is used repeatedly. If you have seen one, however, and have seen it used in testing the human breathing capacity, you will feel less threatened.

General semanticists have provided us with certain insights into the use of words and the concept of meaning, which are summarized in the next paragraphs:

1. Tree (1) is not tree (2). Indeed every tree is different from every other tree. We need to recognize dissimilarities as well as similarities.

2. All objects change constantly, and even those who are talking about these objects and those receiving their messages are in a process of constant change. There is really no such thing as saying the same thing twice.
3. Man is capable of speaking not only of facts, physical objects or things which exist, but also of abstract ideas and things or objects which do not exist.
4. We cannot say everything about anything.
5. The symbol is not the thing for which it stands.

These general semanticists have also provided us with specific devices to help us use these concepts.

1. Index: We cannot assume that every object is like every other object simply because we call them by the same general identifying term. Instead, we might use index numbers such as (1), (2), (3) to distinguish objects with the same "name" from each other. In speaking we would need to provide individual terms which distinguish between several members of the same group or category.
2. Date: Change is probably the most consistent thing in our experience. What exists now did not exist exactly the same way an hour ago, nor will it be the same two hours later, thus a speaker should associate time concepts with the ideas he presents.
3. Hyphenate: There is a tendency to classify things as "black-or-white." Things may not be black-or-white; they exist on a continuum and thus can be shown to be "black-white," including all shades in between.
4. Use quotation marks: This is another device to delay immediate reactions which could trap a speaker into untenable positions. In effect by using quotation marks with a given term in his own mind the speaker avoids categorical statements such as good or bad, by thinking of them as "good," or "bad." Very authoritarian people may think that something "is" or "isn't" when in reality it may have elements of both in it. The statement: "This is true," puts the speaker in a position where he may have to spend all of his time proving such a claim, while stating that something is possibly true, that is, using quotation marks, "true," indicates he will at least consider other possibilities. "Oral" quotation marks are more difficult, but can be applied by emphasis or voice inflection, or by explanations of how we see the term.
5. To be continued: The "etc." following many statements may annoy grammar teachers, but it is a necessity in developing ideas in a public speech. We will never say the last thing about anything until Time itself comes to an end.

These considerations suggest that we need to learn to distinguish between *reports*, that is descriptions with a minimum of interpretation which can be varified by sense data or observation; *inferences*, which are statements about something unknown based on some known concept, thus going beyond reports; and *judgments*, which in addition introduce some specific value judgment indicating specifically how someone communicating this judgment feels about a certain object, idea, or person.

General semanticists also remind us that the word is not the thing for which it stands. If we permit words to become substitutes for things we soon begin to live in a world of primitive word-magic hoping to manipulate events, people, and ideas merely because we are in control of the words representing them. Adolf Hitler, during the final days in his Berlin command-bunker moved whole armies on his maps even though they no longer existed, and gave orders to officers who were no longer alive.

Another helpful idea is to remember the difference between the *extensional* and the *intensional* meaning of words. Intensional meaning refers to the picture we have in our heads, while extensional meaning is best represented when we point to an object such as a tree, a dog, or a cloud. Obviously, pointing is impossible when we talk about ideas or highly abstract concepts which may have no physical referent, making such concepts entirely intensional.

THE SPOKEN WORD

The oral communication situation presents some special challenges to the use of language or words. Have you ever wondered why your statements were not as effective as you wanted them to be, or why words seemed to sound so different when you used them in formal speeches rather than in day-to-day conversations?

Today we tend to stress a "natural" approach, a "conversational" style in public speaking, but these terms mean very little because what is natural to one man may not be natural to all his listeners. Furthermore, all of us know that standing before an audience somehow changes the usual conversational situation with which we are familiar. For these reasons, we need to spend adequate time and effort looking at the use of language in oral communication. Earlier in this book, the term "code" was mentioned in our discussion of communication methods. All of us have grown up using a language code almost every day but we usually do not pay very much attention to some of its features.

Why do we emphasize the spoken word as compared to written material? Language is language, according to some people. We certainly use many words in speaking which would also be included in a written report, but most of us can tell when someone makes statements which sound "written" rather than "spoken." First of all let us consider some distinctive features about vocalized-verbal communication. The spoken word came first. Any rule of grammar we now use was developed by man in accord with his observations of the effective use of spoken language. In many ways, we have put into written form what we have found to work in oral communication. Ideas which have never been tested in oral discourse may indeed remain difficult in spite of the fact that they are perfectly developed grammatically. They are abstract, or difficult to relate to readily observable features of our world, and difficult to clarify orally.

Even today, when a flood of printed matter seems to overwhelm most of us, spoken communication is used far more frequently by man than its written counterpart. Yet we tend to neglect the study of the more common activity, and often do not learn how to use words effectively in speaking. Small children serve as examples of what happens all too frequently to our mode of oral expression. They relive the history of language, learning to speak long before they learn to write. Consider how effectively, and often creatively, children express themselves, although little of that spontaneity and creativeness may remain in later life.

A CHALLENGE FOR THE SENDER

Until I ate in a Chinese restaurant I really did not know what the word "chopsticks" meant. After I had finished my first meal there, I knew what the words stood for, but I still did not know how to handle those two little wooden sticks. Even today, I can handle the word better than I can the implements, and that is one of the interesting things about language symbols. They often make things deceptively simple. I could "talk" pretty good chopsticks, even if I couldn't use them very well.

We handle words with relative ease because they are *abstractions* of larger ideas or realities. Basically, by abstraction we mean that we have to leave out details, that we use some relatively simple word which stands for another much larger, much more complex concept, or reality. The more abstract a word, the more information is left out about the thing it represents. The process of abstraction is necessary because no speaker can say everything about anything, so he abbreviates concepts. In addition, many words have no actual physical referent. For instance, carrying around the American Constitution would not make the word "liberty" any clearer. Yet, if we are to communicate through the use of words, we somehow need to relate them to our own experience, background, and ability. Only half of the process is completed when the speaker has made sure that he understands the terms he uses. Meaning has to exist also in the minds of listeners if communication is to take place.

There are at least three factors about oral communication which need careful consideration: (1) visual and vocal clues, (2) the immediacy of the spoken word, and (3) the meaning of words. The chapter on nonverbal communication is devoted to the first point. One great advantage the speaker has is the fact that people *see* as well as *hear* him. The simple combination of two written words, "You liar," leaves the meaning open to a number of possible interpretations. But when we observe that wide grin on the speaker's face while he slaps us on the back, it helps immensely in understanding what he has in mind. Gestures, facial expressions, and the speaker's total appearance offer clues which no printed page can provide unless long and laborious explanations are included. Thus, the communication of the total person assists the spoken word.

The spoken word also has an immediacy which is a vital factor in the reception and acceptance of any message. Listeners cannot readily go back to what has been said. They either understand it right now or they may never understand it. If an immediate negative impression is created because of a lack of understanding, the speaker may have difficulty in erasing it, and the entire communicative effort can be slowed down or abruptly and drastically altered.

We learn many things through the use of words. Yet, we usually learn words by the use of other words. Looking up a new word in a dictionary will illustrate the point. One word points to another, which points to another, which points to another, and finally one can hardly remember the first word he tried to look up. Most vital is the concept that words do not have an inherent meaning of their own. They are merely sound or letter combinations which possess little or no intrinsic meaning. If someone does not know the common meaning of the food we call "bread," he cannot react to the word unless there is present some visible object he can recognize.

As a result, in the oral communication situation, few if any people will search for meaning merely in the words a speaker uses. Therefore, all of the available techniques should be used to make meaning clear and to accomplish a given purpose in the allotted time. In addition, any statement we make will be interpreted by listeners on the basis of their past experience. The words "Jew" or "Negro" are not merely combinations of letters, they encompass experiences real and imagined; they trigger prejudices both for and against people to whom these terms are assigned. The speaker may have no negative feeling toward Jews at all, but his listeners will look for anything that offers them a clue as to what he "means" when he uses the term. Fortunately, most of us are well-balanced enough to keep from becoming easily disturbed by words. But all of us, at least at times, may be looking for implied meanings.

When we sit down with a book, we have some physical control over the use of the actual material we are reading; but when we are in a public speaking situation, we have much less control over the development of the total function. Most of the time, we are part of a larger audience whose reactions make us respond differently from the ways in which we would react privately. During a speech, for instance, how often have you laughed at a joke which you did not understand simply because your neighbors did? And how embarrassing was it when they nudged you and asked: "What did he say?" Normal reactions are also increased beyond habitual levels when we are part of an audience, and we find ourselves reacting much more emotionally than we would in the privacy of our own home. A good example are the loud shouts at a ball game which go virtually unnoticed because others are just as emotionally involved and such behavior is accepted in that particular situation.

WHAT DO YOU MEAN?

How many times have we listened to a confused explanation until we finally burst out with the question: "What do you mean?" When the reply came, it only added to our frustration because the speaker said: "Well, you know . . . !" Obviously, we didn't know or we wouldn't have asked. No one was using words effectively under those circumstances. How can problems of misunderstanding be decreased in public speaking situations?

Consider the Meaning Intended by the Sender.   Take a simple sentence: The sun is setting. Scientifically, the statement is nonsense. We know the sun only "appears" to be setting. But even a scientist will use that terminology in daily conversation. The reason is simple: We have decided to ignore one meaning of these words for the sake of communicating on another, more common level.

It is usually not important in a normal conversation whether the sun is really setting or whether it appears to be setting. The importance lies in the entire background of the situation in which we use the sentence. If we must be scientifically accurate, the setting sun could become a major bone of contention. In most other situations, the only disagreement may be caused by someone who uses scientific accuracy as a source for quibbling. However, we need to consider the possibility of quibbling over words when we face hostile audiences, or when we have to overcome objections. Obviously, our ideas must be much more carefully worded under such circumstances than if we present generally accepted information to a group of well-meaning peers.

Consider the Possibility of Differences between the Words Used by an Individual and his Actions. Think about another phenomenon of meaning. We constantly run into individuals like the man who says, "I think our ideas of freedom are great," but who, a few minutes later, advocates that anyone disagreeing with his view of freedom should be thrown into jail. That can be a very annoying inconsistency. All of us are able to verbalize beliefs. We might stand before an audience and emotionally whip them into a frenzy until they readily shout "yes" when we ask: "Are you with me?" However, if we expect them to die on some barricade, our plans may fail because the audience is not ready to go all the way, or never considered all the implications of what was asked of them.

Consider the Combined Use of Reason and Emotion by Man. All of man's actions result from a combination of reason and emotion and words can serve as triggers for action. As a matter of fact, the more we learn about human behavior, the more evident it becomes that we cannot really think of a dichotomy. Reason and emotion are so closely related in human experience that we can only separate them in textbooks to make some points which we consider to be important about each one individually.

Our society tends to place great value on reasoning, which already puts a value base, and thus an emotional foundation, under the reasoning processes we use. Even the statement, "Let's be reasonable!" is frequently an emotional call for agreement in spite of the culturally conditioned reminder of the great value we place on "reason."

WHAT THE VERBAL-ORAL MESSAGE SHOULD ACCOMPLISH

We usually want to bring about agreement between the words which stand for concepts or ideas in our heads and the concepts or ideas formed in our listeners' heads. At times we hope that such agreement will lead to specific actions or convictions.

Overcome Interference

That is easily said, but considering the interference of various types of noise, we have to consider some specific means of accomplishing the basic task of bringing about agreement or consonance.

At all times, sounds, heat, cold, color, and many other things interfere with what we have to say. As we develop our verbal-oral message, therefore, we need to use words and other means of communication which will counter-balance and overcome most of the effects of noise. Sometimes just speaking louder will help, or a different seating arrangement can be used to bring listeners closer to the speaker. At other times attention-getting material, or improved lighting, or the use of visual aids may make an idea clearer.

Develop Agreement

Fortunately, most human beings in a society agree sufficiently on the meaning of most words to enable us to talk to each other without constantly becoming involved in long wrangles about meaning. When we speak to someone, we intend to send him a clear message that can be received fairly closely to our original intent or is closely related to the meaning we have in mind.

Musical reproduction will illustrate the point. High fidelity recordings are closer to the original sound than earlier recordings, and stereo records and tapes copy the original sound even more adequately. We know that there are several hundred-thousand words available to us, yet in every speech in every oral communication we select only certain ones to make our points. Sometimes we have good reasons for picking one word over another, on other occasions we may not even know that other words exist. Sometimes even the *sound* of a certain word may cause us to use it again and again, or we simply fall into the habit of using a certain expression. A favorite line for President Nixon, "Now let me make that perfectly clear," has been picked up by every major cartoonist or comedian in America. A foreigner was once asked, "What is the most beautiful word in the English language?" and she replied, "Cellar-door." Under the right circumstances, a sender could have made quite an impression on that woman if he had known her preference for that particular word. Education, emotion, and previous experiences, are all closely related to the reasons behind our choices and uses of words. A speaker will certainly tend to choose words which will help him develop the overall message he has in mind, but he should not forget that words need also to be selected with the receiver in mind.

Cultural and educational factors, though always changing, play a vital role in the selection of words by speakers. Women had "legs" seventy-five years ago, but no one would have referred to them by that word in public. They were called "extremities" or "limbs." It is easy to laugh at the attitude portrayed by such word choices, yet all of us fairly bristle at certain words, and feel like purring when others are used. The point is, a sender must be aware of emotional reactions to words or the values a given audience holds or he may find it impossible to accomplish the task he has set for himself.

Words should be considered as tools which can either help or hinder our communication. If they are to help us, we need to pay attention to what people think they mean and why. A speaker cannot assume that his own reactions to words are the final standard. Anyone wishing to communicate with other human beings must be as aware as possible of those to whom he is directing his messages.

There is another trap, however. Words are not merely tools. People become attached to them because they associate them with important meanings or values.

If they did not serve some purpose, they would quickly fall into disuse. Consider the word "cool." At one time it corresponded to "detached," but to a later generation of teenagers, it had a meaning closer to "involved," and a later generation used the term to mean "acceptable." Words at times are used to prove that a certain individual is "one of the crowd," even if there is little lasting meaning to such terms. As the crowd and its needs change, words disappear and new identifications have to be found to separate another "in" crowd from what has suddenly become the "out" crowd. Word choice is an important consideration in all groups. It is easy to sneer at the strange attachments people form to words, but it must be apparent that better communication or even acceptance by a certain group will result only if we relate words sufficiently to the experiences of all concerned. One word of caution is needed. Nothing sounds more ridiculous than the sixty-year-old "teenager" who figures he can overcome the generation gap by the mere use of words.

Agreement is based on more than just words, and requires honesty, an acknowledgment of the individuality of both sender and receiver, and the continuing search for common ground which can be only imperfectly expressed by words even when they are used most effectively. That agreement also depends on the fact that the speaker really has something to say, that is, his verbal message is capable of making a contribution to the lives of his listeners.

Make Words Effective Tools

A certain sensitive awareness is called for in the use of language. A so-called expert who has difficulty in making his ideas clear to listeners is not accomplishing his purpose. He may be an expert in one field, but he certainly lacks communicative ability. Formulas and rules can be compiled, but in the long-run, a personal involvement in communication which makes us deeply aware of the needs and desires as well as the abilities of our listeners is much more important. As word usage changes, only a communicator who sees the words he uses as a part of a living, continuing process will truly communicate effectively. Such an attitude will help to do more than keep us from using antiquated language, it will enable us to use words in order to accomplish human communication, human interaction, with whatever words we use.

COMMON FUNCTIONS OF WORDS AND LANGUAGE

Alfred Korzybski, in *Science and Sanity* (1933), first pointed out that words relate to the things they represent as maps relate to an actual territory. Man constantly faces new, unknown territory, and, if he is not personally able to explore it, must rely on others for information. Words help to accomplish that purpose in oral communication.

All of us know what confusion results when we use an inaccurate or partial map. The same thing happens when we carelessly conclude that the words we have heard are an accurate map of territory with which we are not familiar. We may very well act according to the information we possess, but that does not save us from making mistakes, because our knowledge was faulty. The danger is increased if we trust words too much, or take them as substitutes for reality, or if we act consistently as if the word were the thing it stands for. When we speak to others we may be providing verbal maps of unknown territory and many of our listeners may depend entirely on the information we provide. For that reason we will consider here a few of the functions words serve for us in communicating with others.

THE FUNCTION OF WORDS

Words are symbols. In discussing the nature of words, semanticists find the term symbol helpful. It is derived from the Greek word *symbololon,* a sign by which one knows or infers a thing. To make thought possible, man is forced to use brief summaries of facts and ideas he wishes to communicate. Words serve this symbolic function for him.

Words are vehicles. If the term symbol does not adequately describe what words do for us, perhaps the term vehicle is helpful. Words convey ideas or concepts. They are not the things themselves, and meaning is not in the words themselves, but they help to convey our meaning to the receiver of our message.

Words lead to inferences and judgments. Sometimes when we ask "What do you mean by that?" the symbols or words used may be quite clear in themselves. However, we sense from the speaker's presentation that he intended to accomplish more than to communicate the obvious or dictionary meaning of his words.

For instance, the use of the word student could be serving merely a descriptive purpose or it might incorporate a speaker's belief that students can't be trusted, indicated by a facial expression or the vocal stress laid on the word. Words must be appropriate, within the framework of our culture and society. Words which are perfectly suitable for an after dinner speech may not be acceptable in a funeral oration, because they would indicate to the listener a disrespect or lack of concern on the part of the speaker. The sensitive awareness for an audience's possible inferences or judgments caused by the words used on a particular occasion help a speaker in developing his message more carefully.

Words are assigned arbitrary value by man. Certain ideas which we were previously free to discuss may be judged treasonous and detrimental during a war. This is only one indication that man is able to assign arbitrary values to many things, including words, and that he can change those values repeatedly. By common agreement, and with a certain important force backing it, a piece of metal and ribbon becomes a medal of great value. Medals are not the only symbols which can be assigned such values: words such as "honor," "justice," and "peace," have a very similar influence on man's behavior. Or consider the fact that, in order to be called "Athlete Of the Year," someone may forego many comforts and pleasures which most people would consider to be a part of a normal life. Words can stand for things that are of value to us, and thus we need to consider more than their dictionary meanings.

Words open or keep open varied channels of communication. Most of us have been angered by the person who stooped over us after we had fallen, torn our clothes, and bloodied our knees, to ask, "Did you hurt yourself?" From a simple, factual standpoint, the answer was evident. Since we were suffering pain, frustration, and perhaps humiliation by an accident which people could interpret as clumsiness, it was easy to verbally attack the questioner for such a stupid remark.

Ask yourself, "What do we really mean when we use some expressions?" If the questioner is a stranger, he has no other way of establishing a bridge of understanding and sympathy than to use words, and perhaps some limited actions. He needs to find a common basis upon which he and the injured person can establish interaction. His upbringing and his culture probably limit him rather severely in this respect. His entire training may make it seem necessary to start with some polite conversation to break the ice. If the injured person understands that, he can help the questioner move quickly to a more positive and helpful action. If he does not, the injured individual may set up even more severe barriers making it perhaps impossible to get help at all. All words, then, are not important in and of themselves. As we say, "It's really the thought that counts," or the fact that words provide bridges for later vital communication.

Words can be maps to nonexistent territories. Words not only serve as maps of existing territories, but as guides to describe something not yet in existence or which may never exist. Listeners who do not realize that the speaker is talking about something which lies in the future, or exists only in his mind, may be confused. Certainly such confusion should be clarified and *can* be cleared up, since man has the ability to relate not only to the past and present, but also to that which may yet happen, or the future.

Consider again the fact that many businessmen suffer from ulcers, resulting from worries about things which they believe will happen in the future. The results are just as painful as if they were caused by already existing problems. In reality, men worry about symbols, about *words*, because the situations have not and may never develop. Communication and the use of words for the purpose of control has been mentioned before. Our hypothetical businessmen may feel it to be very acceptable to suffer from ulcers, if they can feel assured that they have developed the right word "map" in their minds to help control some possible future event. In a way, such reactions represent a type of primitive "word magic."

SUGGESTIONS FOR USE OF VERBAL MESSAGES IN ORAL COMMUNICATION

We have taken a brief look at some of the factors about language usage in oral communication which should be helpful. Some specific suggestions should facilitate application of these principles to practical situations.

Be aware of differences between concrete and abstract, general and specific terms. Of all the characteristics of meaning, abstractness is one of the worst troublemakers. Words are assigned certain arbitrary values, similar to money. However, if for some reason we cannot "cash in" our word coins, their value to us is at best limited. We may keep them around as collector's items, but they certainly do not help us achieve their intended purpose. For instance, if you asked someone what he means by freedom, and he responds with the term "liberty," he has probably not provided you with a concept you can cash in on your own experience to help you understand the values he has in mind,. But if he tells you, "I mean that I want to be able to choose my own job, choose my own reading matter, and go to church anywhere I please!" he certainly has found some concrete means of providing an understanding of what freedom means to him. He may not have provided an indication of all he considers it to be, but he has at least provided some definite basis for exploring the question further. Usually the more concrete a word is, or the closer it is related to a known physical entity, the clearer it will be. However, the more abstract a term, the more it may tend to express a speaker's emotions or thoughts. Both means of expression are needed, as long as we understand the difference.

The use of specific or general terms must be carefully considered. At times, it may be entirely sufficient to refer to automobiles, a general term, while at other times a speaker needs to say that he is driving a Ford, using a much more specific word in order to bring about the desired reaction. That certainly would be the case if we intend to discuss a specific part found only in Ford automobiles.

Provide a variety of clues. Both the speaker and the listener must consider all factors relating to the use of words. Many different clues to different meaning may be found. It was mentioned that listeners are frequently in a much better position to understand the intention of a communicator than readers. A written passage provides only verbal clues but, in addition to words, the costume, gestures, and look on a speaker's face help us to understand what his intended meaning is. Furthermore, the mood of the meeting may provide clues. Knowing that a speaker will address a patriotic gathering on the Fourth of July provides helpful hints about the meaning of words which an audience might fail to understand under any other circumstances. The title of a speech and the arrangement and background of ideas and similar clues should be consciously provided by the speaker if he wants to be more easily understood, and listeners should be aware of them as they follow a speech.

Language does not merely consist of symbols, but also makes use of syntactical rules to govern the relationship of such symbols. Listeners tend to take

into consideration *all* the words a sender uses, and he should thus consider the meaning of words in context and not merely in isolation.

Consider the denotative and connotative meaning of words. Beyond the *denotative* or dictionary meaning there are also *connotative* or implied meanings which depend on the individual's interpretation for their meaning. The term "nut," for instance, has a number of meanings which a speaker can make clear with fairly little explanation. However, a fruit grower who has just lost a year's crop of nuts will certainly find the term much more disturbing and related to his own vital needs than a housewife to whom they may only mean part of a fruitcake, or Christmas and the other pleasant ideas related to that holiday.

Speakers lose their listeners when they go off on a sudden tangent, their thoughts re-routed by a word whose effect the speaker may not have been able to predict. Even the most cautious speaker cannot look into the deepest recesses of man's mind, but he should try to keep detours at a minimum by careful consideration of a word's connotations.

Choose simple words. The word "nut" also points to another factor. It is a small word, but it can be most expressive. It probably never occurred to you that you might refer to one of your eccentric friends as "that hazelnut!" although that is certainly a bigger, as well as more explicit word. Why not call him a "hnutu" since the dictionary tells us that this is the Anglo-Saxon term from which our word "nut" was derived? Words need to be neither big nor unknown to be impressive, forceful, or interesting. The Sermon on the Mount, the Gettysburg Address, and many other great speeches illustrate clearly the value of simple, direct words.

Define operationally, use examples. Since oral communication depends on the immediate reception of the message by a listener, the listener must be able to reconstruct ideas as closely in agreement with the meaning intended by the speaker as is possible. Many senders are sure that by defining terms they accomplish this end. Unfortunately, definitions are frequently no assurance for the creation of a more precise meaning. Operational definitions and examples which tell us what to do and what to observe, what something does, or how it works, are often much more helpful than elaborate statements used in the false hope that more words will eliminate problems of understanding.

Understand your own ideas. No sender can hope to make an idea clear to any other person if he has not first worked to understand it himself. For that reason, any good speaker will test ideas, will learn from those to whom he listens, will use the tools of research, the dictionary, books from other fields, and anything else that can assist him in formulating his concepts. Such exposure to varied ideas will also tend to help him avoid the temptation of using simple either-or choices, realizing that many more than two possible reactions may exist.

SUMMARY:
USING LANGUAGE EFFECTIVELY

Careful use of verbal messages is not trickery. It provides a sender with the means of accomplishing more adequately the task he has set himself—communicating ideas simply, clearly, accurately, completely, and meaningfully.

Words are among the best vehicles for carrying ideas and civilization could probably not continue without them.

Admittedly we can never say everything about anything, and human language is an imperfect stimulus. The simple fact is that we are stuck with it. Our very awareness of language's imperfections will help us select words more carefully, try to understand their varied meanings more adequately ourselves, and assist our listeners by as many methods as possible to make our intentions clear and effective.

Several major factors about human communication should now be understood. The human system, or organism, is in a state of constant neurophysiological readiness or arousal—at least as long as it is conscious. Responses, reactions, indeed our total behavior, are the results of internal and external stimuli. Language, especially oral-verbal language, is one symbol system which triggers behavior or response, as do objects and other symbol systems. Effective use of language results when a sender has transmitted messages which a receiver not only receives, but "checks" against the cognitive storehouse of knowledge and experience in his system. The effective message results in a manipulation of the cognitive environment of the receiver in such a way that either new input, modification of old concepts, or the strengthening of old associations within the individual human organism results. Verbal-oral stimuli are among the most important means available to man in his attempts to change the behavior of other men, or, in the larger sense, to control his environment.

EXERCISES

1. Assign five students in your class to read the same newspaper report. Have a 25-minute discussion to see if you agree on all the material and implications of the report. Open the discussion to the class after completing the first sequence.

2. Take a newspaper editorial, underline all specific (as opposed to general) statements in red, and underline all concrete (as opposed to abstract) statements in blue. Evaluate your findings in a 300-500-word written report.

3. Give an eight-minute informative speech based on your own research, explaining semantics and its major principles to an imaginary group of ten-year-olds.

4. Give a five-minute speech dealing with instances of people being exploited because of value terms which we associate with "good," "beneficial," or "advantageous" concepts as, for example, in advertising. Use visual aids.

5. Show your class a series of five pictures in rapid succession. Follow this by a discussion with the entire class of the things they saw—or didn't see. With the help of your classmates, try to determine why they reacted as they did.

6. Check the indexes of several books dealing with general semantics and do some research on the meaning and use of the term "two-valued orientation." Give a three-minute report in class concerning your findings.

BIBLIOGRAPHY

Alexander, Hubert G. *Language and Thinking*. Princeton, New Jersey: D. Van Nostrand, 1967.

Allport, Gordon W. "A Five-Volume Shelf about a Sickness of Individuals and Society: Prejudice." *Scientific American* 182 (June 1950): 56–58.

Alston, William P. *Philosophy of Language*. Englewood Cliffs: Prentice-Hall, 1967.

Beardsley, Monroe C. *Thinking Straight*. Englewood Cliffs: Prentice-Hall, 1966.

Chase, Stuart. *The Tyranny of Words*. New York: Harcourt, Brace, 1938.

DeCecco, John P. *The Psychology of Language, Thought, and Instruction*. New York: Holt, Rinehart and Winston, 1966.

Fishbein, Martin. "An Investigation of the Relationships between Beliefs About an Object and the Attitude Toward that Object." *Human Relations* 16 (August 1963): 233–39.

Hayakawa, S. I. *Language in Thought and Action*. New York: Harcourt, Brace and World, 1972.

Johnson, Wendell. *People in Quandaries*. New York and London: Harper, 1946.

————. *Your Most Enchanted Listener*. New York: Harper and Row, 1956.

Korzybski, Alfred. *Science and Sanity*. Lancaster, Conn.: Institute of General Semantics, 1958.

Lee, Irving J. *How to Talk with People*. New York: Harper and Row, 1952.

————. *Language Habits in Human Affairs*. New York: Harper and Row, 1941.

Nichols, Ralph G., and Leonard A. Stevens. *Are You Listening?* New York: McGraw-Hill, 1957.

Ogden, C. K. and I. A. Richards. *The Meaning of Meaning*. New York: Harcourt, Brace, 1936.

Osgood, C. "The Nature and Measurement of Meaning." *Psychological Bulletin* 49 (May 1952): 197–237.

————. "Report on Development and Application of the Semantic Differential." Urbana, Illinois: Institute of Communications Research and Department of Psychology, University of Illinois.

Rapoport, Anatol. "Semantics: The Problem of Meaning." In *American Philosophy*, ed. Ralph B. Winn. New York: Philosophical Library, 1955.

Ullman, Stephen. *Semantics: An Introduction to the Science of Meaning*. New York: Barnes and Noble, 1962.

5

BEYOND THE SPOKEN WORD

The idea we need to keep in mind as we continue our study of human communication is this: Communication is a process, and as we look at its parts it is important that we do not forget the close interrelationship of all its components. For our study we will think of nonverbal communication in the broadest sense possible, defining it as all communication other than vocalized language symbols or spoken words. This chapter will deal with types of messages which differ from the oral-verbal messages discussed and defined earlier.

NONVOCAL OR NONVERBAL?

A number of scholars have pointed out that we have confused the use of the terms verbal and vocal. Dance explained the difference in some detail, but for our purposes a brief summary will suffice.[1]

Any message making use of words, whether it is a written or spoken message, can be identified as verbal. A vocalized-verbal message consists of spoken words, a nonvocalized verbal message is made up of written material. By the same token it is possible to vocalize, or produce sound, to communicate meaning without using formalized language or words.

Verbal communication is a part of any thought process which involves identification or interpretation. Responses to objects in any communicative framework require use of words and thus include some aspects of verbal communication as defined above. Few instances of truly nonverbal communication

---

1. Frank E. X. Dance, "Toward a Theory of Human Communication," in *Human Communication Theory* (New York: Holt-Rinehart and Winston, 1967), p. 290.

emerge, but many communicative situations are not dependent on sound or vocalization. Holding up a banner with the word P E A C E spelled out on it obviously makes use of language symbols, words, and thus it is verbal communication. Our confusion, as the dictionary points out, results from using the term verbal as if it had the same meaning as oral.

There may be some physical reactions which make no use of symbolic-language interpretation processes, but most of the time words and other factors are so closely interlinked in the process that any distinctions between verbal and nonverbal communication become highly arbitrary. The cry of a human being in complete terror, or someone dying a violent death, illustrates dramatically a purely physical nonverbalized vocal reaction. In such cases there will rarely be any verbalization, that is, no distinguishable word symbols will be heard. The emotional experience of terror may even be so great that no symbolization, no interpretation, or thought pattern can emerge. But there is vocalization, there is a sound, which can easily be interpreted as a response caused by fear or pain.

For these reasons a distinction between vocalized and nonvocalized, in addition to verbal and nonverbal, communication is helpful. As a result we will be able to consider vocalized communication which makes use of verbal language symbols or words, and vocalized behavior which does not use symbols but only sounds. There is also verbal communication through the use of words without vocalization, as in written messages.

One final point needs to be made while we are defining basic concepts. It is difficult to conceive of any human oral, vocalized interaction without some form of nonverbal, nonvocalized communication accompanying it. Man will observe other men with whom he communicates, or he will get clues from the voice of someone to whom he is speaking but whom he cannot see. The physical setting in which we send and receive will influence our interactions, and even instruments we use for communication will exert an influence on the total process. There is always some sort of nonverbal communication going on while we communicate orally.

INTERPRETING NONVERBAL COMMUNICATION

Age

There are at least three concepts which deserve our attention. Age is of major importance. Very small children react to any sudden noise in the same way, with fear and crying. It is only with age that they learn to make distinctions between what is an "acceptable" or "safe" noise, and what is a "dangerous" noise. Later in life they may organize that noise into music, and in spite of the fact that it may reach noise levels where it produces physical pain, peer pressure, physical enjoyment, and other factors will be used to interpret the event as "music" and as something which is "fun." Flashing lights, movement and other physical factors will produce a similar neurophysiological response in small children with a minimum of symbolic interpretation taking place.

As we grow older our primary groups, such as our family and peers, will begin to shape a conceptual framework for us. We will no longer react only on a neurophysiological basis but we will begin to interpret events and make culturally acceptable responses to them. "Boys don't cry," even if it hurts, in most of Western culture. Certain physical sensations may be pleasurable, but because of social pressures we will vocalize them as being inappropriate or unacceptable.

Cultural Background

As we grow older secondary groups, including larger segments of our society, and our culture exert a stronger and stronger influence, causing us to react in ways which are "normal," "predictable," in agreement with readily identifiable norms. The vast number of possible responses based on the vast number of potential contacts with other human beings makes it necessary to develop standardized norms of nonverbal communication which require only a minimum of "on-the-spot" interpretation.

Once a child has been taught by his culture, or perhaps one could say, once most of his behavior-patterns have been programmed in accordance with certain cultural norms, there is little originality or personalized response left in most human interaction. Culturally developed standards or norms of nonverbal communication differ so dramatically from culture to culture that most students of such concepts agree that no nonverbal communication symbol is completely the same for all cultures.

On the other hand, certain nonverbal behavior seems to be strictly on a neurophysiological, noninterpreted level and can be recognized by members of other cultures. If we can observe nonstaged, nonplanned responses to physical pain, for instance, we should be able to recognize the nonverbal responses across cultural boundaries. However, it is safe to assume that the physical stimulus has to be intense. The older the person gets the more deeply cultural norms have been ingrained in him, and prevent any kind of interpretation which does not result in a culturally acceptable response. Pain which can be controlled, and thus can be nonverbally interpreted into the message, "I can handle it. See, I am in control of myself," would not fit this kind of intercultural communicative behavior.

Physical Acuity, Physical Contact

This is the third factor fundamental to the reception and interpretation of nonverbal communication. A man who is almost blind will find colors dimmed, outlines indistinct, and even sudden flashes of light which might produce strong physical responses in others produce a much less intense response in him.

The same is true of hearing. Someone who is almost deaf might hear only a slight popping noise when a gun discharges. Another human being with near perfect hearing will be startled, perhaps even frightened, by the sound which has great physical impact on him, and which by sheer volume he interprets as a possibly dangerous event.

Drugs and medication have the same effect of cutting down on the acuity of our reception, as do extreme fatigue or other physical factors, such as severe pain, which might interfere with the reception of nonverbal stimuli. Of course, the same would be true in the case of the word messages we hear. All of us respond differently at different times, depending on how closely we are in contact with communication stimuli and how well our physiological and neurological systems are capable of responding.

FUNCTIONS OF NONVERBAL COMMUNICATION

Knapp very adequately summarizes the major influences nonverbal communication exerts, especially as it is used in support of verbal, vocalized interaction.[2]

Repetition

Cooking demonstrations on television illustrate this concept. After the actual demonstration of the preparation of a certain dish, a list or chart is flashed on the screen to allow the viewer to see the entire process outlined in verbal, nonvocalized form once more. This serves as a positive means of reinforcing the information.

Contradiction

Our actions often speak louder than words. An employer may hear one of his employees stating with seemingly great enthusiasm: "I think that's a great idea, J. B.!" But the agonized look on the face of the employee tells his boss that the actual attitude toward his idea is very different from the vocalized statement he heard.

Substitution

At times a physical act takes the place of verbal, vocalized interaction. The man who storms into your room and knocks you down does not have to say a single word to make you understand that he has some sort of negative feeling toward you.

Compliment

Much of our nonverbal, nonvocalized, and vocalized behavior is an attempt to add some meaningful additional information to help human interaction. Background music, candlelight and a special dinner are signals to a husband that something special is happening. Political rallies make use of music, singing, banners, bunting, signs waving (this includes actually *two* kinds of nonverbal communication, the verbal message printed on the signs, and the nonverbal, nonvocalized action of waving the posters), girls in short skirts, supporters wearing buttons with the name of their favorite candidate, and other similar nonverbal or nonoral means of assisting in the process of selecting a candidate.

---

2. Mark L. Knapp, *Nonverbal Communication in Human Interaction* (New York: Holt, Rinehart and Winston, 1972), pp. 9–12.

Church services include such things as the robes of the minister, the quiet of the assembly, kneeling, and an altar to support the vocalized message indicating that something holy or spiritual is taking place.

Accent

All of us have at times become so involved in a subject that we struck a desk or podium to underline the point we were making. Many men develop easily identifiable means of nonverbal communication to assure that others understand their concern with a given point. President Kennedy's hand movements were distinct, and most other political speakers either by leaning forward into an audience, by making a sweeping hand movement or similar actions, will support a verbal-vocalized point they have made.

A final category used by Knapp could easily be included under one of the above headings. He refers to it as "relating and regulating." It is basically a feedback function which encourages a reaction. These signals tend to help individuals enter a conversation or discourage them from speaking by a nod, frown, or smile, for instance.

TYPES OF NONVERBAL COMMUNICATION

Beginning with the broadest concept, we have to realize that our environment provides a large number of nonverbal factors in human interaction. We seek out a certain spot because it is "quiet," "we can think there," "it is beautiful," "it is romantic." Trees, water, the fragrance of flowers, colors, and temperature help to provide natural settings for us. Human beings, possibly with the assistance of interior decorators, also create such settings for themselves to work, play, and live in. We respond to colors by becoming relaxed or more tense, some types of furniture are "heavy," others "light," some are "masculine," others "feminine." The highest compliment for an outstanding homemaker may be the phrase, "This room is really you." Again, you should note that in all of these cases verbal communication, that is, word messages, were used for purposes of assigning and interpreting meaning.

Within the environment there are specific objects which assist in communication. The interior decorator has to find a specific chair, a lamp, a drape, a painting to create the setting he is working for. If the total message is well developed, observers will pay little attention to detail, at least at first. The overall effect is pleasant or unpleasant, and the message is so strongly integrated that we tend to ignore its parts. At other times such objects become focal points. A peace symbol or a fish symbol on a necklace, especially if it seems incongruous or unrelated to the rest of the clothes an individual is wearing, carries a message to anyone who knows its meaning. However, the response that such a symbol is "beautiful," or that it is "an unusual design" may represent interaction—even if the receiver didn't get the point, or didn't understand the intended meaning of the symbol.

Organizations have consistently developed objects to assist in human interaction. Party buttons, the cross, flags, wedding bands, and myriad other objects are nonverbal means of communicating messages such as: He is one of us. Hands off. We are enemies.

Some nonverbal communication occurs when we have physical contact with other human beings. While that term may be interpreted as being very positive, we should include physical touches of any kind, such as blows, beatings, striking someone, as well as holding or restraining another individual. Touching another individual indicates a fairly close or strong relationship, or a message which is considered to be vital enough to intrude on someone else's personal world as represented by his body. Depending on how private the individual is, and the kind of physical contact, a touch could be interpreted as being nearly meaningless if touching is a frequent experience, or very meaningful in the case of the individual who either craves to be touched or considers touching a violent intrusion on his privacy.

Appearance also is involved in human interaction. Clothes are the most clearly developed system of appearance for man to express feelings, attitudes, and values in a consistent pattern. When we relax we tend to indicate that fact by the comfortable clothes we wear. Formal occasions require that we wear a tie, or even a dinner jacket. Too much make-up may cause some people to pass a moral judgment on a given woman. We judge individuals' tastes and their feeling for what is appropriate by their clothes and their overall appearance. It must be stressed here that first impressions are vital to many human beings. True, we may "grow" on someone if they just get to know us; but such growth takes time, often more time than we are able to give to another individual.

Numerous stories have been told about American presidents who were mistaken for gardeners, ordinary fishermen, etc., simply because their appearance at the time was not that of a president. Such misunderstandings can be funny, or they can be tragic if an individual feels ridiculous, rejected, or unworthy. Sometimes physical disabilities need to be considered under this heading. A paralysis of the face is part of appearance. If it draws the victim's mouth into a consistent smirk, many individuals who come in contact with him will find it difficult to make a distinction between a voluntary, momentary physical activity and constant appearance.

Voluntary physical activity, gestures, body motion—many terms could be found to identify the kind of nonverbal behavior most of us think of first when we discuss this subject. In verbal-vocalized interaction, gestures or motions, eye contact, movement, stance, crossing the legs, hiding hands, or such annoying habits as playing with coins in your pocket when you speak, and twirling a pencil, come under this heading. These are things which we can "turn on" or "turn off" at will. At times we are not aware of what we are doing but a look or statement from the receiver may quickly make us aware of the nonverbal message we are sending and cause us to change our physical behavior. These physical actions do help a receiver in understanding or interpreting the verbal-vocalized messages he receives.

We expect an individual to be in a different state of tension or nontension while having an after-work drink in his local pub than when he is sitting in a witness chair in court. His physical behavior will be influenced by this state of relaxation or tension. Some observers have suggested that the rapid crossing of legs or shuffling of feet may be controlled behavior of what in childhood would have resulted in a swift kick at an offending object or person. We interpret someone's dejection or tiredness from slumping shoulders or a shuffling walk.

We should note, however, that various attitudes can be expressed by very similar physical behavior. A furrowed brow could mean anger or deep thought. A shuffling walk could mean dejection or be part of a teenager's "pouting" behavior.

The more frequently we are exposed to an individual's physical activity, and the more that verbal, vocalized or nonvocalized interaction accompanies it, the clearer the message becomes. Few brothers attempting to enter their sisters' rooms could miss the intended meaning when they are greeted at the door with a scowl, and a finger pointing at a sign on the door which reads: STAY OUT! THIS MEANS YOU!!!

NONVERBAL COMMUNICATION IN PUBLIC SPEAKING

In formal speaking situations nonverbal communication by means of physical activity is important to the speaker because it enables him to accomplish at least two things:

1. It helps to get rid of tension, or to work off excess energy which could result in more tension, and finally speech fright.
2. It helps to impress an audience with the importance of certain ideas by serving as a means of illustrating, emphasizing, or visualizing parts of a speech.

Types

A speaker who is strongly involved in, or concerned with, a subject will find it difficult not to add at least a vigorous nod or some rapidly changing facial expressions to his presentation of ideas, but even more subtle messages are relayed to the audience by the entire "set," the muscle tone, and state of overall tension

of the speaker. As a result it may be helpful to distinguish between two types
of "body language":

1. *Overt* which is readily observable and easy to describe or identify, such
   as a clenched fist, or a sweep of the hand.
2. *Covert* activity, which is much more difficult to define because it really
   refers to the total muscle tone, the physical attitude or state of health
   which causes the speaker to miss timing slightly or be less vigorous
   than one would normally expect. These are clues which tell us that
   a speaker may not really be as interested in his subject as he would
   like us to believe. Again, it is the total man communicating, and his
   attitudes, fears and emotions have a strong bearing on how he acts when
   he stands before an audience.

Within our cultural framework there are specific types of physical activity
which support vocalized message.

1. *Gestures*, or movement of any part but not all of the body, such as
   hands, arms, or the head.
2. *Movement*, involving all of the body, such as walking toward anyone
   receiving the message.
3. *Facial Expressions*, such as smiling, frowning, or raising eyebrows.
4. *Eye-Contact*, which enables the sender to keep up with his receiver's
   reactions, and vice versa, making interaction more meaningful.
5. *Posture* also serves as a signal. A slouchy posture may indicate an "I
   don't care" attitude.

Effective Use

Physical activity supports vocalized messages because it is:

1. *Timed.* As a result of spontaneous reactions by the speaker to the thoughts
   he is developing, physical activity does not occur too late or too soon.
2. *Coordinated.* Physical activity is not stiff or awkward. In effect it is
   expressive of usual physical responses, at least as far as types and amount
   of activity are concerned, and thus it appears to be a natural part of
   the message.
3. *Definite.* The appearance of awkwardness is avoided by making all bodily
   activity as direct and definite as possible. A receiver should never be
   left in doubt as to the intent of the sender. One way to assure definite
   communication is to make all activity lively and forceful. Physical
   activity in support of the vocalized message can add to the feeling of
   empathy, the close sharing of the total communication situation by those
   involved.

PHYSICAL ASPECTS OF NONVERBAL COMMUNICATION

Size

This is a vital factor in nonverbal communication. Large posters, or life-size
pictures, are more readily identifiable than small, post-card–sized pictures. A

small diamond engagement ring, although appreciated, carries a different message, as far as the young man's financial status is concerned, from the "big rock" a millionaire presents to his wife. Large audiences require large gestures. The magnificence of mountains and the relationship man feels to them are partly the results of their overwhelming size. On the other hand miniatures have their own attractions because of their daintiness and tiny detail.

Definiteness

Try this gesture-vocalized message combination: "I am going upstairs!" As you make the statement, vaguely point up while saying the first three words and drop your hand sharply and definitely on the last word. The two messages, vocalized and nonverbal, are obviously confusing. Where *are* you going? Where you *say* you are going? Or where you are *pointing?*

Appropriateness

A tuxedo looks great at a dinner party, it looks strange at 10:00 A. M. if you are riding your bicycle down a busy street. Many valued symbols, such as a flag or the cross, seem to be out of place if they are not found in their usual settings. A dress or a beachbag made out of the American flag causes resentment from some observers who feel the flag is being desecrated. A cross used as a doorstop causes some people to feel that the symbol is not being shown proper respect.

ORAL CLUES IN VERBAL-VOCALIZED COMMUNICATION

How often have you called a friend on the phone, and after only a few words found yourself saying something like: "What's the matter? Something wrong?" The human voice is a remarkably flexible communication instrument, and all of us have learned over years of experience to recognize even subtle changes which indicate anger, tension, happiness, or contentment. We can tell that someone is rushed and would rather bring the conversation to an end. In most instances our reactions are the result of very subtle, difficult to identify clues. At other times a loud voice portraying anger gives us very definite clues. In many situations, especially in public speaking or in formal interviews, we need to recognize the fact that people with whom we are interacting do pick up clues from our use of voice and diction. In order to prevent interference with the message we intend to communicate, we should consider the use of the human voice in some detail. Certain oral, vocal, vocalized verbal clues provide us with many bases for reactions. A Southern dialect or a French dialect may very well influence our attitude toward the sender, especially if we have categorized it as being "charming," a value judgment which may carry over to the speaker and his message. Incorrect usage of words may make us doubt that a person being interviewed is suited for a given position. Nervousness, indicated by the fact that a sender speaks too fast, also may be interpreted negatively by the receiver.

These and other aspects are under our control and we can use them positively to make the message more meaningful and more easily understood. We can avoid letting bad habits or lack of control create the wrong impression of our ability or our desire to communicate with another individual. At times it isn't so much the words we use as HOW we use them, it isn't the dictionary meaning we can assign to certain terms, but the subtleties of inflection, rate, pitch, or force which carry the "real" message.

Voice and Diction in Oral Communication

As is the case with all categories of prescriptive definitions, you will think of examples which appear to defy the rules provided in this segment. For instance, singer Eartha Kitt and actor Andy Devine have very "unusual" voices and yet have gained popularity. It is safe to say that we do not really know when a combination of the factors listed here hinders your interaction with others, but we do know that there comes a point when they combine in such a way to keep you from accomplishing your communication purpose.

The standards an audience or an individual considers important will decide the reaction to whatever peculiar speaking habits a sender might have. If these habits keep him from achieving his purpose, he should seriously consider changing them. Otherwise, two things might happen: Those listening either may not receive all the information the sender wants them to have, or if they receive the information, their emotional reactions to a speaker's voice or diction may keep them from responding in accordance with his purpose. In either case, he has hindered the communication's process. Some of these reactions are so automatic and immediate that a listener may not even be aware of them, and the speaker may also recognize them too late. In our society certain emotional states are associated very closely with types of delivery or voice quality. For instance, it is difficult for a sender to elicit an energetic or vigorous response from an audience if his delivery is lackluster and low-key. Speech is a learned activity, and we may learn to do it poorly or learn to do it well.

Few things about us are so typically our own, so much an indication of what we feel, so much a clue to our background, as our voices. Voice prints are now being used for personal identification in court cases, similar to the way in which fingerprints have been used for years. Millions recognized President Kennedy not only because of his New England accent, but because of the pitch of his voice, its resonance, and its typical inflections which even made it distinguishable from the similar voices of his brothers. In a room full of people, with conversations being carried on all around you, you will nevertheless be able to distinguish the voice of someone you have been waiting or looking for.

We feel emotionally involved when hearing someone speak whose voice portrays depth of feeling. We also, almost unconsciously, find ourselves rejecting the obviously studied and false sound in the voice of someone simulating an emotion. Some of our habits are good and should be developed even further. Other habits are bad and can be replaced by better ones to make communication effective. If we have learned to use our voices in an ineffective way it will take work to overcome the habits of many years.

Qualities of the Effective Voice

Two factors are probably the most vital in making the voice an effective instrument: audibility and variety.

Audibility basically refers to the appropriate use of force. Adequate force is the direct result of an adequate breath supply, not of strain or the raising of pitch. Good resonance is also necessary if a speaker's voice is to be easily audible. Flat, lifeless sounds do not carry well and thus hinder reception. Resonators such as the nasal cavity, the throat, and the sinuses can be adjusted within the limits of any given individual, providing great variety of depth and mellowness. The relationship of distance to loudness or intensity of the voice is geometric. That means that without electronic assistance, we will have to use sixteen times the force at four times an increase of distance from a sender. While some of this problem has been overcome through the use of public address systems, there are still many situations in which such assistance may not be available to the speaker.

Nothing makes it more difficult for any receiver to pay close attention to a sender than a repetitious, monotonous pattern of delivery. Change is a vital factor in our lives. Varied, moving, unusual things catch our attention. However, change for the sake of change is ridiculous and confusing when one considers the human voice. Some comedians have made a career out of routines which made extensive use of this fact. Consider, for example, the confusion which might result if a sentence is ended on a strong rising inflection, indicating a question, when actually the speaker had in mind a forceful, declarative statement. "I am going to town?"—"I am going to town!" Suppose your instructor said, "You are a good student!" Now read the same statement with a strong rising inflection indicating a question, "You are a good student?" The difference in meaning derived from just one change of inflection is indicative of the many clues our voices can provide.

Changes in voice should be a result of a change of attitude, change of thought, or controlled emphasis by the speaker. Such controlled changes become clues to the meaning a sender associates with any given statement, or otherwise they become a hindrance to his overall effort. The four major areas in which controlled change or variety is possible are: rate, pitch, force, and quality.

Rate refers to the speed of delivery, and three major factors should be considered in its careful use:

1. The number of words per minute. The number of words per minute should be regulated in accordance with the size of the audience and physical obstacles. One or a few people at a close distance, all of whom can hear well, can easily follow a fast rate, especially if the subject and the words are simple. Larger audiences are usually far away from the speaker and inadequate public address or other electronic transmission systems, coupled with a difficult subject or a complex vocabulary, may result in the necessity of using a slower rate, adjusted to these difficulties. A sportscaster reporting an exciting ball game or a forceful news reporter probably will speed up their delivery. As long as the sender can be clearly understood, and as long as he avoids a repetitious pattern, the number of words per minute may very well be increased

or decreased as one means of individual expression. Don't forget, although a certain pattern may be the trademark of a famous newscaster, it could be disastrous to someone else who copies it because he considers it to be impressive.

2. The number and position of pauses. Public speakers may be as afraid of saying nothing for a second or a fraction of a second as they are of the speech itself. Pauses are natural. Moments for thought and the consideration of any important ideas are necessary and appreciated by any receiver, and in conversations they usually become a natural part of interaction. The concept of variety requires that we use every available means of reinforcing an idea, and there is no better way of doing this than to set off a vital concept by pausing. One of the most common mistakes made by public speakers and those who read material orally is the use of too great a speed, or rate. Pauses can assist in slowing down the rate of delivery in formal speeches.

3. The duration of each speech sound, or the length of syllables, obviously also affect the rate of our delivery. A very clipped, choppy style of speaking develops when speech sounds are not given their proper duration.

Pitch is the lowness or highness of voice, as one would identify a note to be high or low on the musical scale. Variations in pitch result from the number of vibrations of the vocal folds located in the larynx. The greater the number, the higher the pitch. It is well to remember that major variations from your normal pitch may cause damage to your voice. Our society tends to identify low voices as being "masculine," high voices as "feminine." Thus we may subconsciously or consciously attempt to modify our pitch beyond our normal range to fit into the cultural norm for our sex. When that happens the constant strain may actually thicken our vocal folds or cause them to become sore and inflamed resulting in laryngitis.

Again, flexibility is the key word. Since tension or strain cause pitch to rise in everyday life, it is only reasonable for listeners to conclude from the rising pitch of a speaker's voice that he is angry or tense. Lower pitch, a deeper and more resonant voice, on the other hand, give the impression of thoughtfulness, relaxation, or quietness of spirit. The most frequent changes in pitch are an abrupt step up or down from one pitch level to another, or a continuous glide from one pitch level to another similar to the wailing of a siren.

Force is related to the number of people with whom we are communicating. The same amount of force which was adequate in addressing an outdoor rally would appear ridiculous in a small room with few people. Too much force may actually cause a listener as much trouble in understanding as does the use of too little.

Greater force or volume can be applied in different ways and again should be used to indicate the attitude of the speaker. A sudden shout in the middle of a political speech at a noisy rally is more meaningful and acceptable. A gradual increase in force to a vocal climax, on the other hand, may be much better suited to a persuasive plea for support in a face-to-face dyadic situation. Sometimes this stress may be put on a single word or even part of a word, at other times an entire section of a speech may gradually build up to a vocal climax.

Too much force, and too much change in any of the variable aspects of the voice can be as bad as too little. Meaningful use of these attributes of the voice, never the mere change for the sake of change, is vital.

Quality is another frequently used term. Basically it refers to the overall reaction a listener has to someone's voice. Good quality most frequently results from a proper balance of force and resonance. Many of these unpleasant qualities we notice, such as breathiness, harshness, or stridency, are directly related to poor or inadequate use of the human speech mechanism.

Poor control of the outgoing breath stream, shallow breathing, and tension, particularly in the area of the neck, cause thin, reedy voices, lack of force, and cracking, husky voices. Because you have lived with it for so long, it is difficult for you to evaluate your own voice properly. That is why all of us need to remember the reactions of those who listen to us. The interpretations receivers put on what they hear are vital to the eventual success of any message. Many individuals have worked hard to improve their voices because they realized that listeners rely on the voice as one point of reference to interpret messages.

Diction

When correct articulation, enunciation, and pronunciation are combined, we say that diction is good. Coupled with a voice that has no other defects it will make for clarity of oral expression. No one speech defect, problem of articulation, or difficulty in delivery causes a receiver to reject either the sender, his message, or both. However, a combination of various factors makes communication much more difficult or even ineffective. If it is impossible to understand words clearly and easily, an additional strain is put on the receiver. Both understanding and good will may suffer in that kind of situation. Various concepts can be included under the umbrella of diction, although distinctions between subheadings such as articulation and enunciation, and sometimes pronunciation, are not always clear. The following brief definitions may help you in using or understanding these terms.

> *Pronunciation.* When we speak of difficult words, we usually mean that we don't know how to pronounce them. There are careless pronunciation mistakes, such as saying "pitcher" for "picture," or problems with uncommon words such as niche.
>
> *Articulation.* Basically this refers to the adequate use of our modifiers or articulators. They are the flexible parts of our speech mechanism such as the tongue, lips, teeth, soft palate and jaw, which help us to speak distinctly. Swallowed word endings and indistinct initial sounds are the result of poor or lazy use of the articulators. "En" instead of "end," "goin" instead of "going," are two examples of poor articulation.
>
> *Enunciation.* A confusion of speech sounds often results in poor enunciation. For instance, many people do not clearly distinguish between the following series of words: "pin," "pen," "pan," "pawn."

As you know there are many words in the English language which are very close in pronunciation or enunciation, but whose meanings are very different. Thus, it becomes rather difficult, from the standpoint of meaning, to write with a "pin," although everyone will understand from the context of your statement, "I am going to write" what you mean. However, if you turned to someone and asked, "Would you hand me that pin?" only a finger pointing in the direction of the desired writing instrument will prevent confusion.

Overcoming the habits of a lazy tongue, a frozen jaw, a mushy-mouth, or lazy lips takes effort. There is usually an emotional block because the new way of saying things just doesn't seem "to sound right." At first, any attempt to speak more carefully and accurately sounds stilted and formal. We haven't worn in the new "groove." After a few weeks or months the new habits will take the place of the old ones and any stiltedness will disappear.

SUMMARY

Oral communication involves a combination of factors which interact to produce desired results. Some of those factors are nonverbal messages, both vocalized and not vocalized. Probably the most frequent type of nonverbal clues we use in oral interaction are those provided by physical appearance and body movements.

Clues can be misinterpreted, and the messages we receive from both verbal and nonverbal communications may lead to wrong conclusions. However, through many years of preparation all of us learn to recognize at least the overt, culturally "normed," nonverbal messages, and we use them in agreement with the standards generally applied by our society.

The function of nonverbal messages is either to support or replace oral messages. However, currently available evidence indicates that to be communicative, messages require some sort of interpretation, categorization, and interaction. Our language system provides the most common means of accomplishing these tasks, and thus virtually all communication tends also to be verbal, that is it makes use of words in speaking, writing, or in the interpretation of those stimuli we perceive and interpret as we hear, read, see, or feel.

Understanding the place of environmental factors, including specially designed objects or symbols, helps in the effective communicative interaction of human beings. Many successful sales or political campaigns have resulted from careful use of even one special factor, such as color or the location of rallies.

Reception of a message is a prerequisite if communication is to take place. Reception of a message, however, depends to a large extent on the adequate use of the sending mechanism. In the case of man, his voice is the basic instrument or tool for the effective oral transmission of a message.

Audibility, distinctness, and a flexible use of the speech mechanism to express a variety of meanings can be improved through learning. Communication can be more effective if all the aspects discussed in this chapter are used by man in his communicative efforts in a meaningful interaction of verbal and nonverbal clues.

EXERCISES

1. Attend a political rally or a church service and make as complete a list as possible of the nonverbal factors involved in that communication situation. Distinguish between those factors which served as positive reinforcement to the intended

message, and those which contributed negatively. Distinguish between those factors which were planned to contribute positively to the effectiveness of the message, and those which were either not planned or were not under the control of those responsible for the communication of the intended message, or the overall purpose of the meeting. Write a 500-word paper critically analyzing your findings.

2. Watch an interview and concentrate on the person being interviewed.Note as many of the physical actions in which the interviewee engages as possible. List them under two headings: physical activity while speaking; physical activity while listening. Are you able to find any pattern, any repeated activity? What clues did you pick up concerning the feelings or attitudes of the interviewee? Using the categories developed in this chapter, for what purpose or purposes were these physical activities used? Write a 500-word analysis.

3. In a five-minute speech discuss types and functions of objects developed by some group or organization with which you are familiar. Stress the use of these objects for purposes of nonverbal communication.

4. Develop a five-minute oral presentation, making use of visual aids, dealing with nonverbal communication clues resulting from facial expressions. One subject could center around smiling as a nonverbal response, making extensive use of pictures of smiling individuals from various cultures. Use background information from authors who deal with the subject of the ability to interpret facial expressions or other nonverbal clues across cultural divisions.

5. Develop a rating chart, including the major factors concerning the voice discussed in this chapter, such as rate, force, pitch, etc. Distribute this chart to your classmates prior to your next oral presentation in class and ask them to rate you. Evaluate the weaknesses and strengths noted by your classmates in a 300-word paper.

BIBLIOGRAPHY

Bronstein, A. J. and B. F. Jacoby. *Your Speech and Voice.* New York: Random House, 1966.

Curry, E. T. "The Pitch Characteristics of the Adolescent Male Voice." *Speech Monographs* 7 (1940): 48–62.

Dance, Frank E. X. and Carl E. Larson. *Speech Communication: Concepts and Behavior.* New York: Holt, Rinehart, and Winston, 1972.

Fairbanks, G., and L. W. Hoaglin. "An Experimental Study of the Durational Characteristics of the Voice During the Expression of Emotion." *Speech Monographs* 8 (1941): 85–90.

Fast, Julius. *Body Language.* New York: M. Evans, 1970.

Fisher, Hilda B. *Improving Voice and Articulation.* Boston: Houghton-Mifflin, 1966.

Hahn, Elise, Donald E. Hargis, Charles W. Lomas, and Daniel Vandaegen. *Basic Voice Training for Speech.* New York: McGraw-Hill, 1957.

Hall, Edward T. *The Silent Language.* New York: Doubleday, 1959.

Hicks, Helen Gertrude. *Voice and Speech for Effective Communication.* Dubuque: William C. Brown, 1963.

Knapp, Mark L. *Non-verbal Communication in Human Interaction.* New York: Holt, Rinehart, and Winston, 1972.

McCroskey, James C., Carl E. Larson, and Mark L. Knapp. *An Introduction to Interpersonal Communication.* Englewood Cliffs: Prentice-Hall, 1971. Chapter 6.

Ogilvie, Mardel, and Norma S. Rees. *Communication Skills: Voice and Pronunciation.* New York: McGraw-Hill, 1970.

Ortleb, R. "An Objective Study of Emphasis in Oral Reading of Emotional and Unemotional Material." *Speech Monographs* 4 (1937): 56–68.

Pronovost, Wilbert. "An Experimental Study of Methods for Determining Natural and Habitual Pitch." *Speech Monographs* 9 (1942): 111–23.

Simley, Anne. *Oral Interpretation Handbook.* Minneapolis, Minnesota: Burgess, 1960.

Wiseman, Gordon and Larry Barker. *Speech: Interpersonal Communication.* Scranton: Chandler, 1967. Chapter 10.

6

BASIC CONCEPTS OF INTERPERSONAL COMMUNICATION

All of man's undertakings are indicative of his needs, and are representative of those ideas or concepts which are most important, most meaningful to him. The sciences, the humanities, or the arts throughout the ages serve as indicators of those factors which preoccupied man at any given time.

The field of communication is only one indicator in contemporary life, but it is an important one. We live in an age when we are deeply concerned about the alienation of man from man, gaps between generations, the increasingly difficult struggle of the individual in mass society. At the same time the contemporary experience in the Western world is curiously romantic. There is a search for ideals which another generation thought it could live without. There seems to be a search for roots that can assure the continuity of human experience, and an insistence on such values as hope, trust, faith.

The words of one contemporary song express that romantic longing for a more common human experience and values which bind man together rather than tearing him away from other men: "I'd like to teach the world to sing in perfect harmony." Hundreds of similar songs, styles of dress, resurgence of poetry as a part of daily, human experience, even hairstyles are indicators of that resurgent interest in emotional experiences, and meaningful relations with contemporaries as well as with the past.

In the study of human communication we can see a change from the earlier preoccupation with public speaking to a more balanced combination of concern with public speaking and interpersonal communication. Even the choice of terms, the much more frequent use of the concepts of interpersonal communication, appears to be related in the overall trends and needs of the contemporary individual.

WHAT INTERPERSONAL COMMUNICATION MEANS

A simple definition would be: any situation which makes possible the overt sending and receiving of verbal and nonverbal messages in an interaction involving two or more individuals. The idea of active involvement on the part of all those participating must be included in this definition. That does not necessarily mean an equal amount of participation by all members, nor does it necessarily mean the same kind of communication behavior on the part of all members. Interpersonal communication certainly has taken place when a man says to a woman, "I love you," and the woman follows the verbal declaration with a kiss.

This simple definition does not fully take account of our introductory discussion. Probably the values seen in the term interpersonal also need to be considered. In other words, the very fact that our emphasis has shifted in many speech or communication courses from public speaking to a balance with interpersonal communication indicates that there is an underlying sense of need.

INTERACTION AND INTERPERSONAL COMMUNICATION

Idealistically, we have no problem relating to the concept that it would be wonderful to teach an entire world to sing in harmony. As an ideal the concept has a significant part in man's overall attempts to build his world, to grow, to establish and live by important values. However, there is another side to this entire consideration. Whose harmony would we use? Is it not often true that one man's harmony is another man's dissonance? Who would direct this worldwide chorus? Who would teach them? What about those who are tone-deaf? Would they be left out? Would they be ignored, ostracised, attacked for their lack of musical talent? Obviously, our entire inquiry could be carried too far, but the central concept should be clear by now. When we get down to particulars, human communication becomes complicated. Individual talents, individual likes and dislikes, individual prejudices or capabilities, as well as other factors we could mention make "singing in harmony" a much more formidable task than writing a song about it.

Don't misunderstand—the task may be very worthwhile, the human need may be overwhelmingly important, but only if man moves beyond the glorification of the ideal, or the romanticized version of the world as he sees it, can certain important feats be accomplished. How does this translate into human communication? The following possibilities for interpersonal·interactions illustrate some of the interrelationships between two people. While interpersonal communication in the framework of our original definition is possible in many different situations involving two, three, a dozen, or even more people, we commonly use the term today in referring to one-to-one, triadic, or small group interaction.

Some People Will Not Interact

Figure 4 will disturb the value concepts of many people. It goes against the grain of many of us to think that there may be someone, somewhere, who either does not want to interact with us or with whom for some reason we cannot interact.

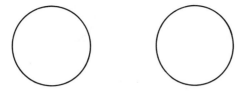

FIGURE 4

One great myth about communication in contemporary American life centers around the idea: If we could just sit down together and talk about it, our problems would be solved. That may or may not be true. As discouraging as it is, there are some people who simply are not interested in our ideas, who are not interested in us. Or, it could also be true that because of physical distance or physical inability we may never be in touch with certain individuals.

Since this is to many a negative concept it was put first in this series of almost progressive graphic representations of human interaction. Will Rogers said many years ago that he never met a man he didn't like. Of course, he did not meet all men, and chances are that Will Rogers, like all other men, found himself in situations which he helped to create and which were in part developed by people to whom he was close already. Thus, Will Rogers and all of us help to predetermine whom we will meet. Our own cultural setting, our own education, and our own personal likes and dislikes tend to create situations in which we meet or do not meet certain people. Few of us have even a chance of breaking out of that framework in an attempt to consciously come into contact with very different people. Even then, whether or not all the people that met Will Rogers liked him is another question. After all, by definition interpersonal communication depends on interaction, and that takes a minimum of two people. There is one other factor. Our culture in many ways requires us at least to make certain "tribal noises" which indicate that we are tolerant, that we like people, that we can get along with others, and that we are willing to cooperate. We tend to "talk" interaction even if it did not take place. This underlying force within our society can lead to an attempt at interpersonal communication which does not result in interaction.

They Touched

Our need for bridging the gaps a complex society has created often finds expression in attempts to reach out, to touch others, or to touch objects in the hope that touching will give us greater awareness, understanding, and a better base for interaction. Figure 5, however, indicates that mere touching does not necessarily result in interaction between two people.

People "touch," they come in contact, but they do not necessarily share enough ideas, thoughts, or experiences to make possible a meaningful interrelationship. They may decide not to bother, not to go on with something that will not fulfill their needs or make a meaningful contribution within the framework of their lives.

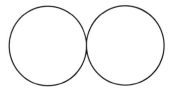

FIGURE 5

Then there are those of us who have heard that interaction or interpersonal communication is the "in thing," and that we really ought to try it. That is like the man who heard that feather pillows are good to sleep on, and so he decided to try one—one feather that is. Pressures for interaction are so great that even those who would rather be left alone experience it as a kind of new, social demand, so they make attempts to reach out. Indeed such individuals touch, but usually withdraw when they find no commonality of interests. It could become a bad experience, and one which would be traumatic for all involved, if such individuals because of social pressure, grit their teeth and continue to touch until an almost inevitable explosion. A sixty-year-old dowager and an eighteen-year-old youth may decide at a party they need to prove that there is really no communication, generation, or any other gap between them. So they start interacting to prove something quite beyond what we normally expect to gain from human communication. They are engaged in a social experiment which may go far beyond what we normally have in mind when we speak of human interaction. True, they may find that they are soul-mates, but because of differences of life style, experience, age and other factors they may find too little in common to truly interact. They touch, take a curious look at each other, and decide that is all they want—unless they belong to those teeth-gritters mentioned earlier whose own insecurities or inner desires to prove something beyond the actual need for communication become a driving force to see if something will "happen." We come into brief contact with hundreds or perhaps thousands of people who all add some small experience to our lives, but with whom we do not really interact because there is no mutual need or possibly no common area of interest.

Repelled

There is a law in physics which says that opposite poles attract while like poles repel each other. Man has tried to cope with that concept in human interrelationships in his own way. He developed two contradictory axioms which represent an interesting means of solving the dilemmas in human relations which he observed. On one hand, man says, opposites attract each other; on the other hand, he claims that similar interests bring people together. Take your pick. As so many other factors in human relationships, it depends more on what man wants, what his needs are. Thus axioms, concepts, and sometimes even laws are changed to fulfill his vital needs.

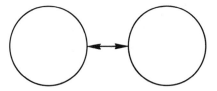

FIGURE 6

Figure 6 indicates a concept in human interaction we do not particularly enjoy, but frequently experience. There are some people with whom we come in contact who for various reasons, such as their behavior, their appearance, their background or our own background, prejudices, experience, and emotional attachments, repel us. Sometimes these reactions are almost automatic, unthinking, and difficult to identify or categorize. Color, hair-style, beard, size, pitch of voice, and myriad other things make us turn away before we have made extensive contact with the person. It may very well be that certain people would "grow" on us if we only got to know them better. If they are important to us, maybe the wife of a new boss, we may make a determined effort to get to know them. That effort may result at least in the touching relationship discussed in the preceding section, or it could go beyond the teeth-gritting, hanging-on stage and develop into a much closer interaction.

If I have no particular need for interaction with that particular person, chances are that I will simply give in to my immediate reactions and feel repelled. All of us have to make selections, have to make choices in our human interactions since there are such a vast number of possibilities. Obviously, choice indicates some standard of appeal, of need, or rational and emotional basis on which we select some human partners for interpersonal communication while rejecting others.

On the other hand it should not be assumed that rejections always result from mere emotional reactions, or that only prejudices lead to rejection. We meet many people within a lifetime who create problems for us far out of balance with any benefits either one of us could achieve. There are people whose values are so different from ours that we may take a look at them and decide that they are "not for us." In other words, all of us have to decide what to add to or subtract from our lives to make it fit the pattern or concept we have of ourselves in our attempt to achieve our final goal of self-actualization.

Common Ground

Figures 7 and 8 illustrate what has been implied in all of the preceding discussion. For human interaction to take place, for interpersonal communication to become reality, there must be common ground, *shared experiences or background,* a *cultural basis* on which to communicate, a *common language and experiential framework, common interests,* or *shared needs.* That may be only a very small amount of common ground as in figure 7, or it may be a greater amount as

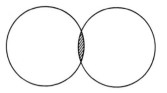

FIGURE 7

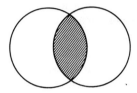

FIGURE 8

in figure 8. Depending on needs, even small areas of agreement or common ground can bring about meaningful, successful, purposeful, and satisfying interpersonal communication. Probably no two people can merge entirely, or become so alike that the two circles representing two individuals completely merge. There are even differences between similar individuals, and there is a need for maintaining self-identity and a feeling of individuality which would not make it possible or desirable for two people to really become one.

Intrapersonal

The only way the self-integrated communication system could really exist would be in intracommunication. Figure 9 represents that concept. It is actually not the overlapping of two or more experiential worlds in interpersonal communication, but rather the communication which takes place within one individual, the integrative processes of thought, meditation, spiritual experiences, and neurophysiological internal reactions to stimuli.

FIGURE 9

The Concept of Growth

One vital idea needs to be stressed. The graphic representations used so far appear to leave room only for rather static relationships. The circles used in these figures seem to indicate that interpersonal communication can only take place if there are predetermined, fixed areas of common ground, and that we go through life searching for those individuals who bring a very similar experiential framework to the communication situation.

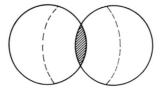

FIGURE 10

Not only is there room for growth, but all of us have had the experience that through long-time association the common ground between two people will expand. Figure 10 illustrates the fact that there are potential areas of growth once common ground has been established. Areas of cooperation and thought which can be built on the relatively "safe" foundation of the original contacts usually open up. Depending on the need for interpersonal communication we may well be satisfied with the original limited areas of common ground. However, since any long-range human interrelationship is not a static event, either diminishing or increasing contact, or possible fluctuations in the area of the contact, will result.

Realignment

Figure 11 illustrates one final very important concept in interpersonal communication. At times we come in contact with other human beings, especially if there is a specific task which needs to be completed, in such a way as to expose nonrelated areas of interest, seemingly making interaction impossible. For instance, a vice-president in charge of reorganizing personnel structures in a large company contacts one of his section foremen in a technical area. The vice-president wants to talk reorganization, the foreman wants to talk about new equipment he needs. A clash seems inevitable, except for the fact that the foreman is also interested in reorganization of the personnel structure as a secondary consideration. If either of the men engaged in this communication situation realizes that by realigning his primary interests he can allow an area of initial contact, he probably will facilitate the eventual solution of the problem he has in mind. In other words, one of the two will have to "turn himself around" to establish common ground for the solution of *both* problems.

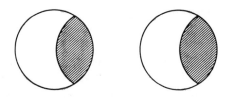

FIGURE 11

THE INFLUENCE OF TASK ORIENTATION IN INTERPERSONAL COMMUNICATION

Let's return to our concept of "making the world sing in harmony" for a moment. As long as I desire to sing in harmony with others only for the fun of it, or as an emotional expression, there is relatively little difficulty in reaching some sort of cooperation which makes all of us feel as if we are singing harmoniously. If we have to engage in that activity for a long period of time and we can begin to notice mistakes others are making, or allow others to determine that we really do not have very good voices, trouble may develop. More specifically, if someone else were to hear us and decide that he wants to start a worldwide chorus which would give scheduled concerts—although that might be difficult if the *whole* world were to sing in harmony, since there would be no one left to listen—suddenly the fun situation would have changed into one in which we need to accomplish a task. We may need to develop and live up to certain standards of excellence or performance. Some of the possibilities resulting from the injection of another dimension into interpersonal communication, through the emphasis on a task which has to be performed, will be illustrated in the following graphic representations.

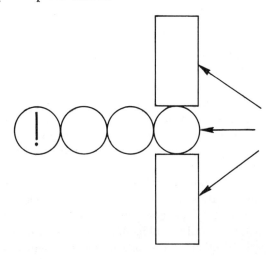

FIGURE 12

My Way, the Only Way

Figure 12 indicates the attempt of the vice-president in charge of personnel reorganization to reach his desired goal which is indicated by the circle marked with an exclamation point. This figure illustrates one possible response which the foreman in our example could make. The only way the vice-president will reach his goal is by first doing all the other things the foreman wants to see accomplished. In this case the vice-president has to do all the giving, all the adjusting. If he wants his task accomplished and if he has enough time or enough flexibility to adjust to the demands, and if he does not feel threatened by the situation, his task will eventually be taken care of. If the demands made by the foreman are meaningful and contribute to the general benefit of the company both partners in this situation will probably be relatively happy. If it is a power play the power balance between the two men may be threatened and resentment by the vice-president could easily result. That will be especially true if the foreman is not careful in his responses and starts bragging about his victory or tries to press his advantage in other matters.

The Trade Off

The second example, illustrated in figure 13, shows a situation which also results in a blocked channel leading to the accomplishment of the vice-president's task.

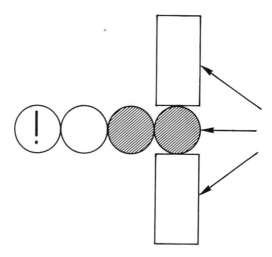

FIGURE 13

However, this time greater flexibility on the part of the foreman is the result of the latter's willingness to use the vice-president's desire to get his own work done by also getting a few matters accomplished which are on the foreman's list. This situation would suggest that the foreman knows he has something the vice-president wants and in effect he is willing to give it to him, if he first gets a limited, negotiable number of other items taken care of. In effect, this is a bargaining situation.

In many confrontations on American college campuses members of the Black Students Union or Students for a Democratic Society presented lists of "non-negotiable demands" which more often than not turned out to be negotiable. Depending on how reasonable the demands appear, how many real problems they solve, and if they allow both partners to save at least a minimum amount of face, such bargaining is often considered to be a very acceptable way of getting things done, especially if both partners feel that just demands had not been met in the past. Members of a society which builds much of its economic thinking on the concepts of supply and demand, trade offs, and bargaining have relatively little trouble accepting such compromises.

Yes—But!

In a very trusting, secure relationship, especially if past experiences have been positive, another situation may develop which is illustrated in figure 14. In this case the foreman readily agrees to personnel reorganization because both he and the vice-president agree upon the fact that this is the item of highest priority. However, the foreman also expects the vice-president to take care of other demands or requests as soon as the high priority problem has been solved. If the foreman in this situation has reason to believe that he can trust the vice-president, and if there is a certain balance of power concerning task achievements, such a situation is likely to develop.

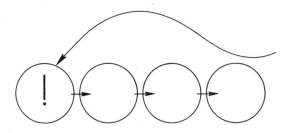

FIGURE 14

No Preference

Figure 15 illustrates another possibility. While the foreman* has a number of tasks to accomplish, all of them forming part of his daily routine or assignment, he has no particular problem which he feels needs solving. Everything is running well in his department, and when he is approached by the vice-president who appears to face a specific challenge, the foreman is willing to pick that specific task out of the many in which he is engaged. Under those circumstances he simply addresses himself to its solution, together with the vice-president, in a cooperative effort not specifically related to any other situation. This attitude may make interaction in the solution of later problems much easier, but it is not planned with that particular possibility in mind.

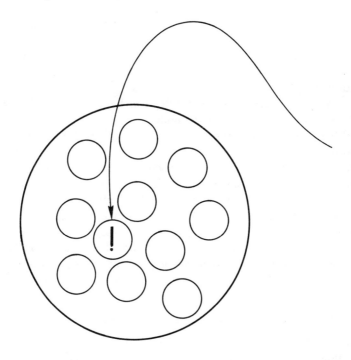

FIGURE 15

THE CONCEPT OF ROLE

All of the ideas discussed in the preceding pages assume that in our relations with other human beings we play, or are expected to play specific roles. What is your reaction to the term role playing? Does it somehow suggest play acting, making believe, possibly even deception, or not being yourself? If you react to the term in that way, it will be necessary to consider carefully the following concepts. For our study we will not think of role playing in the ways intimated above. We will think of it as a means of expressing the fact that all of us come in contact with many different people under many different circumstances, and that each relationship brings about its own peculiar interaction with other human beings.

Any one individual may be someone's boss, someone's mother, someone's sister, someone's friend, member of a given church, member of a certain PTA unit, member of a swimming class, and so on. All of these contacts, or roles as they will be referred to in this book, are indeed part of what we call the total person or personality. It would be unusual if an individual were to react in the same way to everyone with whom he interacts. There are obvious *differences because of convention.* For instance, it would be considered strange if a woman kissed both her husband and her swimming instructor in the same way. And differences *because of involvement or need*—one would not expect the same woman to be as concerned or as involved with matters relating to the local PTA as those relating directly to the health of her children.

There may be some who for reasons of their own suggest an egalitarian attitude towards all men, and in some communes attempts have been made to create that sort of situation. However, it would appear highly doubtful, on the basis of all we know about man, that we can react and respond to all with whom we come in contact in the same way.

What has been said about roles can be summed up by two statements. All of us play various roles depending on contacts with other human beings and the relationship to them which have been established both by convention and by our own needs and desires. Second, all these roles could be theoretically combined to describe our total personality, although they probably can never come together in one large massive block of personality to be observed at any one time. There are very consistent features about our reactions but they tend to be identifiable only as large, general concepts usually referred to by such terms as outspoken, calm, aggressive, dependable. Specifics will depend on specific situations, with decisions constantly being made by individuals as to whether or not their reactions are appropriate to a given situation.

SUMMARY

Each one of us plays many roles depending on self-image, the expectations of others, the tasks accepted, and the cultural framework in which he operates. The most frequent interaction in which we engage with other human beings occurs in one-to-one relationships or very small group situations involving three, four or five people. Such interpersonal communication has become of major concern in contemporary life, because its successful use appears to be one meaningful answer to what many people consider to be a threat of alienation between human beings. Against such a powerful background of personal or psychological needs, limitations placed on the process by varying levels of intimacy, need, and common ground should to be taken into consideration. For man to remain truly human he needs to interact with other humans, but it appears to be equally true that his humanity requires the right to reject or limit such interaction on the basis of his needs and his image of self and others. Furthermore, the roles he must play because he is part of various societal, family, and cultural structures, plus the sheer impossibility of interacting with all other human beings on earth, suggest the existence of processes of elimination or choice. It would appear, therefore, that in order to remain human, man must also develop an understanding of both rational and emotional factors involved in interpersonal communication, making possible thoughtful, purposeful use of both in his interactions with other men.

EXERCISES

1. Develop a continuum of intimacy making use of the following concepts or your own scale: Very Intimate. Intimate. Somewhat Intimate. Not Intimate. During

two 24-hour periods, list the people with whom you engage in interpersonal communication under the appropriate category. Use two time periods which are somewhat different; for instance, a regular school day and a day during the weekend. Write a 500-word evaluation of your findings.

2. Present a three-minute oral report in class detailing reactions by authors of other texts on interpersonal communication, which either prove or disprove the theory advanced in this text that emphasis on interpersonal communication is the result of special needs in contemporary America.

3. Collect 15 to 20 ads from newspapers and magazines, providing some indication as to whether commercial advertisers depend more on an "interpersonal" or "mass" image to communicate their messages. If you notice differences, attempt to indicate any discernible patterns or areas of difference. Present a five-minute oral report in class using visual support material.

4. In a 500-word paper list and discuss various roles you play as roles are defined in this chapter. Describe and evaluate each role from the standpoint of its cultural framework, need or task orientation, expectations of others, and your self-image or need for self-evaluation.

5. In a three-minute oral report summarize factors which would make interpersonal communication difficult in a public speaking situation before a large audience of 200 or 300 people. Explain and illustrate each major point.

6. Write a 500-word evaluation relating to you and your social role. Answer such questions as: How do I relate to my peers? How do I feel about my background when I do not belong to a majority group? Am I comfortable with adults, younger people? What groups do I belong to, and do I approve of what the groups do, believe in, stand for? How strong is my need to "belong"? Do I feel I "belong"? Do I feel rejected and by whom? What do I have to offer to others? Can I start conversations or contribute to them?

7. Ask one of your classmates who does not know you very well to give you a verbal description of how he "sees" you, what feedback he can give you as he observes your nonverbal behavior, clothes you are wearing, etc. Do not ask for interpretations but write your own evaluation or interpretation of the statements your classmate made. Did his statements strengthen your behavior or cause you to want to change?

8. From the following, pick one emotion you think is difficult for you to express nonverbally, and without informing your classmates, try to interpret that emotion nonverbally. Get their reactions. Did they interpret what they saw you doing in keeping with the emotion you tried to express? *Emotions:* approval, love, fear, hate, serenity, failure.

9. Stand close to several of your friends and classmates during the course of conversations during a given day. When does each of your conversational partners move away from you? How quickly, how far, what other nonverbal actions go with the move? At what distance do different individuals seem to feel that you have invaded their territory? Report your findings in a three-minute oral report in class.

10. Bring several (3 to 6) objects to class. Reveal them one at a time to your classmates, and let each one describe the objects individually on a piece of paper. Require each one of your classmates to use some value statements, ask them to state how the object makes them feel, or what it makes them think of. In a discussion compare their observations and attempt to analyze what caused different or similar reactions.

BIBLIOGRAPHY

Brooks, William D. *Speech Communication*. Dubuque: Wm. C. Brown, 1971.

Davitz, J. R. *The Communication of Emotional Meaning*. New York: McGraw-Hill, 1964.

Gibson, James W. *A Reader in Speech Communication*. New York: Mc-Graw-Hill, 1971.

Gruner, Charles et al. *Speech Communication in Society*. Boston: Allyn and Bacon, 1972. Part 3.

Miller, Gerald R. *Speech Communication: A Behavioral Approach*. Indianapolis: Bobbs-Merrill, 1966.

Mortenson, C. David. *Communication: The Study of Human Interaction*. New York: McGraw-Hill, 1972.

———. *Explorations in Communication*. New York: Mc-Graw-Hill, 1972. Part III. A workbook to accompany the above text.

7

DYADS AND TRIADS
IN INTERPERSONAL
COMMUNICATION

Certain underlying assumptions make the concept of interpersonal communication very appealing to many contemporary Americans. In a society which expresses high regard for individual preferences and individual involvement, even if there is extensive involvement with the mass media, mass production, and mass psychology, a strong association between individual expression and interpersonal communication is easily formed. There is less that can "get in the way" when two or three people communicate. There is more of a chance to let the "real you" be seen, or to observe the "real you" in someone else. One feels less threatened and thus more able to control the environment if there are only a few people, or preferably if there is only one other person involved in the communication process. Sharing oneself with others, being open rather than playing games, putting on a false front, conforming, or engaging in similar, supposedly deceptive strategies as part of human communication, is frowned upon in a society which desires closer rather than less intensive contacts. Interpersonal communication encourages those who feel getting together on a one-to-one basis resurrects important values or assures the survival of the individual in a mass society.

Employees in contemporary America do not merely want to be told what to do. Many people consider interoffice, written communications to be inadequate. Instead, employer and employee seek opportunities to sit down together and discuss problems of mutual concern. Young people deride members of the establishment for lacking insight into the affairs of the people whom they are to serve. Demands for "eyeball-to-eyeball" rap sessions are commonplace in all situations involving contact between human beings. The cry of students during the 1960s that they wanted to be more than IBM numbers has become an almost universal demand for recognition of the individual. As a matter of fact, the concern with interpersonal communication has become so overwhelming

103

that there is almost a mythical quality about it, probably representative of the average American's conviction that if he can just get to the other fellow on a one-to-one basis he can solve most of his problems.

The opportunity for feedback and an empathic relationship is greater in a face-to-face situation. Interpersonal communication suggests that we can more readily receive all the verbal and nonverbal cues from anyone sharing the communication situation with us. The opportunity to concentrate on fewer stimuli, and especially those which we judge to be of primary importance, is a positive factor to be considered in such human interaction. Obviously feedback does not have to be positive; it can also be negative. Agreement or very positive responses will not automatically result simply because the relatively "close" situation suggested by the term interpersonal communication has been developed. One common American myth about communication can be summed up in the statement: If he has all the facts, he will make the right decision. By a "right" decision usually we mean the one which agrees with our own point of view. But people may have all the facts, or the same facts, and still be capable of individual preferences and differences of choice.

One other factor will extend the idea developed in the previous paragraph. We cannot assume that interpersonal communication results only, or is sought only, as a means for cooperation or agreement. Ours is a competitive society. Even if it were not, individual human beings would be engaged in many forms of competition for position, power, love, influence, a "place in the sun," or similar matters of importance to them. Interpersonal communication thus may be one means of expressing personal hostility, warning an enemy, or of exploring dangerous enemy territory for the purpose of eventually destroying the opposition. The idea that people communicate only for purposes of cooperation or to create a positive relationship may be very intriguing, but it is hardly representative of the total picture of human interaction.

One of the most important factors in establishing positive, purposeful interpersonal communication is a definition of the role each individual is playing in the process. Much of the ultimate outcome of interaction depends on the interpretation participants put on their own roles and those of others with whom they are communicating. Like all others, this human process of communication does not take place in a vacuum but is used, evaluated, and otherwise interpreted against past experiences, task needs, and personal needs.

As indicated in the previous chapter, interpersonal communication commonly is used as a term describing interaction between two or three people or within small groups. Since the latter category will be discussed in chapter 8 we will direct our attention to the two remaining categories of interpersonal communication.

DYADIC COMMUNICATION

One-to-one oral communication situations, frequently involving face-to-face interaction, represent one of the most frequent kinds of human contact.

Intimate Dyads

This kind of communication is representative of the most revealing and most personally satisfying contacts we can think of. A man and a woman, a husband and a wife, through countless opportunities to observe each other, to respond to each other's needs whether they be physical, spiritual, or intellectual, evolve a network of contacts that lead to understanding and cooperation in the fulfillment of needs which represents much of the idealized, hopeful side of interpersonal communication. The intimacy of such contacts will result in relationships which make possible observation of the other individual without distortions caused by the environment. In other words, such interaction permits us to ignore environmental interference in our understanding and observation of another individual.

It is also obvious that such constant exposure will tend to magnify weaknesses—caps left off toothpaste tubes or stockings hanging in the bathroom. Depending on the overall purposes for which communication is being used in a given situation or in the overall relationship, these irritations can be used as a means of attacking the other individual, or as a means of expressing latent and hidden hostilities which cannot be easily brought out into the open because of cultural norms, social amenities, or an unwillingness to face underlying problems. On the other hand, depending on individual attitudes, these challenges can be seen as opportunities to develop closer contact with a communication partner. They can become opportunities to understand him better, to be of assistance, or simply to provide an opportunity for communication that is enjoyed by both partners.

What is true in a more intense way for a married couple is also applicable to other dyadic situations. Contacts between teacher and student, between father and son, between two friends, between individuals in all the varied ways of interacting during a normal day's activity, are probably the most frequent types of communication. The difference between these various situations is really the amount of intimacy or the amount of personal involvement and willingness to expose hidden feelings, needs, and attitudes. While we may insist that the world would be a better place if all of our contacts were more intimate, it must be remembered that there are people who merely use information about other people to control them, to take advantage, or to destroy them.

Intimacy depends on trust. The value of intimacy lies in the fact that it is a very personal, limited experience. There would be nothing very special about constant intimacy with everyone. It would become a norm, a very common standard. Such norms are usually very dull and after a while tend to be ignored by man for other factors which are unusual, different, more easily brought into an experiential framework because they are more readily distinguishable from the normal, usual things we do. There was a time when a woman's ankle peeking out from under a long skirt would be noticed immediately by any man. Not too much attention has been paid to ankles during the age of mini- or-micro-skirts. Same ankle—maybe—but the general setting, and certainly the exposure from the standpoints of frequency and degree, changed sufficiently to make the object noticeable in one situation, readily ignored in another.

Debates: Dyadic Communication for Controversy

Verbal confrontation between two individuals making use of formal, carefully developed rules often plays an important part in settling issues, determining the tolerance of opponents to certain ideas or actions, venting hostile feelings, and providing an intellectual basis for making decisions. The presence of judges, observers, or a critical audience distinguishes the formal debate from other forms of dyadic controversy, as does its use in decision making by nonparticipants.

Verbal Fights

Verbal fights between two people remind us of a jingle children repeat in very unpleasant dyadic communication situations: "Sticks and stones may break my bones but words will never hurt me." Obviously, words are used at times to hurt. Sometimes they are even intended to take the place of physical violence in which we are not physically strong enough to engage. A 230-pound policeman facing a 100-pound freshman girl on a college campus presents a rather formidable physical obstruction to the girl. Physical violence would be futile, but she knows that certain words may cut more deeply than any rock she throws at her adversary. Often obscene language and profanities are used in confrontations. The sender feels that while he or she might miss the target with a rock, as long as these aggressive, taboo words are heard there is no way the receiver can really avoid a verbal barrage of terms which shock his sensitivities. More than that, if the policeman in our example decides to react physically, he is still the loser. Our society has established the norms of free speech in such a way that we have a difficult time accepting physical violence as a response to mere words in spite of the fact that the psychological impact or pain produced by words may be more lasting and make a deeper impression than a missile hurled at an opponent.

As long as man holds to certain values or believes certain factors in his life to be important, there will be words and other symbols he cherishes or values. Our value systems may be different but we all use symbols to represent them or to speak of them. As long as that is true, there will be other men who will see in these values and the symbols that represent them opportunities for attacking others in their most vulnerable spots. Somehow man must care about something if he is to remain human, but if he cares he is vulnerable to verbal attacks. Vulnerability is one of the by-products of dyadic communication where man cannot hide in a crowd but must face his opposition alone. He can probably be desensitized as Black Power advocates attempted to do in special schools set up for their children. In the classes, epithets which could be used by other racial groups to attack them were repeatedly hurled at the children.

Conversations: Dyadic Communication for Cooperation

The most frequent cooperative dyadic interaction takes place in conversations. Conversations are generally the result of a need for information sharing, reinforcement, or relaxation and enjoyment. In information sharing, the most important factors would be that one partner possesses information and the other partner wants that information. The appropriate choice of time is one vital component in this situation. A phone call from a friend indicating, "I have that recipe you wanted. Let me read it to you over the phone," could very well be stopped right then and there if the response was, "Sorry, Johnny is in the bathtub. Call you back later." More negative yet would be the response, "Sorry, I already got the recipe from Jane, since I thought you had forgotten about it." In the first case there is still a chance for information sharing, in the second case more serious interruption of the interaction between the two partners probably will result. The least that will probably happen is that they will both just forget about the entire matter. On the other hand the one offering the recipe may try to interpret whether her friend is angry about the delay.

Another situation concerns a conversation between a wife and her husband about a certain job that needs to be done around the house. One interpretation of this situation could lead to a discussion of the specific factors involved in the job, the cost of it, the importance of having it done, etc. However, the wife may only want reassurance that the job is going to get done and that her husband appreciates her thoughtfulness in remembering the problem. One's value as a communication partner or as a marriage partner is at stake in cases such as this, since the purpose of such conversations has little to do with information sharing, but rather with reinforcing or accepting an individual or strengthening his self-concept.

At other times conversations are opportunities to "put up your feet," to relax verbally, to enjoy each other's company. No information is sought, no message is contributed for its informational value, no one feels insecure or needs psychological shoring up, and the conversation may ramble without anyone becoming particularly concerned about it.

Conversations at times present the challenge of finding some common ground, some basic agreement as to their purpose. Take the case of the young man parked with a girl friend in some particularly romantic spot. She says: "Isn't it a beautiful moon?" He has to figure out if she wants to discuss factual information concerning the moon, or if she would prefer a philosophical discussion of the meaning of beauty. Does she on the other hand want to discuss matters of romance, or does she perhaps expect a more direct action, and is she in effect asking for a kiss? Whatever the response in answer to her question, it will certainly determine in part the future relationship between the two.

Successful, meaningful, satisfying conversations thus have been shown to require:

1. A shared need, interest, or subject matter, and agreement on the general purpose of the conversation
2. Responsiveness by both partners and active participation which does not allow the conversation to turn into a monologue.
3. Direct verbal responses, which provide sufficient clues for adequate feedback, overcoming the feeling of uncertainty which results when we don't really understand what our conversation partner means
4. Directness in nonverbal responses involving eye contact, and alert meaningful physical responses such as frowns, smiles, or touches
5. Physical closeness or at least electronic means such as a telephone which create a feeling of physical closeness
6. A lack of preplanning and specific agenda.

Interviews

This type of dyadic communication is frequently used to determine whether or not a certain individual fits a need, a task, a position, or can provide desired information, or to determine a problem. As in the case of all dyadic communication situations nonverbal clues, appearance, dress, and mannerisms form part of the final evaluation. It would be unusual, for instance, if a bank in Beverly Hills hired a slovenly dressed, dirty individual to work as a bank teller. Preparing for an interview includes understanding the requirements and expectations of the interviewer, as well as understanding the general framework or setting in which the interview will take place. For employment interviews, specifics concerning the job offered, training required, employer expectations concerning appearance and dress, potential colleagues, physical requirements, age requirements, and communication skills need to be taken into consideration.

Preparation for information-sharing or problem-sharing interviews consists mainly of information gathering and mentally relating, organizing, or identifying the data which will most likely be required. Interviews conducted for therapeutic purposes, or in order to reprimand or praise an employee obviously are difficult to prepare for, except that the interviewee should enter into them as relaxed and rested as possible, with an open mind or attitude. In such situations the direction of the interview will be strongly determined by the interviewer. The interviewee needs to be mentally alert and quick to pick up verbal and nonverbal clues to respond effectively, especially in the initial stage of the interview.

Two types of questions generally are used in an interview.

1. Directive Questions for Factual Information. Relating to the specific purpose of an interview such data as age, specific illnesses, home addresses, previous employment, references, height, weight, academic training and degrees may be asked for. Answers will usually be given in response to short, precise questions.

2. Open-Ended Questions for Personal Reactions, Evaluative Statements. This category includes questions asked in an attempt to accomplish two things: (1) to help the respondent be more relaxed, and cooperative, (2) to get some impressions that could serve as an indication of how the person being interviewed will react to other people, what his likes and dislikes are, how effectively he can communicate verbally, and perhaps to gain some insight into his values or other concepts related to a given situation or job.

Choosing Effective Questions.   The first category requires brief, precise, definite questions. The most frequent mistake made in interviews probably results from indefinite statements which were intended to secure specific, factual information. "What about your birthplace?" is an inquiry which could be interpreted in so many ways that it may take one or two other questions to straighten out initial misunderstandings. "Did you go to high school?" provides very different informational input from the question: "Did you finish high school?" It is the interviewer's responsibility to understand what information he needs and wants before he can ask meaningful questions. If he starts an interview with the request, "Tell me about your family," he must be ready to be presented with a large amount of data and reactions forcing him to do a great deal of listening.

If the interviewer intends to stay in control of the interview and direct it in specific ways he must be very specific even in his first question. Asking for the name of the father and mother, and the number of brothers and sisters keeps control over the interview in the hands of the interviewer. If, on the other hand, the interviewer is interested in reactions, if he is interested in the way the interviewee handles himself in a dyadic communication situation, the question should reasonably provide opportunity for more than a yes or no answer.

The Use of Follow-up Questions.   An interviewer may use probing questions which insist on more information, or more detail, or some reactions which were not completely expressed. In such cases the respondent is specifically encouraged to "tell more." Another major use of questions is to bring out specific points which are either being avoided by the respondent or which he misinterpreted. Such leading questions seem to insist, however, on a specific answer, and may cause a respondent to tell the interviewer what he wants to hear. The question, "You really did not need the new equipment, did you?" allows very little choice in answering it. Of course, the reply may be an indication of how easily the respondent caves in under pressure. Such a reply could provide important information, but frequently it is only an indication of how well a respondent has learned to go along with the expectations of those in authority or power. In all interview situations a balance has to be created. Inadequate or incomplete answers often require probing by the interviewer. Incorrect answers caused by misunderstanding questions have to be corrected if information input is vital. An interviewer needs to decide if he is more interested in getting hard facts, impressions, or interpretations relating to the interviewee's capabilities, emotional stability, or attitudes, and how that information is to be used. As the interpretation of data becomes more complex, obviously the skills of the interviewer also have to be more complex.

Eye Contact.   It is true in all dyadic communication, but in the case of the formalized interview situation we become even more dramatically aware of the importance of eye contact in human communication. Americans tend to distrust people with "shifty eyes," but also get uncomfortable when someone "stares" at them. The compromise most of us make is the culturally acceptable means of solving the problem. We look at the face of our partner in dyadic communication, frequently looking into his eyes but not fixing our eye contact mechanically. We remain free to move our eyes, blinking at different intervals, and at times briefly looking away at related objects such as notes, pencils, watches, or charts. In that way we indicate interest and personal contact, without intruding too much. Other cultures, such as the Turkish, actually require a constant "eyeball-to-eyeball" contact, while conversation with a Japanese, especially a woman, tends to include much less eye contact.

Time.   Interviews are usually very clearly and definitely time bound. They are intended to accomplish a specific purpose in a specified amount of time. For that reason they will be most successful if both partners respect each other's time concepts by neither extending an interview too long, nor cutting it short, thus giving the impression that the interviewee has "failed the test," or that the interviewee has become impatient and wants to have the whole thing stopped.

Roles.   In most interviews there is a dominant personality, usually the one who called for the interview, the one who has the job to offer, or the one who asks the questions. It was already mentioned that interviews include such experiences as being reprimanded or praised for a job, information sharing with an expert on a specific problem, counselling, information sharing concerning a new product, a new experience, or some significant change in an organization. As a result they usually come about because of a feeling that two people share a significant need which can best be met by limiting the interaction to those immediately affected.

Purposes.   Interviews are task-oriented, they can provide means of evaluating one's position, of evaluating future needs, current trends or receiving some relevant data from the person best qualified to provide them without having to go through complicated channels. They may also turn into persuasive attempts to stimulate someone into changing his approach, to make more meaningful contributions, or to deal more effectively with a personal problem.

Formats.   Formats may range from highly formal question-and-answer sessions in the case of job interviews, to opportunities for a client or patient to say whatever comes to his mind in a therapeutic or counselling session. The former is more effective when specific, predetermined data which require little interpretation are needed. The latter is more effective when both partners in the communication situation cannot be certain what they are looking for, or when specific questions would exert too much control or give too much direction to the answers supplied.

Conversations and Interviews: Comparisons and Contrasts

Differences between conversations and interviews are often only a matter of degree, so much so that unskilled interviewers may find themselves almost imperceptibly slipping into an easy conversation with their interviewees. Only when it becomes evident that the predetermined purpose is not being accomplished may they become aware of the change. The opposite also may happen. Consider the example of the husband who engages his wife in a pleasant, relaxed conversation after dinner, only to find out that she has had an accident with the car that day. The relaxed conversation quickly turns into an interview trying to determine some of the standard facts in the matter. Before long the interview may even change into an interrogation, as the husband begins to assign guilt to his wife and questions her with little choice for reply except to supply yes or no answers.

The difference between conversations and interviews can be summed up by restating two major considerations. Interviews depend to a considerably larger extent on preplanning and predevelopment of questions. A specific direction for the interview is planned, time limits are set, and a specific outcome is, in most cases, taken carefully into consideration. In the case of conversations there is little preplanning, no specific direction is predetermined, and instead of a task orientation most conversations are really only means of socializing, or of keeping communicative channels open while relaxing and enjoying the company of others.

Conversations provide opportunities for reinforcing self-concepts, and at times in information sharing they come close to being interviews. Two students, who during the course of a conversation in the cafeteria discover that they are taking courses from the same professor, undoubtedly will share some information about their experiences with the teacher. While they may question each other, the formal structure, the predetermined direction, and the specific prepared questions of the interview will be missing.

It must be remembered that some individuals have worked with the interview method so much that even their conversations turn into formal interviews or interrogations. Speech professors have similar experiences when they try to enjoy a lecture, but find their role of professional critic spilling over into their private lives. In other words, techniques and their repeated practice can sometimes become such an overwhelming influence that a man confuses his roles out of habit.

This is a good place to consider another important difference between conversations and interviews which centers around the concept of roles. In interviews the role of the interviewer as the individual setting the tone, getting the whole interaction started, and keeping the overall direction of it under control, is a very formal contribution. Interviewers determine by the mood they set whether the interview will be relaxed or tense, friendly or filled with animosity. A smile, a handshake, a relaxed stance, or a relaxed way of sitting behind a desk, will provide positive clues for every interviewee as to what he may expect. On the other hand, the interviewee also plays a rather formal role. Information input, and thus to some extent the specific direction of the entire interview, is under his control. Confused or incomplete answers, hidden meanings, unwillingness or inability to understand questions posed by the interviewer, will all contribute to poor interview results. In a conversation, on the other hand, there are no formal roles. Both partners tend to contribute almost equally, although they may not contribute the same type or kind of communicative content. For instance, a "good" listener can at times make for a very one-sided but very satisfying conversation if he throws in only a few reinforcing words such as, "You don't say." "Is that so." "My, wasn't that brilliant." Of course, that is only true if that kind of one-sided exchange does not last too long, *and* if both partners enjoy their individual roles. In some situations, such as parties, conversations between two people may be discouraged because even that relatively unstructured interaction is too specific, too limited. Involvement of more people, and casual changes of roles and involvement are much more desirable under those circumstances.

TRIADIC INTERPERSONAL COMMUNICATION

Interaction involving three, four, or five individuals begins to change the context or environment of the interpersonal communication situation. It still allows direct contacts, with less interference from objects, settings, or the influence of large audiences. However, such interaction contributes one major new concept which is almost absent from dyadic interactions. In effect, the involvement of others in what may have started as a one-to-one communication makes possible various "escape" routes for participants. In case of a question directed to one individual who does not wish to answer it, he may simply turn to a third party, ignoring the question or playfully asking him to respond. A dominant personality may even interject himself into a one-to-one exchange and submit his own contributions without being asked to do so. Eye contact becomes less direct as participants have an opportunity to shift their attention from individual to individual, and sometimes points are lost as they are passed around an expanding circle of contributors in such interpersonal communication situations.

The triad can, of course, become a problem-solving rather than a problem-creating interaction. In labor arbitration, marriage counselling, or fights between brothers and sisters we tend to introduce a third person who is "neutral." Being caught in the middle is not always a pleasant, nor successful, experience for the third person. Frequently, the role falls to professionals who are paid and have been taught to keep their professional distance while serving as catalysts in the problem situation. They are not really full partners, however, in such triadic communication situations, rather they have stepped, or have been invited to step into a dyad because it is faced with a breakdown of communication.

As the size of groups increases, the opportunities for escape from face-to-face confrontations or cooperative efforts increase. As was pointed out earlier, intimacy is achieved more easily by two people. The interjection of other personalities, their value systems, their background, their experiences, tends to add so many new features to interpersonal communication that common denominators for communication will tend to become more and more general. With the development of more generalized areas of contact, a very personal exchange of ideas or coverage of very personalized ideas and concepts becomes less and less likely. An individual's purposes or needs are, of course, an important consideration when we evaluate the usefulness or appropriateness of interpersonal communication. Greater coverage and more general areas of agreement applicable to larger numbers of people may actually be desirable if they are not merely the result of accident or the desire to hide important communicative content.

SUMMARY:
REACHING OUT TO INDIVIDUALS

Few of us are called upon to make public speeches. All of us, however, constantly interact with one or two other individuals in the course of our daily lives. The influence of environmental factors and large numbers of other people disappear or are greatly diminished in dyadic and triadic interaction. As a result we can discover more about others and about ourselves.

The more frequently we are exposed to the same individual, as in the case of a marriage, the greater are our opportunities for self-revelation, intimacy, and understanding. With greater exposure comes also greater vulnerability. The more we allow other human beings to enter into our private lives, or the more we interject ourselves into the world of personal values and images, the more intensive become our opportunities for either harming or helping an individual.

In addition, many problem-solving or information-gathering tasks are based on dyadic communication, as represented by interviews. In all cases of such human interaction both verbal and nonverbal clues take on considerably more "personalized" dimensions since they cannot be as easily overlooked as in larger groups.

EXERCISES

1. Develop questions for a ten-minute interview to involve you and one of your classmates. Choose some problem, possibly on your campus, and attempt to get as much information concerning the attitudes or reactions of your classmates as possible. Conduct the interview in class.

2. During a one-week period try to listen to or view as many interviews on radio and television as possible. In a 1,000-word paper evaluate these interviews. Citing specifics, indicate strengths and weaknesses. Did you notice any significant, constant differences between radio and television?

3. Read conversations in three different books or short stories, one contemporary, one written about 50 years ago, the third from a book 100 years old or older. In a five-minute speech inform your class about differences and similarities of conversational style and content in these three examples, and summarize any conclusions you may have drawn on the basis of these limited samples.

4. Try to recall one of the most enjoyable or meaningful conversations in which you have taken part, and write a 500-word paper listing and evaluating those specific features which you can recall.

5. Same exercise as (4), except that you should recall the same type of information about an individual with whom you had a memorable conversation.

6. Set up two categories: interpersonal communication—mass communication. Under each heading list situations, purposes, needs, or tasks which you think are best suited to that category. Write a brief summary statement reacting to your own selections, and any pattern or lack of pattern you can observe.

✳ 7. During a regular school day engage a friend in a fairly detailed and personal conversation in a place where you can reasonably hope that other friends will pass by. As soon as you spot another friend call him over and pull him into the conversation. What happens? Immediately following the event write down your impressions about those factors which entered into the interpersonal communication situation with the introduction of a third participant.

✳ 8. During an interview the instructor may sudddenly bring an unknown third party into the situation. After continuing the discussion for some time to allow establishment of a new pattern of interaction, the class can discuss what took place, what changes were observed, what differences in both nonverbal and verbal-oral behavior developed.

BIBLIOGRAPHY

Berne, Eric. *Games People Play.* New York: Grove, 1964.

Bois, J. J. *Exploration in Awareness.* New York: Harper and Row, 1957.

Culbert, Samuel A. *The Interpersonal Process of Self Disclosure: It Takes Two to See One.* New York: Renaissance Editions, 1967.

Goyer, Robert S. et al. *Interviewing Principles and Techniques.* Dubuque: Wm. C. Brown, 1968.

Johnson, Wendell. *Your Most Enchanted Listener.* New York: Harper and Row, 1956.

Keltner, John W. *Interpersonal Speech-Communication.* Belmont: Wadsworth, 1969.

Lee, Irving and Laura L. Lee. *Handling Barriers in Communication.* New York: Harper and Row, 1956.

Menninger, Karl. *The Vital Balance.* New York: Viking, 1963.

Wiener, Norbert. *The Human Use of Human Beings.* Garden City: Doubleday, 1956.

8

SMALL GROUP COMMUNICATION

We use the term group quite frequently, and usually we are speaking of audiences, congregations and other aggregations of human beings whom the communication scholar would not consider to be a group. For that reason it might be well to start with brief definitions in an attempt to develop some perimeters, while remembering factors relating to interpersonal communication discussed in earlier chapters.

DEFINING THE SMALL GROUP

For our purposes we will think of a small group as a number of human beings, three or more but small enough so that the members can personally interact and are aware of each other, aware of a common purpose or problem. They are consciously engaged in a cooperative communication effort which provides a maximum opportunity for participation by all members of the group. Such groups often continue their efforts over an extended period of time.

Since we have discussed dyadic and triadic communication in the previous chapter, we will concentrate here on groups that have more than three members. There is a kind of "upper limit," however, beyond which the interaction between all members of the group becomes difficult or even impossible. Any group with more than nine members tends to become cumbersome. The group size needs to be considered in relationship to the amount of time available to the group, and the magnitude of the problem which a group may face. However, it would seem almost self-apparent that interaction will be considerably slowed down if a group consists of more than five, six, or seven members, especially if each member has important contributions to make. In such cases it has generally been found that task-oriented groups which are too large function more adequately if they are divided up into smaller groups. To synthesize all views or findings each group then sends a representative to participate in a final discussion or meeting.

Casual, Informal Groups

Since we are primarily concerned with purposeful, task-oriented group communication in this chapter, it will suffice to mention briefly that there are casual, or informal groups. They tend to lack an agenda or a specific purpose which has been defined prior to the meeting. Usually there are no clearly definable results which involve all members of the group after a meeting has concluded. The purpose of such groups is usually social, they exist for the enjoyment of their members although at times specific problems may be discussed quite seriously and at length. However, such informal groups frequently develop into more formal group efforts.

It may very well be that a group of neighbors meets at a backyard party with the understanding that one of the things they wish to do is to discuss the upcoming election. In the process those attending decide that they want to develop a formal neighborhood political study circle which will meet regularly, invite candidates, and discuss political questions of importance to the community.

Groups Without Formal Leaders

Whether or not there is such a thing as a leaderless group has been debated for some time. The answer seems to depend on how one defines a leader. From experience and on the basis of most studies, there appears to be no such thing as a truly leaderless group. While many groups never select a formal leader, it is equally true that the leadership functions which will be discussed later in this chapter are necessary if the group is to continue existing and if it is to accomplish any kind of specific task. We could say then that groups can exist without formal leaders, appointed or self-appointed, but that group efforts require that a number of functions, which we will define as leadership functions, will be taken care of. Various individuals in the group may share these functions or take care of parts of these functions at different times to assure that the group can fulfill its purposes. By the same token, most groups either appoint a leader or one emerges in the course of the group interaction, since the catalytic function of a leader is deemed important to the smooth operation of the group, a sense of cohesion, and a sense of accomplishment. Leaderless group efforts usually result in: (1) inadequate exploration of the subject; (2) prolonged personality clashes; (3) lack of overall direction leading to (4) no definite conclusion or solution.

Small Groups in a Free Society

While we chuckle about such tongue-in-cheek jokes as, "A camel is a horse which was put together by a committee," most of us realize that a free society depends on the participation of individuals in all of its efforts. Stop to think for just a minute about the large number of charitable, civic, religious, political, and educational groups meeting every day of the week in your community. A good deal of our time and effort is directed toward work in small groups. There are few if any other nations in the world where this kind of citizen involvement and group participation is as highly developed as in the United States. As a matter of fact, after World War II, Germany and some other European countries developed educational, civic, and political study groups when they came in contact with the American example, since they had had little prior experience with such groups.

In every society there have been individuals who view the efforts of small groups with some disdain. They tend to believe in an authoritarian or elitist system, and thus feel that interaction in small groups is wasteful and really does not produce the same outstanding results one would get if decisions were made by experts. It is true that small group efforts are time-consuming. Whether or not that is wasteful, however, depends on one's philosophy of life and government. If the goal of a society is not merely the achievement of tasks, but the involvement of as many individuals as possible, then time is a commodity which in many instances is of only secondary importance. Underlying the entire idea is, of course, the belief that two heads are better than one, that even an expert can learn something from another expert or even from a layman who brings detachment but intellectual ability to a certain problem.

What has been said in these introductory pages could be summed up by definitions: Small groups depend on cooperative verbal and nonverbal interaction, in a face-to-face communication situation, involving three or more individuals who have come together in order to understand or solve some problem. Frequently a leader is appointed or emerges during such discussions, or leadership roles and functions are shared by a number of group members.

TYPES OF FORMAL GROUPS

Distinctions are frequently made between learning and problem-solving groups. However, the former can readily be included in the second category. The gathering of information and resulting learning can be defined as an attempt to solve a problem, namely that of ignorance or lack of knowledge. The steps involved in solving that problem are very similar to those used in other discussions. The major difference lies in the fact that group members are left to make their own decisions as to what they wish to do with the information they have gathered.

In effect, learning groups deal with some specific problem. The members gather as much information as possible, or involve experts who have the information, and then interact purposefully to understand and prepare themselves to make adequate use of the information they are sharing and discovering. The vital feature is one found in all group activities: All members are involved, all members interact and contribute. This last point is what makes a classroom discussion a meaningful learning experience rather than turning it into a conversation between two or three individuals. Just as obviously shared ignorance will result in ignorance, the mere fact that everyone is contributing does not assure that learning is taking place or information is being shared. Such learning groups often have little continuity beyond the immediate information-sharing experience. There is usually little incentive provided for the group to act on the information or knowledge which has been gained. Specific problems involving the entire group in their solution tend to tie us together for longer periods of time, and thus produce more easily discernible group action.

Therapeutic groups are similar to learning groups. They really are intended to help an individual understand himself. In role-playing groups or encounter groups of various types, there is undoubtedly some general learning which takes place by observing other group members and their responses. However, the final outcome of group efforts is usually individual development, individual understanding, individual self-assurance, rather than some goal the group in its entirety wishes to achieve.

In a highly organized, complex society such as ours, many people also become designated members of groups. Faculty members are assigned to specific committees as part of their academic workload. Members of political parties are assigned tasks which make them parts of groups. There may be no real feeling of need on the part of this kind of designated member, although he or she may make important contributions. Group membership, in other words, is not always a question of personal choice, but frequently becomes a question of necessity as a result of other choices we have made.

Much of what will be said in the following pages centers around the central fact that people tend to come together in groups, at least as we have defined groups, because they feel the need for interaction with other human beings. There is a felt need, a problem, which we believe can best be taken care of by working within a formal group. For that reason the problem-solving group, allowing for recognition of features which relate to learning and therapeutic groups, will be of major concern to us.

John Dewey is credited with developing the steps of a "reflective" thinking process, in his book *How We Think*.[1] In oral communication his ideas have found their most consistent practical application in problem-solving discussions. As this chapter develops you will see how Dewey's five steps can be used when interacting with other human beings as we explore or attempt to solve problems.

1. Define the problem.
2. Analyze the problem.
3. Suggest the solutions.
4. Evaluate the solutions.
5. Put the solutions into effect.

PROBLEM-SOLVING DISCUSSION AS A GROUP PROCESS

Ask yourself what would make YOU a member of a group? Probably the first thing that would come to your mind is the concept of a *common purpose*.

1. John Dewey, *How We Think* (Boston: D. C. Heath, 1933).

People are brought together in various organizations or groups when they decide to accomplish certain things, reach certain ends, or if they want to produce certain changes in cooperation with others. That means, in effect, that no successful discussion will result if the members of the group cannot agree upon a common subject. Merely because we all talk and listen to each other does not mean we are applying our information, experience, and efforts to the same goal. Therefore, a discussion group does not merely have a common purpose, but it goes beyond the purpose of the moment and sees some sort of goal or outcome for which all the individuals are striving.

For example, much vagueness in discussion results because participants get together and say, "Hey, let's talk about parking here at the college. It's a mess!" Look at that statement for a moment. Can any assumption be made that a common purpose or a common goal exists just because five other people immediately respond, "You are so right!" To some of them it may be a question of bungling by an administration they have already judged to be inept, others may consider it to be the fault of undisciplined students. Some may be interested in finding a solution because they get caught in an on-campus traffic jam every day. Others who live on campus and thus have no parking problems only want to find a subject to gripe about because they feel like griping.

A group has to be realistic about the limits within which it can operate. The students mentioned above might decide in a discussion that purchase of two hundred acres of land and construction of several dozen parking lots on this new property should take place immediately. Unfortunately, the college they are talking about happens to be in the middle of New York City and no one can find, much less pay, for two hundred acres of land for parking. All of us are limited by many things: laws, regulations, our roles in society, money, etc. Therefore, one of the first efforts by a small group engaged in a problem-solving discussion is to find out what its limitations are, because only such a realistic evaluation will lead to meaningful solutions. In order to function as a group, a common purpose and an understanding of the limitations of the group are vital.

Another vital factor in any group effort is the changing role of the individual. In order to get group backing, or in order to share in whatever benefits a group can bestow, we may have to give up certain privileges or rights. Let's think, for instance, of the right to free speech. A member of a small group is certainly free to speak, but so are the other four or five individuals who are involved. In other words, if cooperation is desired and if the contributions of the other members are important, each individual has to curtail his own participation.

Highly insecure individuals will be crushed by groups and overpowered by the strongest members. Highly authoritarian members will either learn to cooperate or will finally become so frustrated and unhappy that they will leave the group if they cannot run it their way. If individual group members are truly concerned about the final outcome of this process of oral communication, if the projected end is vital to them, adjustments will be made rather easily. However, if they see the discussion only as a means of gaining status, then the demands made upon them in this cooperative effort will cause them great difficulty. Basically there are three ways of responding to this challenge. Two of them positively contribute to any group's efforts in discussion.

1. Assumption of group task roles, that is behavior which assists the group in carrying out its purposes;
2. Assumption of roles which result in behavior that helps to build and maintain the group itself.

And third is the negative behavior which results strictly in a self-centered role, producing self-gratification but no discernible benefits to the group.

It is well, then, to find out *before* a discussion how an individual sees himself in relationship to the group within which he must function. If he considers the aims of the group important to him personally, or to the purpose he has in mind, he will be more willing to adjust to any standards, norms, or regulations the group must impose on its members to accomplish the task. Don't assume that violation of these rules or norms is the result of disagreement, however, because sometimes it is caused by misunderstanding. In a free society a significant challenge is to assist the individual group member in fulfilling his personal goals as well as those of the group.

PROBLEM SOLVING IN THE SMALL GROUP

Small group communication benefits from the contributions that men and women of different backgrounds, experiences, and feelings can bring to a situation or question. Human beings very seldom make decisions solely on the basis of "facts." Our feelings, attitudes, and background have a significant bearing on which facts we select from among those available to us. That is one of the reasons why an answer to a given question which occurs to you may not appear desirable to someone else. But it also is the reason why scrutiny of a possible solution by several people may be far superior to one limited, and perhaps prejudiced reaction. In effect, the concept of interaction is at work here. Ideas can be modified, explored, developed, and vicariously tested.

People Who Have Shared in Making a Decision Tend to Assume Responsibility for Carrying It Out

Decisions made by others and forced upon us usually result in very little voluntary cooperation on our part. While we may not always give our enthusiastic support to decisions we helped to make, the very fact that we have a personal stake in them often results in much more cooperation. In carrying out any plan or solution the efforts of at least several people are needed. The more individuals there are who have had a voice in the initial interaction, the easier it will be later on to find those who will work diligently at carrying out the decision of the group.

Cooperation Produces More Lasting and Meaningful Results

As opposed to the technique of debate, which is basically founded upon the premise of advocating an idea against all opponents, small group efforts are based on mutual respect and cooperation. There will be disagreements concerning the merits of a given point as perceived by various members of a group. However, the underlying purpose or the overall aim is to come up with an agreement or a solution reached by the group, rather than by any individual. Either the group wins or no one wins. While debate may often follow such initial explanations or problem-solving efforts, the two are seldom compatible when employed at the same time. If a small group has interacted according to the concepts discussed in this chapter, no one's feeling should be hurt to the extent that he will actively work against the group's final decisions. In other words, room should be left for compromise and a participant should not be required to stand or fall with his original opinion.

Listening and Speaking Are Combined

Public speaking, oral reading, and many other forms of oral communication play a vital role. Most of them, however, require silent participation on the part of listeners. In the small group, on the other hand, it is possible both to hear what others have to say and then to react audibly. There is no better opportunity for us to learn to think quickly and to state ideas clearly than in the small group situation. It is also a good testing ground for our ability to hear and understand the statements made by other group members.

There are those who believe that the terms discussion and democracy are inseparable. For that reason they will give lip service to the idea, but will not use the small group processes honestly. They are saying in effect: "In order to appear fair, I'll call my subordinates or co-workers together to explore and possibly solve a problem, but I have already made up my mind about what needs to be done and they had better not give me much trouble in accepting my views." When the small group interaction is introduced into tightly structured, authoritarian systems, such as the military, that sort of attitude can severely hamper its effectiveness. No second lieutenant who appears on a panel with a superior officer can diplomatically forget what their relationship is. By all definitions applicable in such a situation, the older, more experienced man is in a position to make his subordinates accept his views—and thus possibly lose the benefits of all the experiences, learning, and insight others could provide.

The General Situations

Private. This type of group effort depends on the involvement of a limited, usually very small number of people who are attempting to understand or solve a problem involving them personally or involving another very limited number of people. Involvement of others or presentation of the problem to a public assembly would hinder rather than help in solving the problem. A discussion between a father and son in a family situation or use of discussion in a therapy group between a psychiatrist and his patient are specific examples. Dyadic situations, explored earlier, best fit this category.

Public. Groups which are formed to deal with public problems, on the other hand, depend to a large extent for the implementation of their suggested solutions on public recognition of their work. In the initial phases they may still meet in private homes, or have little exposure to anyone except the members of their group. However, the nature of the problem they are exploring, and for which they may be seeking solutions, requires that they eventually involve other individuals who were not part of the original group. For example, a group of students which meets regularly to discuss problems related to the curriculum or grading procedures at a given university finally may ask for implementation of its suggestions by the appropriate administrative officers of the school.

As the terms private and public are used here, they do not mean that the initial interaction takes place in private or in public, but rather that the eventual results of the interaction which has taken place will be a matter of more limited private involvement, or the involvement of larger groups with a certain amount of public awareness. The larger the group of people involved in such group interaction, the more automatically will they be in contact with a larger public, and the more public will their efforts become. Such public discussions or small group interaction will also tend to be structured according to rather formal, conventional systems or methods.

At times severe problems arise when confusion develops between public and private interaction of the types considered here. If a psychiatrist were to write up a report for some medical paper dealing with his patient, without the latter's consent and identifying him by name, a severe loss of confidence by the patient may result. On the other hand, public discussion is by nature intended to have its results become known, to have the decisions used in some larger setting. For that reason, confidential or secret information will have to be clearly labelled by the one providing it, otherwise the group will undoubtedly feel free to use the information in any way it sees fit. Even our laws make provisions for that distinction, when they allow public bodies to go into executive session for the purpose of discussing personnel matters which otherwise might become embarrassing to an individual.

THE LEADER AND OTHER MEMBERS
OF THE SMALL GROUP

As was pointed out earlier, all participants in small group interaction play certain roles.

The Leader

The leadership role can be judged, evaluated, or described along a formal continuum. In their dealings with others, leaders range from highly authoritarian on one extreme to laissez-faire on the opposite extreme, with other categories in between. Depending on specific situations, groups, or the personality of the leader, each individual may consistently use one type or a variety of these leadership types.

A highly authoritarian leader will dominate the members of his group, giving them little opportunity for doing anything but agreeing with him and supporting his decisions. A supervisory leader will tend to modify that control and be less demanding, stringent, or categorical in his approach. The democratic leader seeks and encourages participation by members of his group, and will serve primarily as a facilitator by assisting members of the group to achieve both the task and their own purposes. Laissez-faire leaders are actually mere figure heads, they allow the group members to do what they want to with virtually no control, assistance, or special concern on their part. At times individuals are chosen for the purpose of lending dignity or authority to a proceeding while interfering to a minimum degree with the outcome already predetermined or desired by the group.

In the following paragraphs discussing the role of a leader in formal panel discussions, you will notice a distinct preference for the democratic leadership type. However, that should not be interpreted to mean that other types are not desirable under other circumstances. The needs of the group, the specific situation, and the task to be accomplished dictate the preferrable type.

Whether a leader is chosen prior to a discussion or whether he emerges in the course of its development, he must fulfill two basic functions. On one hand the group, or those who have assigned the group a certain task, expect him to serve as a *facilitator* in accomplishing that task in the quickest, most efficient, and most meaningful way. In other words, he is expected to play a major role in rallying the resources of the group to get the job done. However, there are also group needs which he has to help fulfill. Such needs include a feeling of success, opportunities for participation, a feeling that the effort is worthwhile, a feeling that the valuable time of individual group members is not being wasted, and a meaningful distribution of rewards. On the basis of these factors, how can the role of the leader be described?

He does not dominate the discussion or other group members. Put more simply, this means that it is the leader's job to assist every member of the group in making his most useful and valuable contributions to the group effort, without putting words in another person's mouth. He must be comfortable in letting others speak, although he might have had the same idea or could have said it better. He is not some sort of father-figure who sits enthroned over the group permitting others to speak. A truly outstanding discussion will provide opportunities for the leader to contribute, but his role in controlling, guiding, and involving others will blend in smoothly with the efforts of everyone else on the panel.

He guides the discussion to its intended goal or purpose. Here the leader's role becomes most noticeable. Basically, it is his job to keep people from overworking any one point, to summarize what has been said up to a given point, and to aid the other group members in moving ahead to the next idea. He assists quiet members in making contributions, clarifies the lengthy or indefinite contributions of others, keeps track of the vital ideas expressed or discussed, and finally brings the discussion to a well-rounded conclusion.

If a leader is to be appointed the following questions serve as guidelines in choosing an individual who can most successfully fulfill the basic chores discussed above.

Does he possess self-control?

Can he listen attentively without either becoming bored or confused?

Does he have a certain analytic ability which makes it possible for him to keep the total question in mind, while showing some insight into all contributions group members might make?

Can he speak clearly, loudly enough, and without offending group members?

Does he have the ability to inspire respect and a willingness on the part of other group members to cooperate with him?

Does he seem to understand the problems to be discussed?

The Leadership Role. Some of the following steps are part of the normal preparation for a discussion and some of the specific aspects of the role played by successful discussion leaders.

1. A discussion leader makes sure that he understands the problem and the purpose of the discussion. It may even be necessary to meet with group members before the discussion in order to develop a specific question. For instance: Should our college build a new gymnasium? That's a question of policy—some specific action is called for or rejected. Other types of formal discussion frequently center around questions of *fact* and thus call for understanding a certain problem, its identification or definition. For instance: Who is the best player on this year's football team? The more definite the question the more definite is the answer likely to be and the group will be less likely to get off the track, a constant danger in small group communication.

2. The discussion leader prepares the physical setting and gets things ready for the discussion. If a blackboard would help in spelling out details, a leader should make sure it is available. Physical comfort of the participants should be considered, especially as far as temperature and seating is concerned. The leader should not make things too comfortable, though, since one expects participants to remain alert and active. Very important is a seating arrangement which makes it possible for all panel members to be in face-to-face contact with each other and the leader. Semicircles or arrangements around a table are usually most satisfactory. If at all possible, avoid having the quietest members of the group sit next to each other or on the extreme ends of the group. In either case, they may be "lost" to the effort. They may be comfortable keeping each other silent company, or just fading into the background.

3. The discussion leader introduces the subject briefly and meaningfully. Long introductions slow down the discussion before it gets moving. He briefly

states the subject, introduces the group members to each other if that is necessary, and immediately starts with some statement or question relating to the first part of the subject. One word of caution should be included here. Questions such as, "Do you agree that we have a parking problem?" can too easily be answered by a simple yes or no. From that point on, only more questions by the leader will elicit further responses, and the discussion will turn into a painfully dull question-and-answer game. The leader's first statement usually sets the pace; that is why it is so important to consider it carefully. A leader might ask, "What does our parking problem consist of?" More informative answers can then be supplied by the group members, and others will be more likely to react to the ideas expressed by the first respondent.

4. The discussion leader does not let any segment of the discussion be overworked. If a point has been covered, if a kind of plateau has been reached and the panel members begin to go around and around on the same ideas, time is being wasted. At that point it is best to summarize briefly, using any notes the leader has made on that part of the discussion. What has been accomplished can then be used as a jumping off point for the next part to be covered. Leaders are expected to deal fairly with other people's statements, however. This is not the time to "get even" with group members or to tell them what they should have talked about.

5. The discussion leader helps group members stay on the track. Broadening the subject to include relevant material does not mean the group members are going off the track. If members bring in irrelevant material, or go off on a tangent, a simple reminder can bring them back to their task: "I believe we have moved away from our subject. Could we come back to the question we are dealing with right now?" This attitude will also make it possible for members who feel that their leader doesn't see the relevance of a point they wish to make to respond. However, if everyone agrees that the group is off the track, the leader has provided the opportunity to get back to the assigned task.

6. The discussion leader helps the quieter members of the group make their contributions by asking them direct questions, preferably while some interesting point is being vigorously discussed by others. This can be a challenging test and the leader needs to look for nonverbal clues indicating that the quiet member is ready to contribute. Otherwise, a sudden question could frighten him into silence for the rest of the discussion.

7. The leader helps clarify the statements of group members if they are too lenghy or vague. Again, fairness with the ideas of others is the key word here.

8. The leader keeps more outspoken, wordy members from dominating the discussion. Usually a gentle reminder that others need to be brought in, or that contributions should be kept brief and to the point, is sufficient. More autocratic group members need to be made aware of the fact that the leader is watching them, and that he will exert control to provide more balanced participation.

9. The leader keeps track of the time and makes sure that all portions of the subject matter get a fair chance to be discussed. When the end has been reached he summarizes the total discussion. The final statement is not intended to rehash everything that has gone on during the entire discussion. It should clearly be an answer to the original question developed by the group.

Any truly relevant points which make the solution clear or give information important to understanding the answer would be included.

Hopefully, a clear-cut conclusion or decision will stand at the end of a problem-solving or learning discussion. However, if a problem remains, a mere statement of agreement will not suffice. If the group members feel that another discussion is needed or that no answer can be supplied at that time, the leader should not disregard that point of view.

Alertness, a spirit of cooperation, but also one of using control over the process of discussion for the purpose of helping the group achieve its goals are vital to being an adequate leader. The successful group leader will be as well or better informed concerning the question as the other group members, without feeling that this information must be used except to allow him to summarize more adequately, and to provide information which group members might be lacking to reach a meaningful conclusion. In debates between two individuals we look for a "winner" but no one "wins" in a discussion unless the entire group wins, and the effective discussion leader constantly works toward that end.

Other Group Members

Some of the attitudes and contributions of group members have already been indicated briefly. In some ways the leader's job is the most important factor in a formal discussion, but the attitudes and abilities of other group members are also vital. Interaction in the small group is a cooperative effort, and the role played by any member of the group can only be adequately evaluated in relationship to everyone else's role.

If positive interaction is sought, group members will constantly strive to show a spirit of cooperation. Even the little device of using a question, rather than attacking point blank, can help accomplish that. Cooperation means that all members keep the accomplishment of the *group* effort constantly in mind.

Effective participation by group members is based on the fact that they are alert and physically active in their participation. The first of these terms refers to a mental alertness which makes group members aware of all that is going on, eager to follow, and striving to understand what is being said. The second term represents an inward attitude which is portrayed in our outward actions. A slouchy physical attitude is likely to be interpreted by other group members as disinterest.

Members can help the group to stay on the track. Vigorous responses to statements by others, even if this means a rapid-fire exchange of ideas between several members of the panel, are helpful, but they should also be clear, concise, meaningful statements. Rambling remarks, poorly phrased ideas and wordiness tend to confuse other members of the group. If group members go back to points already covered or ideas which have already been completely stated, the discussion will not move ahead to its goal. Preparation is the foundation for all contributions by group members if they are to be meaningful and worthwhile. Unless a participant knows what he is talking about, no one else will.

Failure of leadership does not mean that the discussion is doomed. If that problem arises, any well-prepared, alert member of the group can take over the leadership, or leadership may pass from group member to group member depending on his knowledge, background, and abilities.

Since we are focusing our attention on formal, task-oriented, purposeful small group interaction, there is a great temptation to overestimate the role of the leader and to underestimate the roles played by all other participants. Many small groups just "happen." Just as certainly as we tend to be more frequently involved in interpersonal dyadic or triadic communication rather than public speaking situations, we tend to participate more frequently in informal small groups than in formal panels. It would be wrong to jump to conclusions at this point, and assume that formal public speaking or formal discussion groups are less important. Both fulfill specific purposes, both play a part in the overall structuring of our world, in the control of our environment, in the development of the individual, and in the development of our society. It is a question of which form or type of communication helps man to accomplish his purposes, not which is best or preferable under *all* circumstances.

While the formal discussion group seems somewhat dominated by the leader, the roles played by individual participants should be discussed in detail. Formal, appointed leaders can be found only in certain situations, usually when some force outside the group has an influence, or when specific tasks loom so large that we do not dare leave the outcome of small group interaction to chance. Truly "leaderless" groups do not seem to exist, on the other hand. What we tend to find in informal or less formal small groups is a constant exchange of leadership roles by participants, an attempt to make up for the less formal structure by using the talents available within the group for the achievement of long-range or short-range goals.

There are undoubtedly circumstances under which individuals simply sit around, "shooting the breeze," "rapping," or whatever the current in-term is. In such cases we frequently have only interlinking conversations with other people sitting-in, listening, or perhaps an unpatterned exchange of ideas concerning no subject in particular. These exchanges frequently are more therapeutic, or perhaps they are for enjoyment, or for the purpose of keeping channels of communication open for later, more important events. Such small group communications are indeed "happenings." These happenings are important to human social behavior or action, but their very lack of structure and task orientation tends to remove them from the legitimate concern of this book, and its emphasis on purposeful, planned communication.

In all groups, however, the members appear to fulfill the following major roles:

Resource Person. This is the individual who has available and is capable of sharing some knowledge, experience, or information which is important to the other members of the group, and possibly the purpose of the discussion.

The Questioner. In much small group communication some points are not made very clear. A participant who asks further questions can help to overcome that problem. Not only can he help to clarify a point, but he can help bring an idea into clearer focus by expressing doubts about some claim made by a prior speaker.

The Conciliator. In the actual heat of discussion many situations develop which cause opposing or differing points of view to turn the original cooperative effort into a debate. The contribution of any group member who can help to bring opponents together, or who can help them to see relationships between ideas which make cooperation possible, can be extremely helpful.

The Synthesizer. Some individuals have the ability to look at the most complicated puzzle and see the relationship between all of its parts almost immediately. In any group interaction many ideas, concepts, and statements tend to add up to confusion because participants no longer see relationships or the ultimate purpose of their interaction. At this point someone in the group who has that special ability to organize ideas pulls together what has been said and gives it sharp summary focus.

The Sounding Board. Especially in informal groups, but also in other small groups, some have trouble making clear, definite statements. Often, in the course of interaction we come up with an idea which is not fully developed, not even clear to us. Someone in the group helps us develop and shape that idea by listening and asking brief pertinent questions and makes a vital contribution while helping to avoid great frustration.

The Analyst. Some group members have the ability to look at parts of the subject matter being discussed, probe deeply, and discover nuances and facts which no one else has been able to see. Such insights help others to understand the question or the point they are discussing more adequately.

The Explorer. New dimensions, new fields of endeavor, new vistas, new territory are the realm of the explorer. This individual has the ability to help members of his group go beyond their normal horizons and see different possibilities.

The Temporary Leader. Any group member becomes a leader if he gives direction or some form of control to the group effort. Even when a formal leader is appointed there is no need for the discussion to fail if he does not do his work adequately. The major benefit of the small group is that there are other capable individuals who can take over if only for the moment.

Obviously, these are overlapping functions. Different terms may describe the same basic concept of cooperative participation, but they should help us understand more clearly the variety of possibilities with which small group interaction provides us. The group is fortunate which, either by design or by chance, finds itself with all or almost all of the resources in human capability for interaction which are mentioned on the preceding pages.

LIMITATIONS ON THE SMALL GROUP PROCESS

Any subject which requires clearer understanding or which needs to be explored in search of a solution is suitable for discussion by a small group. But certain limitations to this process should be noted.

Time

If action is needed "right now," as may be required of a company commander in battle, there is simply no time to call a meeting of the men to discuss future action. The involvement of several people takes time, and that fact must be included as we study interaction in small groups.

Expertness or Background of Group Members

Unless group members know what they are talking about and have available the necessary information, the discussion method itself will not create results.

The Type of Problem

If a question can be answered simply by looking up a given fact, or by saying yes or no, the economy-of-effort-principle would tell us that discussion is a wasteful way of handling the subject. The question "Did Russia launch a Sputnick in 1956? " would be an example of a subject that can be dealt with simply by checking any encyclopedia.

If several people can develop a question more meaningfully and help to clarify it by subjecting it to various tests in a group discussion, the subject is probably well-suited to the approach discussed in this chapter.

HOW TO PREPARE A FORMAL DISCUSSION

The best starting point is for each group member to ask himself, How much do I know? This information should not be spotty or indefinite. Once a group member has determined the base from which he can work, he can begin doing research to fill in missing data. For panel discussions every member usually prepares for the entire subject, although each individual will probably come up with some information which others on the panel do not have.

Formats

The subject matter usually determines the format of a discussion. Depending on how many people need to be involved, and if sufficient information is available to all participants, one of the following formats can be chosen.

Forum.   Most frequently this term refers to the period after a meeting, a speech, or a discussion, when an audience is given the opportunity to question speakers or challenge ideas. However, at times a forum is the sole activity to discuss mutual problems such as new zoning laws or taxation and may involve large audiences.

Symposium.   A symposium is made up of a group of experts who are each given a limited amount of time to deliver prepared speeches about some problem. There is little or no interaction between participants, although a symposium is often followed by a panel discussion or a forum.

Panel.   This is the most frequently used type of formal discussion. usually a panel is made up of a group ranging from three to seven members and a leader. Each panel member is expected to interact with every other panel member, exchange ideas, question statements made by others, and explore the entire subject in keeping with the steps of a previously determined outline or agenda.

The next step is to look for the inherent structure of the subject. In the case of panel discussions, which will be considered here in some detail, a rough outline will help all the participants in researching the subject. However, flexibility is the key word. It is very likely that this outline or agenda will later be adjusted as the group becomes involved in the discussion. The greater insight group members have gained into their subject while doing research will probably lead to adjustments of any preconceived structure. As the need arises various areas can thus be added or subtracted in the course of the discussion.

Formal discussions usually have a time limit which requires that the group cover only as much as possible without confusing the issue and broadening the subject too much. Cooperative interaction requires that group members will be ready to respond positively to any suggestions for changes or additions their fellow panel-members make on the basis of information they have obtained. At the same time, groups should be realistic in selecting or accepting tasks. To discuss the evolution of mankind from the dawn of existence to the present in thirty-five minutes is simply not possible.

It is best to bring as much information as possible to the discussion, and then to depend on the interaction of panel members during the exploration of the subject to develop the specific areas or subject matter to be covered. In this way the best possible understanding of the question or its solution can be achieved by a group. No one will be entirely objective in any discussion, but such objectivity is more likely if few firm decisions or solutions are brought to the discussion.

Discussion Pattern

The most frequently used discussion pattern centers around the steps originally developed by Dewey. They can be readily adapted to a particular subject and situation.

Locate the Problem.   Once the group has established that a given problem is real and not merely imagined, members should make sure that they understand it in as much detail as possible. This is an important part of any discussion—like the solid base of a pyramid. In addition the group needs to make certain that it has the authority or competence to deal with the problem. A group can make life-long enemies if it tackles a subject which is someone else's responsibility, or group members can become thoroughly discouraged if they discover that no one will respond to their suggestions. The group needs to identify all the component parts of the subject under discussion, define them adequately, and make sure that it has listed all the factors involved. If the group does not know what the problem is, any later solution will be inadequate.

Analyze the Problem.   At this point causes and relationships need to be examined. This is the second level of the broad base of the pyramid. The group will probably spend most of its time on the first two or three steps. Standards of evaluation can be meaningful only if group members know under what conditions they are operating and what the minimum requirements for any good solution would be. All conditions which could influence later solutions must be considered. Necessary standards of achievement as well as basic values which cannot be violated should be listed.

Utilize All the Available Information.   If some data are weak, either more research needs to be done, an expert needs to be consulted, or the point can be left for some future study if it is not a vital part of the discussion. If the group members understand the problem and all its component parts, if they know its background, and have developed the various criteria or areas that need to be considered one at a time, the group can profitably move along to the next step. Step three really is a kind of intermediate summary, an attempt to make sure the group has all the necessary tools for developing the solution or providing the necessary information.

Explore Solutions.   At this point the group members suggest solutions based on the various data they have brought together in the prior steps. This is the first time the concept of a solution should even be mentioned.

Choose the Solution.   After checking, discussing, and perhaps tentatively testing several of the proposed solutions the group can reach a decision as to which solution will solve the problem most adequately while creating a minimum of new problems or undesirable side effects. No solution which leaves a bigger problem at the end of a discussion than existed at its beginning is desirable. Thus a discussion trying to solve a specific limited war may end up by considering the use of atomic bombs. But group members may completely reject that one possible solution because of the results of such an act which could possibly end the war but might create a worldwide conflict.

In problem-solving discussions, group members should work to understand all factors involved so that they can find out on which ideas they agree, on which ideas there may be partial agreement, and on which points they completely disagree. It is the purpose of a discussion to come up with a group consensus. It is the aim of any cooperative group effort to eliminate as much disagreement as possible so that the members can come up with an answer which represents the best possible solution or compromise.

SUMMARY:
GROUP INTERACTION

Two ideas form the basis for the use of small group interaction by free men. First, there is a belief that contributions from a number of individuals will be more helpful in understanding or solving a problem than if its solution is left to only one person. Second, cooperation is important in any free society, and individuals are more likely to play an active part in solving problems when they have been involved in the entire decision-making process.

A sense of active cooperative communication between members of any group is needed. This should never become a mere pooling of ignorance, but rather a determined effort to gather and present as much relevant information as is necessary. Discussions provide us with opportunities to test our own ideas, to have them challenged by other members of our group, and to develop a basis for further cooperative work in the actual solution of important problems. Such group efforts may provide more insight and understanding even if actual problem solving is not the task of the group, as is true in learning or therapeutic groups.

Preparation for and participation in formal discussions provide the fringe benefits of practice in formulating ideas quickly and accurately, as well as opportunities to modify existing ideas in a face-to-face oral communication situation.

EXERCISES

1. Check your library for published discussions, such as the *Northwestern University on the Air: The Reviewing Stand*, a popular radio series, or consider current television panels presented in your community.

    a. Analyze the leader's role in keeping with the concepts summarized in this chapter. Write a 250-word evaluation.

    b. Analyze the role of various participants in keeping with the concepts summarized in this chapter. Write a 250-word evaluation.

    c. Compare three different discussions and analyze their individual merits and weaknesses in a 500-word paper. Use the standards discussed in this chapter.

2. Your instructor will divide the class into discussion groups.

    a. Prepare a 25-minute discussion dealing with a specific question of fact relating to your school. Appoint a chairman, word the question, do research, and go through all the steps listed in your text.

    b. Develop a 40-minute discussion of policy, go through all the steps described in this text. The question may either deal with some problem on your campus or one relating to your specific community.

3. Your instructor will assign groups to write 200-word critiques for each of the discussions taking place in your class.

4. Conduct a 30-minute discussion on the basis of your written critiques, evaluating all discussions that have been held in your class up to this point, and suggest improvements for another series of discussions. After the panel discussion conduct a forum with the other members of your class.

5. Present a five-minute speech in class analyzing your participation in a variety of small groups. Distinguish the purposes of the groups and your reasons for joining them.

6. In a five-minute speech discuss the role of the individual in the small group. Consider individual versus group goals, and concentrate on possible problems or conflicts caused by the two.

BIBLIOGRAPHY

Barnlund, Dean C. and Franklyn S. Haiman. *The Dynamics of Discussion.* Boston: Houghton Mifflin, 1960.

Brilhart, John K. *Effective Group Discussion.* Dubuque: Wm. C. Brown, 1967.

Cathcart, Robert S. and Larry A. Samovar. *Small Group Communication.* Dubuque: Wm. C. Brown, 1970.

Cortright, Robert L. and George L. Hinds. *Creative Discussion.* New York: Macmillan, 1959.

Ewbank, Henry Lee and J. Jeffrey Auer. *Diccussion and Debate: Tools of a Democracy.* New York: Appleton-Century-Crofts, 1951.

Gibson, James W. *A Reader in Speech Communication.* New York: McGraw-Hill, 1971. Parts two and five.

Gulley, Halbert E. *Discussion, Conference, and Group Process.* New York: Holt, Rinehart, and Winston, 1968.

Harnack, R. Victor and Thorrel B. Fest. *Group Discussion: Theory and Technique.* New York: Appleton-Century-Crofts, 1964.

Keltner, John W. *Group Discussion Processes.* New York: Longmans, Green, 1957.

McBurney, James H. and Kenneth G. Hance. *Discussions in Human Affairs.* New York: Harper, 1950.

Phillips, Gerald M. *Communication and the Small Group.* Indianapolis: Bobbs-Merrill, 1966.

Rosenfeld, Lawrence B. *Human Interaction in the Small Group Setting.* Columbus, Ohio: Charles E. Merrill, 1973.

Smith, William S. *Group Problem-Solving Through Discussion.* Indianapolis: Bobbs-Merrill, 1965.

9

AUDIENCE ANALYSIS

In chapter 3 we considered the roles an individual may play in the communication process. Many of the specific ideas brought to your attention apply to an individual whether he is involved in a one-to-one exchange with another individual, or whether he plays his role as sender or receiver within a small or large group situation. However, the temptation is great to consider audiences in a formal speaking situation merely as a collection of individuals or on the other hand to assume that in a formal audience the group automatically adds up to more than the sum of its individual parts. Rather than drawing these simplistic conclusions, we will attempt to mention some factors the speaker needs to consider when he faces such an audience.

THE INDIVIDUAL AND THE LARGE GROUP

Joining together with a group of other individuals in a more formal listening situation creates some new dimensions for the expression of ideas, emotions, or attitudes which may be suppressed or handled quite differently in one-to-one communication. We join other human beings for a variety of reasons, but usually because we cannot accomplish satisfaction of certain needs or desires without such an association. We may seek companionship, we may want to feel less exposed by joining a crowd of people, we may feel that more meaningful action can be taken by a group of people rather than an individual, or in a capitalistic society, group rates make it possible for us to participate in events which we could not afford individually. For the purpose of communication groups of people, or audiences, also are desirable for some important reasons. The obvious, major advantage is that a speaker can reach a larger number of people in less time than one-to-one communication requires. However, groups of listeners also play other vital roles to be discussed in the following pages.

The Social Purposes of Communication

The formation of large audiences, often with very little awareness of other human beings engaged in the same activity, has at times led to less concern for the individual and more concern for mass psychology and mass communication. We speak of the fact that some seventy million people were in the audience listening to the now famous Nixon-Kennedy debates on television. However, there were only certain very limited factors, most of which had been rather arbitrarily defined by students of mass communication, which molded them into a national audience. More realistically there were thousands of small audiences throughout the nation consisting of one, two, or maybe half-a-dozen viewers congregated in the same room, reacting to each other as well as the television message. Undoubtedly some members of these smaller groups interacted the next day with individuals who had been members of other, similar small audiences assembled before a television set. However, they no longer interacted in the original communication situation.

All of this means simply that we must consider audiences and their purposes for listening in many ways. An advertising agency trying to sell a national automobile manufacturer on a certain television program will attempt to lump together as many people as possible into a meaningful audience, making the large expense of such a program appear reasonable. The President of the United States, presenting a message to all of the American people, will couch it in words and will keep the message general enough in hope of finding a kind

of generalized audience for it, while probably leaving a lot of individual questions unanswered. The man running for political office, however, knows that in order to win votes he has to do more than present a generalized message to the largest number of people. He has to buttonhole individuals and either convince them to vote for him or to go out and get others to vote for him. He needs, in other words, a clear target. However, it must also be acknowledged that in both of these last situations the speaker may purposely be vague when he speaks to large audiences.

Existing data seem to indicate that large audiences will seldom be persuaded to engage in specific long-range activities. Persuasion is not a one-shot effort in any case. The successful call for action or the successful attempt to change someone's mind most frequently results from follow-up on a one-to-one or in a small group situation.

Individuals in a Large Group

We tend to react more emotionally in crowds than we do as individuals since we can blend in with the emotional outbursts of others engaged in the same activities. We tend to react more in keeping with the group norms, that is we respond more consistently to the expectations of everyone in the audience with us. We tend to become less involved in long-range actions unless such calls for action are reinforced by more specific interpersonal contacts. No successful political campaign will ever be waged by means of television alone. Phone banks, house-to-house "blitzes," and similar devices must "get the vote out" on a one-to-one basis.

Relationship of Speakers to Audiences

Audiences provide important means for public speakers to develop common goals or to develop social action. Every society and every form of government needs in the long run some concerted efforts involving many people. It comes as a shock that both President Kennedy and Adolf Hitler asked their fellow citizens not to think of what their country could do for them but what they could do for their country. Not only do such appeals touch the spirit of unselfish dedication in man, but they are important if social cohesion between individuals is to be achieved.

Unfortunately, and this is especially true in dictatorships, audiences some-times serve speakers as "claques," or public orchestration in support of anything their leader wants to do. These demagogues actually count on the fact that members of an audience will be happy to leave the emotional situation which has been created as long as no specific follow-up actions are required of them. They are content that someone else will take care of the details. That is why again and again it is stated that democracy requires participation, not merely in communicative acts, but also in the processes which follow. It is not enough to say "we have communicated," or "we have discussed the matter," because we need to think of public communication and public discussion as merely starting points. Confusion and disagreements may still result after discussion, after communication, has taken place. Talking to each other because we want to continue to think and work together is one thing, talking to each other to stop thought and to prevent cooperative action is quite another matter.

As we have seen, everything we do and everything we say communicate something to someone, but we need to remind ourselves that when we use that term in the pages of this book we will think of it as a purposeful activity on the part of the communicator to which a purposeful, thoughtful response by a listener or by a larger audience is sought. Most public communication seeks response on the basis of understanding as well as feeling. Communication is not, by definition, a one-way street through which only the ideas of the communicator travel to be eagerly received and "swallowed" by his audience. Chapter 3, for that reason, combined the roles of the sender and receiver under one heading to make sure that there would be no exclusive division between the two.

Most of us join groups or audiences with certain expectations. Few human beings enter any situation without some purpose, just wanting to see what happens or permitting the group to control them completely. As a result we program ourselves, we get ready to respond. When members of an audience are affected by what a speaker has to say, individual effects as well as group effects result depending on the individuals' readiness to respond and the factors which have molded all the members of the audience into one cooperative interacting unit. There are, of course, degrees of response. For instance, someone at a basketball game always yells louder for the home team to win than anyone else. Participation in some group activity could be judged incorrectly, however, if we go only by appearances. When the contribution plate is passed after a stirring speech, group pressure may be strong to put something in the collection. Yet an individual is still free to slip in a slug or a button, appearing to take a part but in reality refusing to do so.

In analyzing any audience, therefore, the speaker must carefully consider the expectations and values of the audience. After all, he has a message which he wants his listeners to receive. The most obvious concept in that regard is that the audience must be able to hear or receive the message, which means that the speaker must speak loudly enough and use a language his audience can understand. Other less obvious factors will be detailed in the following pages.

THE AUDIENCE

The terms group or audience can be misleading if we let them become too broad and all-inclusive, making distinctions between various groups and audiences difficult. As the tasks which groups have been assigned or which they assign themselves vary, the nature of groups obviously varies, and so do the specific roles which individuals play within the group or audience.

Audience Dimensions

Three obvious, but helpful dimensions of audiences can be charted as follows: formal–informal; small–large; long-term–short-term. Between these extremes there is a variety of possible designations. The three dimensions are also related. For instance, a small group backing a charity bazaar may be quite formal in its organization, the way it conducts its business, and it may have some sort of formal charter. Another, larger group meets on a weekly basis to listen to a speaker discussing the hobby of horticulture. The meetings are informal, members may or may not attend, there is no membership fee, the group has no charter, no officers are elected, and no specific conclusions affecting the group are reached at the end of the weekly meetings. Some audiences, such as college lecture classes, are formal, structured, carefully planned and long-term, while most audiences are one-time or very short-term groups.

One noticeable feature about formal groups is the fact that they usually have some sort of specific routine or ritual. Anyone who has made the "chicken-and-peas-circuit" of men's service clubs can pretty well predict that there will be a flag salute, an opening prayer, the singing of some rousing songs, or whatever else constitutes a formalized way of making the group act together as a unit. Such groups also tend to exist for long periods of time, and they have regular, scheduled meetings. Audiences, of course, keep changing, though the same basic group forms them.

Probably the most indefinite audiences are those which are formed in response to the effects of mass communication media. Everyone who has read *Love Story* or *The Population Bomb* is in a loosely defined way part of that book's audience. Everyone who tunes in Johnny Carson on the "Tonight" show is part of an audience. However, contact or interaction between all the members of that audience, even in a physical sense, is never possible because of its size, and they frequently are one-time or short-term audiences.

Audiences tend to develop a situation, a context, a climate of which speakers need to be aware. Addressing an assembly of the Daughters of the American Revolution is usually a very formal ritualistic situation. Introductions are carefully prepared and read, wording is less than conversational, and certain patriotic value terms are frequently repeated. To refuse to consider this setting and the resulting context for a speaker's message is sheer folly if the communicator is interested in purposeful communication resulting in a specific positive response. The final task of any communicator is always to discover that channel or those channels through which he can send his message. There is no faster way to block such channels than to assume that everyone else feels exactly as he does, or to assume that everyone has to draw the same conclusions about life and its basic values as he does. Communication calls for adjustments between sender and receiver, between a speaker and his audience. As one public speaker used to point out: "Remember there are always more of them than there are of you." While a certain feeling of self-assurance helps a speaker, that attitude should not become the sole reason for expecting an audience of hundreds of people to change its fundamental beliefs and accept those of the speaker. Audience analysis, in the long run, requires of the communicator that he discover the aims and purposes of his audience. These he should fulfill or help to fulfill as much as possible, while at the same time accomplishing his own purposes.

No human being, and thus no speaker is ever entirely unselfish. One could point to Franklin Delano Roosevelt's famous Fireside Chats or Martin Luther King's speeches on behalf of the Civil Rights Movement in our country. Their speeches had important effects on the total society, but both men were part of that society and thus personally influenced by the decisions their audiences made. In other words, Franklin Delano Roosevelt, as President of the United States, needed the support of those who listened to him in order to carry out his plans, and his own historical role depended on those who cooperated with him. Both men not only spoke on behalf of causes, but they also were highly respected by many individuals who gave them important status and personal satisfaction. They received personal honors as a result of what they did and had to say, they were given important positions, illustrating the fact that no human being is capable of entirely separating his personal fortunes or his personal position from the general welfare, even if the latter is of primary concern to him.

One vital dimension relates to the predominant audience mood or attitude. If maximum adjustment by the sender is to be achieved he has to ask himself whether his audience is *hostile, disinterested or apathetic,* or *friendly and cooperative.* Obviously, any public speaking situation incorporates a number of objects or sources toward which these attitudes can be directed including the speaker, the message, and the occasion. Even the attitudes which the members of the audience have toward themselves can be vital.

We know that a positive relationship to a speaker can cause members of an audience to modify their views toward a subject which they do not like or with which they do not agree. For that reason the selection of a spokesman for unpopular causes becomes very important. Political candidates often "import" leaders of their party to assist them in their campaigns because they hope for a positive identification. At the same time we must also be aware of the fact that identification with an unpopular cause has an effect on how the audience sees the speaker. Even a highly positive image can stand only a certain number of identifications with a negative cause.

Audiences see themselves in specific relationships to the other component parts of the communication situation. If they feel "defeated," "misunderstood," or "dejected," if they are attending a meeting under coercion or because they know someone is checking their attendance, they are in effect programmed to look for all that is bad, boring, disgusting, deceptive, and otherwise negative about the speech, the speaker, and the occasion. As every stage performer knows, an audience which is feeling good, happy, cooperative and ready to enjoy itself can hardly be stopped. The entertainer can even be only moderately good or moderately funny, and yet his audience will literally "roll in the aisles" with every joke.

The dimension of time should not be forgotten. An audience which has been forced to wait for a speaker beyond the announced hour may have to be prepared all over again for a positive reception. Being the last speaker in a group of ten puts anyone in a difficult position. Because such a large number of speakers may cause an audience to become bored or disinterested, experienced program chairmen often put the most short-winded, sparkling, exciting speaker last on the program. This assures in most cases a happy, positive ending to lengthy presentations. Even one speaker should consider the old rule, however, that the brain tends to give out at about the same time—or earlier—as the posterior. Some excellent twenty-minute speeches make terrible one-hour diatribes. The time of day also needs to be considered. Late evening speeches have audiences which are usually more tired than groups meeting at midday. By the same token, considering audience expectations is vital. The speaker who takes ten minutes when his audience was set for an hour's presentation may leave his listeners with a feeling that they have been cheated. It must be evident that the speaker who has not taken time to consider these various dimensions of the audience and occasion may find himself in considerable difficulty.

Occasion is a term which includes many of the concepts we have discussed in chapters 3 and 5. Settings create moods, and a subdued setting can be shattered by a boisterous individual or a joke which is out of place. Audiences get clues from the environment. Lively, light music prepares the audience for a light, entertaining speech, and a scientific lecture on nuclear physics may come as a negative surprise in such a setting. Audiences, as is true of most human beings in one-to-one situations, do not like to engage in constant emotional and intellectual "flip-flops" which leave everyone confused and perceiving an unstable situation. Even introductions to a formal speech provide such indicators for the audience—clues by which they can judge the occasion. It is difficult to shift gears when a speech starts with a series of several jokes and is followed by the speaker's request, "now let's get serious."

Locations for any speech are important. The atmosphere for the old-time brusharbor religious meetings lent an air of excitement, fellowship, and enjoyment which made for some rousing religious experiences. A small audience which finds itself in a large auditorium may interpret the setting as "failure," "lack of interest," or "defeat." A careful speaker makes sure that he has clearly defined the occasion for himself so that he can clearly define it for his audience as he structures or develops the setting. He also shapes his messages in such a way as to prevent disturbing the mood he needs.

One of the major factors about any audience is the crowd atmosphere, the enjoyment of a common experience, the heightened expectations, and the constant stimulus of other human beings who provide us with clues as to what to expect and what to feel. The physical setting is important, and usually culturally predetermined. Americans like to be close but not too close. Being crowded makes for greater closeness but also for irritation and discomfort, especially if it is hot or raining during an outdoor meeting. Americans have a sense of "personal space" which makes them keep a comfortable distance from other individuals in communication situations. They like to sit across from people, rather than sitting next to someone with whom they are communicating. Many of our public buildings, such as churches and meeting halls, have long narrow rows of pews, benches, or chairs. Speakers can often be seen only as tiny figures a hundred or more feet away from us. The ancient Greeks, and even the Romans, had a great sense or feeling for the need to be close to others in their speaking or public performance situations. Circular seating arrangements, which make a sender much more a part of his audience, even today are preferred by many experienced ministers or public speakers.

The importance of audience size has been intimated. It is especially of concern when specific tasks await members of the audience. A charity drive often depends upon large numbers of people. In other situations smaller audiences actually help us to be more casual, informal, and develop a closer relationship in both physical and emotional terms. What is a good size for an audience?

There is no way that that question can be answered without knowing the number of people required by your specific purpose or task. But it is a truism that size is only important in relationship to task and purpose and the physical distance which is created for a speaker, especially if he needs close contacts to accomplish his purposes.

The size of audiences is often related to both the time of day, depending on how convenient it is for people to attend a meeting, and time from a historic, sequential point of view. Since most men work during the day, PTA audiences on a weekday morning will consist mostly of women. At the same time historical events or the sequence of events preceding a speech will have much to do with audience size. Peace rallies as a war is winding down, for instance, will have smaller audiences.

AUDIENCE EXPECTATIONS

Audiences, and thus individuals within audiences, look for at least three things from public speakers and their messages, as well as from other members of the audience.

1. They look for an opportunity to keep their actions consistent with their value systems. Human beings like to think of their beliefs and actions as being well-integrated and consistent.
2. They look for a reward or satisfaction. Such rewards may be strictly emotional, they may consist of gaining new knowledge, or they may consist of opportunities to better one's life. Regardless of what forms such rewards take, members of any audience would like to feel that they have not wasted their time.
3. They would like to have some clear awareness or definition of their positive relationships to others. People judge their actions in part by the reactions of other members of valued groups to which they belong. If they are rejected, or if they feel that they look like fools, their anger will be directed against the communicator who put them in that position. Giving a caustic answer to a question raised by an audience member may make the speaker look brilliant to some people, but if it causes the questioner to lose face before his peers, the speaker has made an enemy.

Oral communication, including public speaking, is one of the most direct communicative confrontations between human beings. One can accept ideas presented in a book without taking them as a personal affront. The same words addressed to an individual before an audience make it more difficult for him to remain anonymous or consider the question on a strictly intellectual level.

Sometimes unfortunate confrontations between speaker and listener are the results of carelessness, because the speaker did not adequately judge the mental capacities of the members of his audience or their attitudes. At other times confrontations result when a speaker confuses the unwillingness of a given audience to recognize or deal with an existing need with a lack of knowledge of the existing situation. Consider the following situation: A student challenges his professor and when disagreement results, he blames it on a "communication gap." The reply made by his teacher, "No! I fully understand what you are saying. I simply disagree with you," may be a very unexpected and thus unnerving reaction.

By now it is obvious that audience analysis requires the awareness and gathering of information, before, during, and after a speech. Information about the consistent reactions of an audience in the past can be a valuable help in the preparation of a given speech. In order to make a speech clear and identify the specific points which a speaker wants his audience to understand, accept, or reject, he ought to know as much about his audience's expectations as possible. At the same time any effective speaker is conscious of the importance of feedback and encourages it. Much vital information thus reaches the sender and causes him to modify his message while he speaks. Staying in visual and empathic contact with his audience helps any speaker clarify previous statements, adjust his language and prevent both overreaction or lack of reaction.

ANALYZING AUDIENCES

There are some generalized categories which represent a good starting place for the analysis of any audience. A speaker should get these specific data as soon as possible before developing his speech.

Important Audience Factors

The following list consists of broad, general, easily obtainable data.

1. Age. Predominant age, as well as range of ages, or differences in ages should be considered. There may be tensions in the audience because of age differences, or difference in age between the speaker and his listeners could become a barrier.

2. Sex. Predominant sex, as well as the relationships between members of the sexes. A man speaking before an all female audience has an easier task in most situations than a woman speaking before an all male audience. If women in attendance are the wives of the male members of the audience, references to certain male-female relationships may have to be considerably tempered.

3. Education. This includes not merely the formal education we usually think of, but all knowledge gained in all possible ways. Obviously, a group of farmers may be very knowledgeable about agriculture, even though they do not have master's degrees in agronomy. The language and structure of the speech will be strongly influenced by consideration of this factor.

4. Membership in Groups. People join groups because they feel a need to do so. If a speaker can determine what groups members of his audience belong to he may gain some of the most meaningful insights into their belief and value systems.

5. Economic Status. In our society many opportunities depend on our financial ability to take advantage of them. In addition, the economic status of members of an audience may result in the acceptance or rejection of a plea

for support of the project in which a speaker wants them to become involved.

Other factors can either be categorized under the above headings or can be considered separately, such as race, family status, occupation, politics and religion. Many speakers are so anxious to say what they have to say that this rather perfunctory look at their audience is judged to be enough. However, once a speaker has gathered information concerning these basic factors a look at other aspects is important to his preparation.

Subgroups within Larger Groups

Members of an audience may have been identified as Democrats. What does that really mean? Are they all of the same mind concerning political concepts? They could all be addressed as Democrats and the speaker would get a certain general response from them, but once a specific item of national or international politics has been mentioned the speaker may find his audience split along very definite ideological lines. The same fact holds true in other groups. In addition to considering the major groups, possible differences in position within those groups must also be recognized: liberal, moderate, conservative; or anarchist, revolutionary, reactionary; or very fanatic, fanatic, not fanatic. Many similar categories could be listed, depending on the specific groups considered. In other words, it is not at all sufficient to identify someone in very general terms as a Communist or a Bircher. To understand him we must know much more about him.

The Degree of Involvement.   There are revolutionaries who by reason of age or exposure are no longer as involved as they once were. There are inactive liberals and there are active liberals. There are conservatives who will tell you of their conservatism any chance they get, and then there are others who will supply that information only when asked. Just belonging to a group or to a specific subgroup is not always an indication of the amount of involvement. A stirring speech may be entirely lost on an audience which considers its involvement to be on merely an intellectual level. They may nod their heads vigorously in agreement, but refuse to engage in any other overt acts.

Attitudes.   A very involved conservative Republican may nevertheless have so much experience with people who hold different beliefs that he is capable of being tolerant of other views. That does not mean he will not oppose these views or that he will not work to defeat them. On the other hand he is capable of listening to others, discussing subject matter with them rather than becoming emotional, and he does not assume that simply because a person is his opponent on one question he has to be his lifelong enemy. Other people may be incapable of personal tolerance because of their dedication to ideas. Attitudes, after all, are consistent, learned bases for our responses including cognition, emotion or feeling, and action.

Membership in Specific Reference Groups.   A dedicated church member may also be deeply involved in certain social or political causes. He may keep these various roles in his life distinct and separate, possibly not even mentioning his relationship to one group while working with the other. Deep internal conflicts may result when two or more roles become antagonistic and at times this conflict may result in bitter reactions to anyone who forces the individual publicly to make a choice. One example would be that of a minister who decides to join a civil rights march in his clerical garb. He cannot "hide" in a crowd under these circumstances, and confrontations with his parishioners may result. The minister's choice to take a public stand may become traumatic.

Level of Interest. We cannot assume that human interest in any subject is always the same from moment to moment. A woman who is about to have a child may love her husband very much, indeed may love him more than she did previously, but the birth of the child, for the moment, becomes more important. A tired or even exhausted audience may be concerned with a subject, but simply not have the physical ability to show great interest at the moment. Some subjects require only a momentary interest while others require a sustained interest. Many speakers destroy their own impact by insisting on continued involvement when a certain problem has been solved or the audience no longer sees a reason for continuing a certain effort. The relationship of level of interest to degree of involvement is obvious.

Relationship to Speaker, Audience, Occasion

As was made clear earlier, even after considering all these factors, a listener or an entire audience may still respond in such a personal way to a speaker that his subject or the occasion make no difference. What the speaker has to say is accepted or rejected merely because of his personality. At other times the subject is so important that the influence of the speaker is minimal, or the speaker and subject may be highly acceptable, but the occasion is judged to be wrong. All these and other possible relationships of speaker, speech, and occasion are to be taken into consideration, with heavy emphasis on the analysis of the audience. The typical speaker must rely on inquiry, personal observations, and also past experiences in similar situations, to supply him with valuable insights.

After these vital data about the audience have been gathered the speaker must make his basic decision: What am I going to say to them? It helps to break the question down into several parts.

1. What *should* be said? What are the things the situation and the audience require to create a positive response?
2. What *must* be said? In other words, what are the minimum requirements to accomplish the predetermined task?
3. What *can* be said? Considering the time limit and all other limitations what can the speaker reasonably hope to say to his audience?
4. What would *I like* to say? The speaker should identify clearly what his own desires, motives, and hopes are.
5. What *could* be said? If some last minute changes take place, either as far as the time limit is concerned, or the inclusion of an unplanned question-and-answer period, the speaker should be ready to have additional meaningful material in mind to assist in accomplishing his overall purpose.
6. What *might* be said? These are certain questionable, dangerous, provoca-

tive ideas, which the speaker should have explored in his own mind. If some specific challenge or some very unexpected turn of events forces him to develop an entirely new approach from the one he had planned, he will be ready.

It should be obvious however, that a speaker cannot answer these questions meaningfully unless he answers them with a specific audience in mind. Otherwise, he is merely preparing what he considers to be important, and chances are excellent that his message will miss its target altogether. The basic drives of human beings such as hunger or sex may differ very little, but the ways in which man satisfies them vary greatly depending on cultural, societal, and situational differences. Merely to assume that all men are alike because they have certain basic needs, and then to formulate a speech on that vague basis could become disastrous. At times, differences may be much more important cthan similarities between human beings, and human beings cherish these differences for the security and the status they provide.

SUMMARY:
THE SPEAKER AND THE LARGE GROUP

This chapter has provided you with an opportunity to view the relationship of a speaker to his audience in formal public speaking situations. After the speaker has considered the role an individual plays when he becomes part of a large group, after he has considered the group as a whole, after he has considered all the factors which help to describe or identify that specific group, and after he feels that he has done an adequate job of analyzing and adapting to those to whom he purposefully directs his message in order to gain a specific response, he should be ready for the rhetorical situation. A final task will be to create interest, while speaking, in something the audience needs and should be informed about, the content of the message.

Audience memberships vary from a casual to a consistent, dedicated relationship. Members of any given audience could either have walked into the hall where the speech is occurring to get out of the rain, or because they had planned to attend the meeting for a long time. Audiences vary from very purposeful groups which may have worked for months to set up a political rally, to groups which decided only the night before that a pressing matter required an immediate meeting. People become parts of audiences because they want to be informed, stimulated, convinced, or because it is the only place they can get a feeling of togetherness. People go to specific meetings because they want to, because their wives or husbands hounded them into it, because they want to be seen by those who may vote for them during the next election, because the subject fascinates them, because they hate the speaker and want to attack him, or for many other reasons.

A well-prepared speaker has considered objectively why people are in the audience, and if their group membership is of a permanent nature or whether their relationship to the specific communication situation is more casual and of momentary importance to them.

EXERCISES

1. Select a specific speech, speaker, and occasion. On the basis of the concepts provided in this chapter, develop a careful analysis of the audience involved. Write a five-hundred-word report. If possible, discuss your analysis with the speaker before and after his speech.

2. Present a three-minute speech on the subject: "The Most Challenging Audience." This could either be a real audience you have spoken to, or an audience which you would consider to be a challenge to you for different reasons.

3. Conduct an informal panel discussion before your class, 25 minutes in length, followed by class participation, discussing the question: "What are some possible conflicts which can arise between a speaker and listeners as a result of inadequate audience analysis?"

4. Check a collection of speeches and select one speech in which the speaker faced unusual difficulties as far as his relationship to the audience was concerned. Present a three-minute speech summarizing your findings and giving summary information concerning the speech, the speaker, the audience, and the occasion.

5. Assume that you are scheduled to present the informative speech required for exercise 2 to your speech class. Carefully analyze your audience and the occasion and present your analysis to your teacher in written form for his evaluation.

6. Present a three-minute speech to your class on the subject: "The Influence of Group Size on the Communication Situation."

7. Write a three-hundred-word paper taking one of the major categories discussed under the heading of "Important Audience Factors" (age, sex, etc.) and list as many ways as possible in which that one factor could influence a public speaking situation. Read the paper to your class.

BIBLIOGRAPHY

Anderson, Kenneth E. *Persuasion.* Boston: Allyn and Bacon, 1971. Section II.

Auer, J. Jeffery. *The Rhetoric of Our Times.* New York: Appleton-Century-Crofts, 1969. Section I.

Bosmajian, Haig A. *Readings in Speech.* New York: Harper and Row, 1965. Section I.

Cathcart, Robert S. and Larry A. Samovar. *Small Group Communication.* Dubuque: Wm. C. Brown, 1970. Parts I and II.

Giffin, Kim and Bobby R. Patton. *Basic Readings in Interpersonal Communication.* New York: Harper and Row, 1971.

Hoffer, Eric. *The True Believer.* New York: Harper and Row, 1951.

Oliver, Robert T. and Rupert L. Cortright. *Effective Speech.* New York: Holt, Rinehart, and Winston, 1970. Chapter 10.

Phillips, Gerald M. *Communication and the Small Group.* Indianapolis: Bobbs-Merrill, 1966. Sections I, II, and V.

Turner, Ralph H. and Lewis M. Killian. *Collective Behavior.* Englewood Cliffs, N. J.: Prentice-Hall, 1957.

PUBLIC SPEECH PREPARATION

Public speaking becomes a more satisfying experience if the speaker is adequately prepared for each particular situation, and if he has something significant or meaningful to say to the audience he is addressing. Fundamentally, the task of analysis before giving any speech consists of five interrelated approaches:

1. Analyzing the audience and occasion
2. Critical and thoughtful evaluation of the speaker's own knowledge
3. Critical and thoughtful observation of the work or activities of others
4. Interviewing those who can supply additional information
5. Note taking and careful, critical consideration of printed material.

On the basis of his understanding of the audience and occasion the speaker attempts to integrate his own experience, that of people whom he can observe and question, and material contained in written records. Past experiences in similar speaking situations can also be valuable. The entire period of preparation and public speaking can be a learning experience, not merely consisting of prior analysis but also requiring the speaker to evaluate his performance critically after the completion of a speech. Debriefing periods with thoughtful critics who heard the speech can be helpful.

COLLECTING AND RECORDING RELEVANT MATERIAL

In most public speaking situations listeners have no way of checking sources for accuracy or even existence. The integrity and commitment of the speaker to be a "good man speaking well" thus becomes vital. An important part of any preparation is, therefore, the selection of material by the speaker. It is best to have as many sources as necessary with varied information rather than to decide at the start what will be proved and then ignoring all facts to the contrary.

After completing his analysis and research the speaker usually has more data than he needs since it will be easier to discard some information than to try to stretch inadequate material. Planning research is not a waste of time and taking short-cuts in the recording of material only causes more work later on. A speaker is not expected to be an expert in every field, or even in one field, but he is expected to be able to find available information and then to use it fairly, giving credit to whom credit is due.

Narrowing the Subject

A common mistake made in public speaking is trying to cover too large a subject in the allotted time. A clear, limited and precise purpose sentence will help overcome that problem. Consider the following statement: "I am going to inform my audience about atomic research." Just a little thought indicates that the subject is much too broad; it would take many hours to discuss it, and an audience would never be able to absorb all of it in one sitting.

On the other hand, consider the sentence: "I am going to inform my audience about the use of atomic power stations." The subject has been narrowed, and the statement itself is much more specific. For a longer speech, this subject may be acceptable. A shorter speech may require even further information. "I am going to inform my audience about California's atomic power station in San Onofre."

The Starting Point

The most effective speeches are those which cover some subject or area with which the speaker is familiar and in which he is interested. Familiarity will help in the smooth and lively delivery of the speech, in gathering additional information, and in making the material clear to the audience. Interest will help the speaker to work more diligently in the preparation of the speech; it will help to make the presentation of the material more vivid and meaningful, and it will help the speaker to feel self-assured as he presents a subject which he considers to be important.

In addition to his own knowledge and interest a speaker may also ask himself: How expert are the members of my audience on this subject? Am I contributing anything new? While meaning will be assigned to any message by the receivers, the speaker needs to consider carefully what he wants to convey. Adequate preparation for effective public speaking will always take into account the *speaker*, the *audience*, the *speech* and the *occasion*.

Sources of Information

One of the most important concepts in gathering information for a speech is economy of effort. There are a number of ways in which a speaker can gather information, but one of the most economical, from the standpoint of time, is to interview the experts. Any expert may not wish to discuss with a speaker a subject that has already been adequately covered in a book or article he has written. Therefore, questions should be avoided which can easily and quickly be answered by consulting other sources such as books, articles, or recordings. The simpler the question the better the chances are for a reply. For that reason it is inadvisable to ask questions which require long discussions. Good speakers tend to be good listeners, and they are almost constantly engaged in gathering information and insights.

Many questions can be answered by listening to discussion programs or newscasts on radio and television, or by attending lectures in the community. Once the habit of listening or gathering data is developed the speaker will get input from many other sources as well. For instance, industrial firms, educational institutions, among them large universities, and many other groups have developed outstanding educational films on a variety of subjects from soil erosion to the use of watercolors. Such films, among others, are listed in the University of California (Berkeley) catalog, and in the University of Illinois catalog. Even movies shown for entertainment may provide information, at least concerning current trends, as can novels, conversations, concerts, art shows, and other sources representative of man's total experience.

Colleges and universities have made every attempt to organize materials in their libraries to make them readily available. Often a speaker will be able to save time by requesting the help of reference librarians either in school or public libraries. In the card catalog books are listed under the name of the author, under the title of the book, or somewhat more laboriously under the general subject matter in which a speaker may be interested. A little prior thought will be helpful, since it will enable a speaker to outline different subject headings under which books or articles may be listed in the card catalog. The *Library of Congress Subject Headings* also can be of help.

Three of the most important indexes of periodicals found in most libraries are the *New York Times Index*, supplying information about articles which have

appeared in this well-known daily newspaper; the *Reader's Guide to Periodical Literature;* and the *Social Sciences and Humanities Index.* Good sources for speeches are *Vital Speeches* as indexed in the *Readers Guide to Periodical Literature,* and *Speech Index* by Sutton. The files or archives of libraries often provide background material which has been collected for many years, as do newspaper "morgues."

Much time can be saved by looking for published bibliographies in the reference room of the library, by checking the books or articles a speaker has already found to see if they supply bibliographies on his subject, and by consulting indexes of published materials. There are many standard reference works such as the *Encyclopedia Britannica.* A list of some of the most important is included in the bibliography at the end of this chapter. They usually provide the quickest, easiest way to get an overview and factual introduction to any subject matter covered. Once a starting point has been found, development of an idea becomes much easier.

Without overstating the case, it can be assumed that books or articles dealing with any subject a speaker may be interested in are available in public or school libraries, including the frequently overlooked pamphlet and rare-book collections.

Collecting Data

Many students become discouraged as soon as they start the actual process of gathering specific data for their speeches. There is so much material to be read or heard that it seems impossible to get the job done. A few suggestions might help. In any case, start with general reference works then, if necessary, go to other books and articles.

Check for Relevant Data. First, you may decide to write down a number of key words, phrases, or ideas representing the subject. Make use of your own knowledge or of information gathered from other sources as you develop these basic categories. Then, you can check the index of any particular book you are considering to see if it deals with any of the subjects in which you are interested. Check the table of contents. Most books and articles contain a kind of purpose statement of their own. Check the introductory sections to see if the subject in which you are interested is covered. For articles or shorter books, you may check the first and last sentence of each paragraph. Good writers, like good speakers, tell you what they are going to discuss; then they discuss it; and finally they summarize for you what they have discussed.

Train yourself to look at whole pages and pick out certain key phrases or words. They serve as signals to check more carefully for a discussion of the subject you have chosen. Some books and articles, of course, must be read in detail and completely, usually because they are standard works in the field or because they provide you with a foundation on which to build your other research. Do not permit yourself to become involved in a book or article merely because it seems interesting. Research discipline demands that you stick with your subject, once you have decided what it is and what its component parts are.

Recording Library Data

A speaker can save himself countless hours of rechecking sources by setting up an efficient system of recording notes before he attempts to find relevant material in books, magazines, and recordings. He needs to have available certain information so that he may include the necessary data in footnotes, bibliographic entries, and quotations.

For books:

1. The complete name of each author
2. The title of each book and possibly the specific chapter
3. The place of publication, the publisher, and the date of publication for all books, possibly adding the number of pages in every book.

For journals:

1. The name of the author and the title of the article
2. The name of the journal or magazine
3. The number of the volume, the date, and the page numbers of the article.

Opposing points of view should be considered. Since this material is being collected for a public speech, generally background information and a number of meaningful, brief quotations which are to be used verbatim will be needed, keeping in mind that different people will be impressed by different approaches.

In preparing for a speech, the speaker needs to make certain that his sources dealt fairly and adequately with the subject, that other authorities agree, and that information is presented in an accurate context. Quotes should be complete enough to give a clear impression of the data, but short enough to make them useful in a speech. Statistics tend to be major trouble-makers in public speaking. Basically, statistics are figures arranged to show a relationship for the purpose of support or proof. They are difficult to present in oral form and should for that reason be used in limited numbers and be supplemented by visual aids.

THE DEVELOPMENT AND USE OF VISUAL AIDS

Many speeches can benefit from the well-planned use of visual aids. The more information listeners must absorb, the more vital becomes their role. One major consideration should be foremost: visual aids must never become more than aids. They are most effective if they do not dominate the speech, or become a substitute for language. A demonstration, for instance, may require little or no speaking. In such a case, it would not be possible to define the situation primarily as public speaking.

The following rules represent some helpful hints resulting from experience:

1. Visual aids need to be built smoothly into the speech and call a minimum of attention to themselves. It is best if they remain covered until the actual moment of use.
2. Visual aids should never be passed around during a speech. Their purpose is not to interrupt oral communication, because long pauses or abrupt

stops may cause breaks in transmission. Timing is vital because visual aids can actually help a speaker remember the major points of his speech.

3. Visual aids should be large enough to be seen easily. Furthermore, they must never be too detailed. Often a single item or idea per visual aid is all that can be made clear. Bright primary colors will serve better than soft pastels or shades of colors so closely related that they become indistinguishable. For the same reason, pencil lines or thin ink lines should be avoided. Small photographs become useless for large audiences unless their quality has first been critically checked.

4. Visual aids are most effective when they are used at different times throughout the entire speech rather than during one brief moment.

Obviously, these points all center around a few basic considerations. Visual aids should not distract but rather focus attention. They are used to clarify not to confuse the issue.

ORGANIZING THE SPEECH

In formal public speaking, time pressures demand almost instant recognition and understanding of the ideas presented by a speaker. Outstanding speakers are not born with the ability to state ideas clearly and convincingly, they learn to establish meaningful relationships between the parts of any message.

Basic Considerations

As stated in chapter 9, it is most important that a speaker keeps his audience clearly in mind. Formal arrangement of ideas is convenient for checking the relationship of material presented in any given speech and helps the speaker remember the sequence of his ideas. There is insufficient proof that such formal structures also help members of an audience remember the ideas, but structure does seem to assist in understanding relationships a speaker wishes his audience to see. We tend to look for patterns, order, arrangement in any message, and a speaker should arrange his material in a manner fitting the patterns of thought commonly used by his listeners. Formal outlines of different types are helpful if they do not force a structure upon the material a speaker wishes to present, but rather if they attempt to discover existing structure wherever possible.

Structure should be flexible enough to accommodate changes while a speech is being delivered in order to assure as much interaction as possible. An arrangement of ideas which causes the message to develop or grow in the mind of listeners as closely as possible to the pattern the speaker discovered and formulated is most desirable.

Outlines

For formal presentations, especially for public speeches, many speakers prefer to develop formal outlines. They range from very complex and detailed formats which come close to being manuscripts, to brief, sketchy key-word outlines.

Outlines, even in their most complex forms, should be only skeletons for which the speaker must supply the "meat" as he speaks. It is best to learn the sequence of ideas, but not to memorize the material as a formal manuscript. A basic pattern for a formal speech may look like this:

INTRODUCTION
BODY
CONCLUSION

In the preparation of an outline the following represents the logical sequence of collecting, evaluating, and using available materials.

1. Develop the body of the speech.
2. Summarize the speech in the conclusion.
3. Develop an introduction which will be both meaningful and impressive. This is the one moment in the speech when a speaker will probably have the undivided attention of all his listeners. The speaker needs to plan the introduction carefully after he knows exactly what he will be talking about and what results he desires.

In the outline, the relationship of all points, major and minor, may be shown by indentation and the use of a set of symbols. The following example illustrates the format.

BODY OF THE SPEECH

(Roman numeral)	I. Statement of a Major Point
(Capital letter)	A. Major Supporting Point
(Arabic numeral)	1. Minor Supporting Point
(Lower-case letter)	a.
(Bracketed arabic numeral)	(1) ⎫
(Bracketed lower-case letter)	(a) ⎬ Details

        B. Major Supporting Point
          1. Minor Supporting Point
          2. Minor Supporting Point

    II. Statement of a Major Point

        A. Major Supporting Point
          1. Minor Supporting Point
          2. Minor Supporting Point

        B. Major Supporting Point
          1. Minor Supporting Point
          2. Minor Supporting Point

   III. Statement of a Major Point
       etc., etc.

Normally if a (I) is used, a (II) follows; if an (A) is used it usually calls for a (B), and so on down the line. More detailed examples are provided in the Appendix.

Rules for Outlining. Make sure the total structure of the outline is clear. Careless structuring might result in the inclusion of unrelated points. Consider the following supposedly major points, which illustrate how easy it is to introduce confusing material:

I. Army
II. Infantry
III. Navy
IV. Marines
V. Coast Guard
VI. Air Force

In checking this basic outline it can be seen immediately that "II. Infantry" is not a major point on the same level as the other five. Depending on the supporting material used for each of the major headings, "Infantry" could possibly be categorized as a major supporting point, subordinate to "I. Army." Careful checking of a rough outline will help prevent confusion later when listeners attempt to understand a speaker's reasoning and ideas.

Any time a speaker includes more than three major points in the body of his speech, he should stop and think it through again. Chances are he is trying to cover too much subject matter. Only if he is certain that he can adequately handle more than three major ideas in the time allotted, or that the subject requires them, should he go ahead.

The first outline often will not be sufficient. A clear relationship among ideas, and the subordination of minor ideas to major ideas in a logical pattern will usually only result from rearranging them, discarding some, and including others.

Neatness and accuracy in the development of an outline are more than "busy work"; they require a speaker to work slowly and deliberately enough to check his progress. Such careful work will assist him in remembering the total structure of any speech.

Each heading in the outline is clearest as a complete statement. While complete sentences are not necessary, each statement should clearly indicate the subject. Statements such as: "I'll explain my point here," or "Use illustration here," are confusing.

Use one symbol for each heading; keep symbols distinct; never combine two or more symbols, such as IA or IIC. If capital letters are used for major supporting material at one point, they should not be used elsewhere in the outline for minor supporting material. The pattern of symbols and indentation given in the sample outlines, if used consistently, will show the relationship of less important to more important material.

No more than one idea should be included under each heading, major or minor. If more than one point is made under one heading, ideas are inadequately subordinated. Use of another major heading could more easily permit incorporation of a number of other points under it. On the other hand, a major idea and a supporting point may have been combined which could hinder clear development of the idea.

Starting at a certain point and moving in a definite direction will be helpful. The following example illustrates a poor habit of structuring ideas which can result in confusion.

I. America's First Colony
II. America's Second Colony
III. British Colonial Policy
IV. America's Third Colony

The third point cannot help but be an interruption in a pattern to which an audience had just barely adjusted after the discussion of the first two areas. Such illogical structural barriers to communication can be readily avoided by careful planning.

ORGANIZATIONAL PATTERNS

Any audience needs to be able to follow what a speaker is saying. It should be able to look back and remember where he has been, and it should have no particular difficulty predicting the direction in which his speech is moving. Some general organizational patterns help accomplish all of this. These patterns are applicable to all types of speeches.

Time Order

This means that a speech starts at a given moment in time and moves in a definite direction, forward or backward. The main problem to be avoided with this type of organization is a break with the established pattern. Movement should be in one direction only.

Deductive Order

In this case the speech starts with a general statement which is then supported by specific instances. Example: "Dams have increased agricultural output wherever they have been built." After that a speaker could list specific dams and the differences in agricultural output before and after the building of the dams.

Topical Order

Sometimes a subject has already been arranged into well-known, convenient divisions. For instance, an informative speech about the manpower of various branches of the armed forces could use their existing divisions: army, navy, air force, marines, and coast guard.

Geographical Order

Using this type of pattern, the speech would start at a given location and move in a specific direction. For instance; top-to-bottom, left-to-right, north-to-south, Texas-to-New York, etc.

Cause-to-Effect/Effect-to-Cause

This order requires statements of a cause followed by a discussion of the effects produced by it, or the statement of an effect followed by a discussion of various possible or probable causes. The problem of air pollution in a major city, using specific causes to illustrate the reasons for its existence, is a typical illustration for use of this arrangement.

DEVELOPING MAIN AND SUPPORTING HEADINGS

Main Heads

Any idea which directly supports any part or all of the purpose statement or subject sentence would be a main or major idea. Main headings provide an audience with the means to look back and remember basic points, and to look ahead to logically related points. Probably the most common, and also most confusing or tiring, pattern any speaker can use is a "string of pearls" type of arrangement. In this case the speaker simply lists idea after idea after idea as it comes to his mind. Under these circumstances it often happens that a listener is presented with ten or more supposedly major ideas which he cannot possibly remember. Consider the following list of items:

    I. Air pollution
    II. Noisy planes
    III. Noisy cars
    IV. Noisy construction
    V. Water pollution
    VI. Oil slicks
    VII. Loss of wildlife

A listener would have great difficulty knowing what to expect next. Instead the speaker might assist those who listen to him by arranging the material under three major headings:

    I. Air pollution
    II. Water pollution
    III. Noise pollution

Other points can be arranged as major supporting points under these three headings. It would be worthwhile, for the purpose of clarity, to drop any idea which does not fit the pattern the speaker has decided upon after considering his audience and the available time.

It is easiest to follow this pattern if one idea clearly leads to another ("Therefore," "The result is," "This leads me to say . . . ," etc.). This happens naturally if points deal with related aspects of one major subject.

Major Supporting Material

The steps taken in the selection and arrangement of supporting points are the same taken for the selection and arrangement of the main ideas of any speech. This time, however, the material must be in direct support of each individual major point, or main head, as it appears in the outline. Specific types of supporting material will be considered in the next chapters.

SUMMARY:
PREPARING A PUBLIC SPEECH

A good speech is usually the result of careful preparation. So-called shortcuts may result in inadequate use of available information, and carelessly gathered or recorded data may result in wasted hours of trying to rediscover some vital point.

At the same time, a speaker can save hours of unnecessary work if he is familiar with information which has been gathered by others and collected in books, magazines, or journals. The economy of effort principle requires that he do all necessary work in preparation but no more than is needed to accomplish a clearly defined purpose. If visual aids will be helpful in making ideas clearer to an audience, they must be developed and used in such a way as to make them readily visible and understandable, without permitting them to become the major attraction of any given speech.

It is important that listeners at all times feel that they know where a speaker is in the overall structure of a formal speech, as well as what he has covered previously, with some idea of the direction in which the speech is moving. Only if ideas have been adequately arranged and only if the speaker understands them and their relationship to each other can he hope to make ideas clear to others. Anyone who has suffered through endless P.T.A. meetings, business meetings, brainstorming sessions, and long, boring speeches has wondered why people cannot organize their ideas more adequately to help make them clear. The formal approach in this chapter represents one means of helping develop the necessary underlying mental discipline.

EXERCISES

1. Outline the steps you would take in gathering information about Franklin D. Roosevelt as a speaker.

2. Take the steps you outlined for project 1, provide brief summary statements, including careful bibliographic entries, for each of ten sources you have checked.

3. In your school library find the most authoritative and complete source listing of last year's graduate theses in speech.

4. Prepare a bibliography of books, pamphlets, and articles on the subject "How to prepare visual aids."

5. Find the following articles in the *Quarterly Journal of Speech or Speech Monographs*. Provide accurate bibliographic information for all.

    1. Riley, Floyd K., "St. Augustine, Public Speaker and Rhetorician"
    2. "J. Q. Adams, Speaker and Rhetorician"
    3. White and Henderlider, an article dealing with Norman Vincent Peale
    4. Brandenburg, Earnest, and . . ., an article dealing with Franklin Delano Roosevent's international speeches, 1939–41
    5. Lambertson, F. W., "Audience Analysis in Early Teaching of Pulpit Oratory"

6. What is meant by the "eclectic" method of studying speech?

    a. Find out what the term means from basic speech texts available in your library.

   b. Compare it to other methods of study mentioned in basic speech texts.
   c. Cite specific support from the textbooks you used and provide footnotes for
      each quotation, as well as a bibliography of all texts used.
   d. Write a 500-word paper summarizing your findings. Be ready to explain or
      defend your paper in a two-minute oral summary.

7. Develop different outlines for a speech, ten minutes in length, on any subject
   with which you are familiar, adapting them to the following groups:

   a. 500 teenagers at a local high-school assembly
   b. 10 college students in a weekly club meeting
   c. a man's civic organization at its weekly luncheon
   d. a woman's club at its weekly breakfast meeting.

8. Read three speeches in a current issue of *Vital Speeches* and outline them. Write
   a brief critique on the structure of the speeches.

9. Select one of the well-known speeches of history, outline it, and comment on
   its structure.

10. Study a number of speech texts for fundamental public speaking courses, and
    give a three-minute oral report on one different approach to outlining you found
    particularly helpful.

BIBLIOGRAPHY

Auer, Jeffrey J. *An Introduction to Research in Speech.* New York: Harper and Row,
   1959.

Backman, John W. *How to Use Audio-Visual Materials.* New York: Association Press,
   1956.

Barrett, Harold. *Practical Methods in Speech.* New York: Holt, Rinehart, and Winston,
   1968.

Bormann, Ernest G. *Theory and Research in the Communicative Arts.* New York: Holt,
   Rinehart and Winston, 1965.

Barzun, Jacques, and Henry F. Graff. *The Modern Researcher.* New York: Harcourt,
   Brace-World, 1970.

Brown, James W., Richard B. Lewis, Fred F. Harcleroad. *Audio-Visual Instruction
   Materials and Methods.* New York: McGraw-Hill, 1963.

Crocker, Lionel and Herbert W. Hildebrandt. *Public Speaking for College Students.*
   New York: Van Nostrand Reinhold, 1965.

Dale, Edgar. *Audio-Visual Methods in Teaching.* Revised Edition. New York: Holt,
   Rinehart, and Winston, 1954.

Dickens, Milton. *Speech: Dynamic Communication.* New York: Harcourt, Brace and
   World, 1963.

Dow, Clyde W., ed. *An Introduction to Graduate Study in Speech and Theater.* East
   Lansing: Michigan State Press, 1961.

Irvin, Charles F. "The Case for Creative Research." *Central States Speech Journal 2*
   (November 1950): 19–23.

McClusky, Frederick D. *Audio-Visual Teaching Techniques.* Dubuque: W. C. Brown,
   1949.

Monroe, Alan H. *Principles and Types of Speech.* Chicago: Scott, Foresman, 1962.

Nadeau, Ray E. *A Basic Rhetoric of Speech Communication.* Mass.: Addison, Wesley, 1969.

Oliver, Robert R., and Rupert L. Cortright. *Effective Speech.* New York: Holt, Rinehart and Winston, 1970.

Scheidel, Thomas M. *Speech Communication and Human Interaction.* Glenview: Scott, Foresman, 1972.

Wilson, Roger P. *Oral Reporting in Business and Industry.* Englewood Cliffs, New Jersey: Prentice-Hall, 1967. Pp. 144–207.

EXAMPLES OF MAJOR REFERENCE WORKS

Applied Science and Technology Index. New York: Wilson, 1958–date.
Biography Index. New York: Wilson, 1947–date.
Book Review Digest. New York: Wilson, 1905–date.
Business Periodical Index. New York: Wilson, January 1958–date.
Contemporary Authors: The International Bio-Bibliographical Guide to Current Authors and Their Work. Detroit: Gale Research Company, 1962–date.
Current Biography. New York: Wilson, 1940–date.
Dictionary of American Biography. New York: Scribner, 1928–40.
Dictionary of National Biography. London: Smith, Elder, 1908–9. 22 vols, Supplements.
Educational Index. New York: Wilson, 1929–date.
Index to Book Reviews in the Humanities. Detroit: Philip Thompson, 1960–date.
Monthly Catalog of United States Government Publications. U.S. Superintendent of Documents, Washington: Government Printing Office, 1895–date.
New York Times Index. New York: New York Times, 1863–date.
Psychological Abstracts. Washington: American Psychological Association, 1927–date.
Public Affairs Information Service Bulletin. New York: Public Information Service, 1915–date (PAIS).
Social Science and Humanities Index (formerly *International Index*). New York: Wilson, 1916–date.
Speech Index. New York: Scarecrow Press, 1966.
Twentieth Century Authors. New York: Wilson, 1942. First Supplement, 1955.

11

THE USE OF INFORMATION IN PUBLIC SPEECHES

Public speaking is intended to bring about some predetermined change in direction, amount, or degree of human behavior in a number of people. Oral communication which fits this category generally attempts to accomplish the task by producing results in one of the following ways, or by a *combination* of two or three of these approaches:

1. An attempt to produce change through a specific act
2. An attempt to produce change through intellectual acceptance or rejection
3. An attempt to produce change through emotional acceptance or rejection.

The first two categories usually make more extensive use of informational material, facts, opinions, and systematic logic. Empirical data tend to prevail in the second approach. The difference is that in the first category the major effort is directed towards a specific act such as purchasing a specific item, or accomplishing a specific task such as painting the houses in a run-down community. In the second case, extensive information may also be supplied, however, in this case only an intellectual involvement or acceptance is sought. For instance, the President of the United States will present specific data in his State of the Union messages. While they may tend to increase his chances of re-election if positive information is supplied, no specific action is expected at the time from the electorate receiving the message beyond acceptance or agreement with the message.

The third category of speaking is based on extensive use of emotional arousal. Some specific types of speeches in this category with which we are all familiar are sermons and patriotic speeches, which are basically inspirational. However, other types of material intended to arouse strong feelings in an audience also fall into this category. One extreme, mob action, is often preceded by this type of speech. In addition to stirring emotional outbursts of the type discussed, many of these speeches strengthen or reinforce already existing belief systems on an emotional level. Listeners under such circumstances are supposed to feel something strongly and to become emotionally involved.

As indicated in the beginning of this book, divisions between informative and persuasive speeches tend to be rather arbitrary. In a way we have returned to Aristotle's definition as we try to discover "all available means of persuasion," by stating that all the material used in any speech *can* be persuasive or used to produce change. Whether a speech is primarily informative or persuasive depends on the reaction of a given audience to the material presented. Information can be highly persuasive, as in the case of an individual checking *Consumer's Guide* before buying an automobile. On the other hand, motivational appeals intended by the speaker to sway an audience may be completely rejected by some listeners who resent this approach as lacking rational, informational data.

We tend to use these classifications in order to identify the purposes of a sender. In some cases a speaker is only interested in presenting information. There is no intention on his part to have the information used by his audience in any specific way. On another occasion, a speaker may use information or motive appeals to convince an audience that it ought to believe something, feel something, or act in a specific way. In these cases the speaker would definitely have in mind a persuasive purpose whether or not he accomplished it. In the long run it is the responsibility of the sender to try to determine what kind of speech material will accomplish the purpose he has in mind, either for short-range or long-range effects.

Individual listener's responses can, of course, change the speaker's intended purpose. For instance, attending an informational lecture on pain killers may result in no other reaction than students' taking notes and "storing" information. However, some of the listeners may decide later, when actually faced with the necessity of finding a pain killer for themselves, to try one type in preference to another based on the original information they were provided. In this case the short-range effect was mostly informative, the long-range effect persuasive. The only time these supposedly distinct classifications really present any problems is in the case of noticeable differences between the purpose intended by the speaker and the actual response by an audience. In such cases we tend to say that the speaker did not fulfill his purpose, at least not while the reactions of his listeners could be observed. We are really not speaking of absolutes but of degrees. As there are degrees of response to a spoken message, we can also think of degrees or amounts of informational or motivational-persuasive material used by a speaker. Depending on the intentions of the sender, but not necessarily the interpretation of the receiver, we can classify the material he included in his speech as informational or persuasive, rational or nonrational, informative or emotional, or possibly in the classical tradition, artistic or nonartistic proofs.

As was stated before, emotion and reason, or intellect and emotion, can either be separated only in a very arbitrary fashion, or on a very specific individual basis. What may be for one person a simple statement of fact used for informational purposes only—for instance, that 65 people died from automobile accidents in our community last year—can be a highly emotional issue for another listener if one of these 65 people was a member of his family. Yet there is some value in recognizing that certain individuals, certain audiences, and certain settings require a more informational and less emotional approach, while at other times audiences need only a minimum of informational material but a great deal of emotional involvement to accomplish a desired change or persuasive purpose.

GENERAL METHODS OF PRESENTATION

Public speeches can be presented in four different ways.

1. *Impromptu.* This means the speech is given on the spur of the moment. Its success will depend on how well the speaker is acquainted with his subject, and how much public speaking he has done to be able to develop ideas clearly and forcefully on short notice.
2. *Extemporaneous.* Many public speeches are of this type. After careful selection of materials, preparation of an outline, and memorization of the sequence of ideas, this type of speech is given with a minimum of notes, in as conversational a manner as possible.
3. *Memorization.* The memorized speech makes use of carefully chosen words presented in a very formal manner. This type of oral communication is more closely related to oral interpretation and acting. It is less a speech, and more an "oral essay."
4. *Reading from Manuscript.* Because it cuts down on eye contact and bodily activity, this type of speech should be used only when accuracy of wording is of maximum importance. Some of the speeches by the President of the United States fall into this category.

INFORMATIONAL MATERIAL

Whether informational material is used to motivate listeners or as a presentation of factual data whose use is left up to the audience, it usually consists of empirical data, observable facts, or material whose existence can be verified through use of the senses. The existence or acceptance of such material is not primarily tied to the feelings, attitudes or motives of any individual.

The purpose for using informational material in public speeches is to clarify or improve understanding. Obviously, once ideas have been clarified or understanding has been brought about a powerful basis for change exists among those who have received the message. However, that is only one side of the total picture. It is difficult to evaluate information adequately unless the needs of both the receiver and the sender are considered. Some people have a strong need to share whatever knowledge they possess in order to feel worthwhile and accepted. Others need information for survival, as in the case of an airline pilot whose plane is in trouble. Most frequently, however, information helps make our lives easier, more comfortable, more meaningful, or gives them more depth.

At times the information supplied may add vital data to an existing store-house of knowledge, at other times it may be new information. Information may result in better understanding and greater knowledge without any specific motivational appeals included in a speaker's presentation, or it may be used for persuasive purposes, for instance, convincing a city council that action must be taken to improve an inadequate system of street lighting. In contemporary American society even the supposedly unemotional terms "facts" and "information" have become concepts whose intensional, persuasive connotations we cannot ignore if we wish to bring about a change or motivate people to think, feel, or act in a certain way.

INFORMATIVE SPEECHES

Certain types of speeches make more extensive use of information or facts than others mainly because the needs of listeners require that approach.

1. *Reports.* Usually this type of speaking requires the presentation of information by an expert or a selected individual to an audience which has requested the information. The report of an engineer to a building committee concerning problems encountered in construction would be one example. Another is the report of a fund-raising committee chairman concerning the specific amount of money needed for the charities the organization supports.
2. *Instructional Talks.* In the training program of the United States Army, instructors give many informative speeches to soldiers. For instance, preparation for overseas duty might include instructional talks on how to behave in a foreign country.
3. *Business Conferences and Meetings.* An informative approach is often used to bring together efficiently a great variety of materials. This helps to familiarize an individual or a group with the various components making up a complex industrial or business organization. The expansion of a certain company may be contemplated. Under such circumstances, the man in charge of that project may bring together leading personnel to provide them with information concerning the current status and future plans of the entire organization.
4. *Demonstrations.* This type of speaking is frequently on the fringe of oral communication. Usually, it involves the use of extensive audio or visual aids, requiring in many instances only a minimum amount of speaking. Working models are frequently used to provide a more accurate understanding of complex pieces of machinery, as in the case of flight simulation for jet pilots.

Information is needed and has been given in almost every conceivable location, hospital rooms, battle fields, schoolrooms, in planes, under the sea, and in lecture halls; involving hundreds of listeners or no more than one speaker and one listener. Opportunities may vary from an instructor attempting to teach a group of Boy Scouts the intricacies of various types of knots on a camping trip, to the impressive ballroom of a large hotel where a speaker addresses an assembly of his colleagues during a professional convention.

GENERAL PURPOSES

Information in public speaking is in many cases clearly directed toward supplying the means for bringing about change. A Peace Corps volunteer may find himself speaking to a group of Africans who wish to improve their economic or educational positions. An instructor may be called upon to teach children how to accomplish a certain task. Perhaps she teaches them how to swim, or shows them how to do arithmetic problems. In an underdeveloped area, disease-ridden swamps may be an obstacle that needs removal before a specific task can be accomplished. Misunderstandings may need to be removed in a business firm. Helping people to develop patterns of cooperation, or teaching them to use their abilities to bring about a more concerted effort may present an opportunity for a psychologist to base his speech on informative material. Sometimes intellectual acceptance, the gaining of knowledge or information, is all that is needed. In such cases, the speaker wants a common basis on which future action can be built.

The general purpose of using informative material in speaking may be stated as follows: The sending of information from one person to another transmits information or data from one area of human endeavor or knowledge to another, or from one individual to another. As indicated earlier, in speaking we use words which merely represent the things they stand for, making the actual "transportation" of even one fact from one human to another difficult. If the informative speech is successful, it will enable an audience to see facts in their relationship to other facts; and it will tend to help members of the audience to develop more adequate points of view on any given subject.

Effectively used informational material may increase the information available to individual listeners, as in the case of a college class. It may help members of an audience to prepare for specific challenges or problems they have to face, or prepare them to function more adequately as a group. If misunderstandings or misinterpretations exist, providing information may result in the clarification of a point, or it may provide more accurate data than previously available. It may provide standards of evaluation and eventually value judgments based on these standards, as in the case of some book reports. The basic concepts of collecting and arranging material discussed earlier apply to all kinds of speeches, but some specific factors are particularly helpful for speeches which make extensive use of information.

An audience seeking information cannot be put off with platitudes. The speaker's confidence, therefore, must be the result of careful preparation resulting in adequate knowledge of the subject. Two of the most common mistakes in presenting information are either to "talk down" to an audience, or to "talk above their heads." An engineer talking to a group of high school students may lose them within seconds of beginning his speech, because his language is technical and his information detailed. A physician addressing a PTA group made up of professional people may insult them by speaking in a condescending manner and by using terms which are obviously directed to people of a low educational level. The speaker must, therefore, determine what he may expect of his audience, based on their capacity to learn new facts and the background information they already possess.

As for all speeches, the speaker should follow some fairly standard procedures. The purpose should be clearly and concisely stated in a *purpose sentence.* The allotted *time* for the speech needs to be fixed in the speaker's mind, then *sufficient material* should be gathered. Finally the speech should be *outlined* as discussed in the preceding chapter and illustrated in the Appendix.

INFORMATIONAL MATERIAL FOR SUPPORT

While major ideas are vital, supporting material will "make" or "break" a speech. Sometimes information is of such immediate importance to people who hear a speech that nothing more has to be done than to give them the facts. For instance, a group of mothers who are aware that a child in their community has recently drowned, may not need anything but brief instruction, followed by detailed demonstrations, to learn how to give artificial respiration. However, in most cases an audience needs to develop some interest in a speaker's subject. Information does not have to be dull. People will retain it more readily if the speaker can relate it to ideas members of the audience have previously held, or compare it to things with which they are familiar. Even an interested audience may find the going difficult when the subject becomes highly involved, and supporting material may be of assistance to them. The time factor should also be considered. A long speech should provide opportunities for the audience to relax briefly, and it needs various methods of stirring up renewed interest. Supporting material provides the means of accomplishing these tasks. The following types of supporting material can be used in all types of speeches, but they are especially useful in a speech relying heavily on information.

Verbal Pictures, Descriptions

A good command of the English language, absolute clarity of an idea in the speaker's own mind, and the ability to visualize the thing he is describing are prerequisites for adequate description. In this case, the speaker depends only on words to make his subject clear. How powerfully descriptive words can be when used by someone who has learned their usefulness in drawing verbal pictures is illustrated by the following brief passage from Karl Capek's "On Literature." "I went into the red-hot hell of the jute-drying kilns and scorched myself beside the stokers at the boilers, wondering at their long shovels, which I could hardly lift." [1]

Comparisons, Contrasts

A pupil in today's schoolroom may have little knowledge of a steam engine, but using comparisons to the tea-kettle he has seen at home, or a cover rattling on a boiling pot, may help to clarify certain points about the power of steam. Sometimes we are required to illustrate a point not by indicating how it is *like* something else, but by showing how it *differs* from another object or idea. "In the United States many farmers own their land, while in the USSR the State owns all the land."

Definition

Especially in informative speeches, it cannot be assumed that the meaning of all key words is known to the audience. A term may be so ambiguous that it produces no sharp image in the listeners' minds. Other words simply may be unfamiliar to them since every area of human endeavor has its own jargon or terminology. The following methods for defining terms are common:

1. Placing the unfamiliar word in a familiar context to show its meaning or its use. For instance, "Chopsticks are used by the Chinese during their meals, instead of forks."
2. Supplying a dictionary definition.
3. Discussing its original meanings or its development. For instance, hypodermic, resulting from a combination of two Greek words *hypo*—under, and *dermis*—skin.

Classification

Often there exist classes which are already known to your audience and will help them to understand a subject. The speaker may illustrate progressive steps in education by reminding his audience of the degrees which represent "steps" on the academic ladder: B.A., M.A., Ph.D.

---

1. Karl Capek, "On Literature," as reprinted in William G. Leary and James Steel Smith, *Thought and Statement* (New York: Harcourt, Brace, 1960), p. 467.

Statistics

These are numbers which have been arranged to show a relationship, a type of classification of material. Often they do not prove anything, although many people believe they have to be factual. Depending on their accuracy and whether they are really relating facts which can be compared or generalized from, they may be very useful in indicating trends, growth, development, spending, and many other facts which require detailed and involved data to illustrate them, especially if they are presented only verbally. It may be interesting to know that twenty people died in a given city of tuberculosis during the preceding year. However, supplying added information, by comparing this figure to the fact that deaths from tuberculosis had steadily declined every year for the last ten years, may help an audience to gain a better understanding of the subject.

Restatement

Sometimes an idea can be made clear to an audience by restating it in different words. It is not enough to say something over and over again. Clarity is achieved if the speaker finds a way of letting the audience look at the same idea in a different light. Maybe a club needs more volunteers to accomplish a certain task. A statement of the simple fact, "We have 45 children who need help from our volunteers," could be repeated in the same words later in the speech. Chances are that the idea will be remembered more readily, however, if you restate it in different words: "We need forty-five of you who are willing to spend one hour a week with the children for whom we are responsible."

Quotations

An idea may already have been made meaningful and impressive because a well-known personality or expert has made a statement concerning it. Unless quotations are clearly related to the subject, however, and help to illustrate or support the point a speaker is trying to make, they are worse than useless, they are confusing. Unfortunately the value of the quotation may depend more on the importance of its originator than on its truthfulness or factual content. The accurate and fair use of quotations should also be stressed.

Supporting material could be compared to the facets an artisan cuts into a diamond. Major points are comparable to the rough stone, supporting material adds sparkle, luster, and brilliance to it. Information should be used objectively. If material tends to persuade an audience to believe certain things about it, the speaker should make sure it is the facts which persuade, not his manipulation of them. And a speaker should repeat, and whenever necessary, emphasize the points he wants to have remembered, but should try to avoid slanting the facts by over- or under-emphasizing certain parts.

A speaker must learn to support a limited number of major points in sufficient detail. He must learn to clarify only as much material as his audience can understand and retain. The educational background of the audience, and the previous knowledge of the subject by members of the audience, will provide a starting point, helping to avoid redundancy, as well as some possibility of judging how much more information listeners may be able to retain. The higher their educational level, the more likely it is that the speaker can expect them to absorb more material. Closer contact with listeners will help the speaker notice any confusion by his listeners requiring him to further clarify his ideas or even to terminate his speech.

The importance of *novelty* should be remembered. Man likes to have things expressed in new and different ways. Most human beings have a yearning for adventure in them. However, there usually exists a dichotomy of interests. The *familiar* is also important. A well-known place or person we meet frequently represents security and the assurance that we are not treading on unsafe ground. The same idea applies to facts. If a speaker tends to become too novel in his approach, his audience may abandon him and his "dangerous" ideas.

No speech can ever be *completely* prepared before its delivery. Wording is a continuous effort which is not complete until a speaker has finished his presentation. Even though he has carefully prepared, he may find during the delivery of the speech that certain ideas have to be further clarified, and that others can be dealt with much more quickly than he had thought possible. A speaker must never simply and blindly follow his prepared outline without adjusting to the actual speaking situation. The purpose is to bring about understanding and the exchange of information, not merely the completion of an assignment without regard for the immediate needs of the audience and the specific situation a speaker faces after he gets up to speak. A speaker should be certain that he knows his subject well enough to be able to adjust every detail on the spur of the moment.

THE GENERAL STRUCTURE OF
INFORMATIVE SPEECHES

Checking the formalized, outlined structure of a speech can be done by asking some specific questions.

Has the speaker created an immediate interest by mentioning such things as significant results he has obtained, summarizing the conclusions the speech will reach, and giving some recommendations? A speech might begin with a startling statement such as: "Seventy-five percent of passengers riding in automobiles were not using their seat belts in a check conducted by the state police at a local freeway entrance." Or it could begin by summarizing the conclusions: "Less money will be needed during the current year to build highways in our state, than during the last year."

Having created an interest and having told the audience what to expect, is the actual subject clearly stated, describing what has been done, discussing specific facts and data of importance to the subject, making clear the relationship between parts? Has unrelated material been excluded? Is a sufficient number of varied supporting points included? Is the stated purpose being fulfilled?

In the summary, under most circumstances, a brief restatement of the purpose of the speech, and a summary of the major points, reminding listeners of the most vital concepts covered, will help to reinforce the message.

SUMMARY:
USING INFORMATIONAL MATERIALS

Whether speech materials are perceived and interpreted to be informative or persuasive depends overwhelmingly on the receiver; whether they were intended to be informative or persuasive depends overwhelmingly on the sender.

Most speeches make use of at least some informative material, and in many cases a speech will consist almost entirely of informative data. Any material which is primarily verifiable by sense data, through observation, or material which we normally consider to be facts, or based on reasoning and logic would fit the broad category of informational input. The purpose for its use centers around two basic concepts: the clarification and the retention of ideas. Even the pattern of most informative speeches tends to reinforce these two general purposes by first stating the intended purpose, then explaining the purpose or ideas in detail, and finally restating both the purpose and the major ideas incorporated in the speech.

A society which depends as heavily on information sharing, and which puts as high a value on education, knowledge, and facts as ours provides many opportunities for the effective use of informative speech materials. Since many data become more than intellectual baggage, since in effect they turn into means for achieving a happier, more complete, or safer life, or at times even become the means for survival, their use depends largely on the needs, attitudes, or motives of the receiver. Information becomes valuable when it becomes useful, when we tend to have some reason or motivation for using it, and at that point rationally based informative material becomes persuasive.

EXERCISES

1. Present a three-minute speech with a carefully developed outline, giving directions for reaching a place at least one hour's driving distance from your present location. Discuss at least two different means or ways of reaching the destination.

2. Give an eight-minute speech with the purpose of securing your classmates' intellectual acceptance of some idea on which they are likely to disagree with you. Make heavy use of factual material and logic. Develop a careful outline with extensive bibliography.

3. Plan, develop, and hold a 40-minute panel discussion exploring the question: What role has public speaking played in the development of America in the second part of the twentieth century?

4. In three minutes, describe the functions or uses of a simple instrument. Develop a careful outline.

5. Give a five-minute speech concerning the current status of America's space program, after developing a careful outline.

6. Develop a five-minute speech concerning some subject which requires the extensive use of statistics. Use visual aids to clarify your points. Develop a careful outline.

7. Give a five-minute speech making use of a working model to explain the functioning of some piece of mechanical equipment, such as a control panel. Develop a careful outline.

8. In a three-minute speech, present a series of carefully developed arguments, with minimum reliance upon motivational appeals and maximum reliance upon facts and logical structure, showing why your classmates should buy insurance. You may select the type of insurance. Develop a careful outline.

BIBLIOGRAPHY

Bosmajian, Haig A., ed. *Readings in Speech*. New York: Harper and Row, 1965.

Brigance, William Norwood. *Speech: Its Techniques and Disciplines in a Free Society*. New York: Appleton-Century-Crofts, 1961. Especially chapter 19.

Bryson, Lyman. *The Communication of Ideas*. New York: Harper and Row, 1948.

Dahle, T. O. "Transmitting Information to Employees: A Study of Five Methods." *Personnel* 31 (1955): 243–46.

Johnson, Wendell. "The Fateful Process of Mr. A. Talking to Mr. B." *Harvard Business Review*, January-February 1953, p. 49.

Mills, Glen E. *Reason in Controversy: On General Argumentation*. New York: Allyn and Bacon, 1968.

Rapaport, Anatol. "What Is Information?" *A Review of General Semantics* 10 (1953): 254.

Redding, W. Charles and George A. Sanborn. *Business and Industrial Communication: A Source Book*. New York: Harper and Row, 1964.

Schramm, Wilbur, ed. *The Process and Effects of Mass Communication*. Urbana, Illinois: University of Illinois Press, 1954.

Whyte, William H. and the Editors of Fortune. *Is Anybody Listening?* New York: Simon and Schuster, 1952.

Consider also chapters on informative speaking in the basic speech texts listed for earlier chapters.

12

THE USE OF PERSUASION IN PUBLIC SPEECHES

Through the ages, bitter statements have been made about man's attempts to manipulate his fellow man. The fact that human emotions are involved in motivational speaking is often cited as proof that something inherently evil and detrimental is the result of any such discourse. However, persuasion is an important part of a free society and it is doubtful that a society can remain free for very long if all kinds of ideas cannot be shared through free speech. Persuasion is the very antithesis of coercion, for it depends on the ability of a communicator to reach both the minds and hearts of his listeners. Attaching arbitrary values to either "reason" or "emotion" is misleading at best. As we have stated repeatedly, no human being can have a meaningful existence without both reason and emotion playing important parts in his life.

PERSUASION AND FREEDOM

Sometimes we become frustrated in a society in which we are constantly under pressure from other people to buy their products, people who want to influence us, who want to persuade us to act, think, and feel in certain ways. Human beings working, planning, and living with other human beings in any kind of societal structure are dependent upon each other. This dependence results in the necessity of an interchange of ideas and, finally, in some sort of persuasive effort. Notwithstanding the statements made by some who resent this sort of manipulation, we cannot really leave one another alone if we insist on living as part of an organized society.

Generally speaking, it is not the act of persuasion that causes us difficulty, but the unethical, unresponsive, or unstable persuader abusing the art of persuasion. As this chapter, and this entire book, attempts to show, the best way of dealing with any problem arising from human communication (especially speech communication) is to prepare *both* the speaker and the listener well, so they can do an adequate job of their specific task in any given situation. A free society depends on free speech, but not just any free speech. Responsibility to oneself and to one's listeners are part of the overall standards by which we must judge public speaking. A good speaker should be a good man skilled in speaking. Especially in persuasive speaking, with its heady mixture of appeals to human reason and human emotion, all of us need to keep that concept in mind. Effective persuasive speaking is important, especially if we consider its alternative in our societal interactions, coercion. If we are to avoid manipulation of man for mere personal gain, or manipulation which results in the degradation or deprivation of the individual, we need to find and internalize standards of persuasion which we can justify.

ARTISTIC PROOFS

For our purposes, three timeless categories of persuasive proofs can be identified. First of all there is Aristotle's classification of *logos*, that is evidence selected and arranged by the speaker in patterns of logic and reasoning commonly used in a given culture. Second, there is the speaker, or the impact the sender has on a given audience. Aristotle called such persuasive impact of the man, *ethos*. Today we often refer to it as credibility or as charisma. Included in the category are such things as the appearance and the impact of the physical behavior of a speaker while he speaks, as well as an audience's prior knowledge about him. Finally, there is material used by a speaker which is basically emotional in nature. Aristotle called it *pathos*. Appeals to the emotions, motives, or drives of a given audience may make use of informational material, factual material, or empirical data, but wording, use of voice, and overall approach will serve the specific attempt by the speaker to make the material as emotionally appealing to the audience as possible. An emotional response or persuasion is not left to chance in this case. There is a specific purpose in the mind of the speaker to involve members of his audience emotionally, or to motivate them.

Intentional, purposeful persuasion or motivation depends on factors residing in the speaker and his audience related to needs, drives, motives, and emotions. Their skillful use in public speaking depends on the artistic proofs Aristotle defined many centuries ago.

ETHOS

One of the major available means of influencing an audience is the speaker. If an audience trusts him, that is, if it feels his previous behavior as well as his speech indicate that he is an honest person and one who sincerely seeks the truth, his job of motivating will be made much easier. However, it must not be forgotten that a person's intentions are often judged on the basis of stereotypes. So-called "con artists," who want to talk someone out of their money, will go to great lengths to appear respectable. Judging the character, the reliability, and the ability or wisdom of a speaker is not easy. Usually, we depend on our observations as well as on the statements provided by others, maybe newspaper stories, books, or other second-hand reports. But whatever sources we rely on, the man and the message combine to motivate us. Since many aspects of pathos and ethos are closely related, specific ways of increasing ethical appeal will be discussed in more detail in the next segment, specifically in the discussion dealing with the influence of attitudes.

Earlier discussions of interpersonal attraction should be recalled at this point. Some people simply "look good" to us. We may be unhappy over the television images which are created for politicians but the truth is that we judge people to some extent by their appearance—the clothes they wear, facial and other physical features, and the way they move, walk, or gesture. A certain amount of adjustment, at least in such a way that an audience will not be offended and thus refuse to receive the speaker's message, may be needed and audience analysis serves as a basis for decision. If, for example, long hair bothers an audience, a speaker may have to decide what is more important to him, a responsive audience or long hair. Whatever his decision, it may have an important bearing on his ethical persuasion.

PATHOS

A speaker will be interested in finding out what emotions exist in his audience already, or to which motivational appeals members of the audience are most likely to respond. Words are some of the most important means we use in a public speech to create emotions or, more accurately, to touch upon emotions already existing in the audience. Take the word "pink." Used in a ladies' fashion show it may refer to something fluffy, soft, attractive—something a woman "ought to wear." If the same word is used before an audience of Birch Society members, their concern with Communist activities in the United States will make them respond as if the speaker has automatically meant something danger-ous, underhanded, confused, which may have to be eliminated.

In this area, the concepts of *feedback* and *empathy* need consideration. If a speaker notices many people sinking deeply into their seats, slowly falling asleep or polishing their nails, he should be aware that they are trying to tell him something! Feedback can be a factor in strengthening or improving a speaker's total approach. On the other hand he may elaborate on a certain point or build up a certain emotion because his audience is signaling him by its eager anticipation of every word he speaks that they are "with him," and have set up a chain reaction of responses which have turned audience and speaker into a team trying to accomplish the same purpose—an empathic relationship.

The impossibility of separating pathos and ethos as if they were two completely different aspects of persuasion should be apparent. Consider again the point that the reputation of a speaker may precede him. The audience will already have developed an emotional response to him, his looks, his charac-ter, and his reputation, before it sees him in person. The speaker's ethos becomes a direct means of creating pathos.

Motivation and Attention

Basically, all human drives and motives and all motivational speaking centers around *self and others*. An effective speaker will try to understand both, as we discussed in chapters 3, 5, and 6.

Gaining attention is a relatively easy thing. Sometimes a speaker merely has to strike the podium in front of him. Having an attractive girl walking across the stage will at least cause some attention among the male members of an audience, although women may be apt to check over the "competition." Undoubtedly, these devices and many others create interest, cause initial attention. However, holding attention is a different matter. It is at that point that the question of sufficient motivation, which will cause listeners to continue to be involved in what a speaker has to say, enters the picture.

Fortunately there is a certain amount of predictability about human actions. Some of these factors depend on our cultural background, our experience, and our education. Others are based on more fundamental human drives or motivations. Predictably, human beings who have been without food for many days will tend to forget about their normal concern with laws and property rights. They may break into a foodstore, or overturn a truck they hope is carrying food and steal the contents. Depending on their relationship to other people, however, what will be done with the food they have stolen cannot be as easily predicted. Man sometimes does not merely steal for his own needs, but may actually reject the food himself so that a child or spouse may have the needed nourishment. There are basic human drives such as hunger, self-preservation, the continuation of the species, but cultural and educational factors, as well as spiritual values, sometimes become of much more concern.

The *primary motives*, as they are often called, or the basic human drives which all center around the continuation of our existence and the safety of our persons, are primary only when they are not satisfied. When satisfied we may be influenced by other, for the moment more important motives. Comfort, the new, the challenge of adventure, beauty, and many other factors may come to the foreground, as we saw in chapters 3, 4, 5 and 6.

A group of people may be driven to explore a new continent by a variety of motives. There may be a basic drive for survival by those whose former homelands can no longer support their existence. Others may be driven by the promise of riches or fame which will provide them with enough money to buy the things they really want. Others are concerned about new knowledge or the conversion of "heathens." Consider these last two motives. We may think of this kind of motivation in overly simplistic terms. The priests who came with the Spanish conquistadores were interested in saving souls, but they believed that salvation of souls also benefited them, the teachers, on the Day of Judgment. Some who assisted conquerors of other lands and people, although they appeared more interested in gaining knowledge, may have dreamed of fame and fortune among their peers, their fellow scientists, once they returned home.

Holding attention and providing lasting motivation require that a speaker arouses the interest, curiosity and involvement of the listeners. At times he may even have to shock them into taking a look at a proposal because they may lack interest, understanding, or concern. While there is danger in the approach which says that many people do not know what is good for them until they are told, there are many cases where that holds true. A medical doctor who has the cure for a certain illness in his hands may have to break through superstitions, racial barriers, or ignorance before he can administer his medicine.

In any case, whatever stimulus we use, it must be something which crosses the cognition thresholds of the individual listeners. It must be something on which they will focus attention from among all the other available stimuli which their senses help them perceive, because it is important, vital, interesting, familiar, challenging, new, dangerous, or in other ways related to their experiences and needs.

The Bases of Motivation in Public Speeches

In order to catch and hold attention all speech materials should be *varied* and *clear*. Whether or not they are accepted by listeners, however, is usually the result of highly complex needs, drives, or motives which can form a difficult-to-interpret, internal puzzle of human interactions. For our purposes in this chapter we will categorize human motives and drives under three headings:

1. Biological, such as sex, hunger, self-preservation. These are probably our basic drives.
2. Social, which depend heavily on the culture, and center around social norms such as standards of success and fair play, justice, law, order.
3. Ego, which involve questions of pride, self-improvement, respect, dignity, acceptance, and also depend on cultural values.[1]

As you prepare your persuasive speeches, it is in these three areas that you need to discover your audience's prevailing motivation, or combination of motivational factors. On the basis of your decision, specific appeals can then be developed as you attempt to help meet the perceived needs of audience members.

Motivation and Freedom

Our earlier example of the physician and his cure illustrates both the dangers and the importance of persuasive motivation. In a free society man can never afford to give up his vigilance toward those who would determine for him and others what is supposedly best. However, it is equally true that in order to maintain freedom any human being must be granted an opportunity to use his or her persuasive powers to convince people that a certain solution to problems is most beneficial. People will not always respond to such motivational appeals. Indeed some people, using the above example, will die within reach of the medicine which could have cured them. But if they rejected its use on the basis of their own beliefs, on the basis of their understanding of all the factors, then a free society has a duty to consider the right of every individual

---

1. Consider also Maslow's hierarchy of motives discussed in chapter 3.

to make his own choice as he sees fit, as long as he does not hurt anyone else in the process. Freedom of speech, freedom to persuade, does not mean that others have to agree with us. Nor is it true that the art of manipulating the minds and emotions of men through persuasion is so highly developed that man cannot resist it, and that, as a result we have to insulate him from persuasive efforts by others.

Pathos, Ethos, and Attitudes

Members of any audience, as well as speakers, bring their total emotional and rational "equipment" to any speaking situation. What we refer to as attitudes really are those personal constructs relating to our world which every individual develops and carries with him as part of his cognitive storehouse, and which he uses for the evaluation of any situation, including public speeches.

The *attitudes portrayed by a speaker* may have an important effect if, for instance, he leaves an audience with the impression that he is not truly interested in them or their problems in spite of the barrage of data and emotional terms he uses. An audience could reject such a speaker, while being in complete agreement with the ideas he presents. The close relationship of audience emotional responses, or pathos, and ethos becomes once more apparent.

The *attitudes of the audience* toward the subject matter, even before a word is spoken, could have a significant effect. If there has been a particularly brutal murder one day before someone is scheduled to speak in a community on doing away with capital punishment, he may face a crowd daring him to advocate easier punishment for murderers, possibly defying even the efforts of a highly respected, trusted speaker. If an audience's attitudes toward the speaker and his subject matter are very positive, they may still not respond favorably if they feel it is the wrong occasion or if members of the audience have a very negative attitude toward each other or their role in the situation.

The speaker's task would be much easier if he could assume that *all* human behavior is easily predictable, or even that attitudes toward his message will be consistent. However, messages will be judged by members of an audience from a variety of standpoints and combinations of factors, based on attitudes which they bring to the situation and which they develop in the course of a speech.

We cannot assume that individuals who have joined an audience have done so because they all share the same attitudes toward the speech, the speaker, and the occasion. Yet in our society there are some factors which tend to be part of any audience's expectations. Some of these concepts relate specifically to the speaker and form a basic kind of *ethic*. While ethical considerations or values are among the most individualized bases for human responses, most of us would expect speakers to be fair in dealing with the data they present, and we would expect them to be open, rather than devious, with their audiences. Admittedly, these are very general terms, but it is most difficult to find specific, limited ethical concepts to which all of us would subscribe. The two basic ideas mentioned above appear to form the foundation for specific, varied, individually adjusted evaluations of what we consider to be ethical or unethical in oral communication.

Many listeners resent a speaker who tries to confuse them with an overwhelming barrage of data supposedly presenting all the facts, alleging to be as truthful as possible, while he hopes that the sheer amount of information will emotionally and intellectually overload them. Audiences usually want speakers to be truthful, but they do not want them to use that value concept for their own hidden agenda, or hidden purposes in an attempt to deceive. An attempt to get audiences to accept a proposed solution without giving them an opportunity to understand it may be resented as much. Sometimes this can be an abuse of the speaker's ethos or ethical appeal. In effect the speaker is saying under such circumstances: "Trust me even if you don't understand what it is all about!"

The introduction of irrelevant, highly emotional material which does not really contribute anything to the audience's understanding is a frequently used device. Referring to someone's ethnic or racial background, or the fact that he is a cripple is usually an attempt to avoid rational appeals or reasoning while making use of negative attitudes or prejudices which will tend to short-circuit the rational processes of audience members. Personal attacks fall into the same category. Many public speakers have refused to address themselves to legitimate questions raised by opponents, and instead attacked the questioners because of some factor in their backgrounds or personal lives, unrelated to the point under discussion. This kind of attack has been quaintly described as "drawing a red herring across some path." The idea is that the bad smell of that fish is hoped to hide the trail of someone who fears revelation of misdeeds.

We must also realize that persuasion is influenced by a number of other common factors in the experience or background of the listeners which help to shape their attitudes. The consideration of counter-persuasive material before a speech, for instance in newspaper editorials, may cause listeners to reject the arguments of the speaker. Even overexposure to the same material prior to the speech can lead to negative results, since listeners may no longer be stimulated by the speaker's arguments, or simply consider them to be "old hat." Such inoculation effects are important, and they show that the persuasive speaker who gets there first with the most can possibly prevent his listeners from being as easily swayed by later messages.

No public speaker can be ready for all possible problems. However, from our consideration of concepts relating to interpersonal communication, it should be evident that there are some very positive things a speaker can do, even as he deals with a large audience, to strengthen his ethical appeal, and thus assure more positive emotional involvement by his listeners. Most listeners, even if they are among hundreds or thousands of audience members, will provide a speaker with a better chance to reach them or persuade them if they feel personally involved, if they feel as if they have been personally addressed. The choice of specific, personal words directed to individuals in the audience and close eye contact are important means of accomplishing this task. An effective speaker responds to the nonverbal demands of his listeners: I want you to talk to *me!* I want you to convince *me!* I want you to look straight at *me!* I want to know why this is important to *me!* I want to be sure that you know what you are talking about! I want to feel involved! Not only does the speaker purposefully counteract the impersonal aspects of public speaking by his positive responses, but he also provides himself with a much better chance for recognizing and responding to feedback information with which his audience is trying to supply him. It may not be easy to define what we mean by being credible, sincere, or ethical, but it is certain that any audience which has judged a speaker not to possess these qualities will either fight him or turn him off. If we want our messages to be received and accepted, we need to consider the points summarized in the preceding pages. As speakers we cannot prevent the formation of negative attitudes before a speech, but we can positively counteract their development or reinforcement during a speech by being fair and open in our use of data and our approach to the audience.

Influence of Imagery and Sensory Appeals

I will never forget an afternoon in the middle of the Nevada desert. The car was overheating, we had no air-conditioning, our small children were very unhappy, and cold drinks had run out several hundred miles back. There, in the middle of some grotesquely piled up rocks, was a huge billboard. The picture on it was of an overhanging ledge, draped with sparkling icicles, and below, deeply nestled in a layer of snow, was a frosty bottle of Coca-Cola. All the billboard said, at least as far as its printed message was concerned, was: COKE   THE PAUSE THAT REFRESHES. I don't believe I ever wanted a Coca-Cola as badly in my life. The right moment, the right circumstances, and the right message combined to motivate me by appealing directly to my senses.

Messages to which we can form a sensory relationship, which reach our emotions through the senses of touch, smell, taste, seeing, and hearing, can help to stimulate us or cause us to perceive some stimulus more deeply. Colors are used by movie-makers in order to produce a stronger sensory involvement. At times, of course, they use black-and-white films for contrast, because variety and change offer great opportunities for attracting attention. Similarly, a carefully planned change from colorful language to stark, simple, realistic words may produce a highly persuasive contrast. Consider also how important other sensations, such as touch, can be. It is difficult to estimate what effect touch has in the purchase of a fur coat or some other article of clothing. The rich, silky texture of the actual fur usually has a strong sensory influence on the buyer.

Because of his unique, symbol-using ability, man is capable of experiencing all sensory stimuli without actually having an object present. Listening to the detailed description of a thick, red, juicy, sizzling steak can make us salivate almost as easily as the actual presence of food, especially when we are hungry and when the speaker has aptly chosen his words. We can relate experiences, we can describe sensations, and share emotions through the use of words. We react to word symbols as well, and reading a Hitchcock thriller can produce strong sensations of fear, discomfort, or suspense, accompanied by rapid heartbeat, nervous twitches and perspiration. Probably nothing helps the speaker more than reading voraciously in order to learn as many different ways of expressing ideas, thoughts, feelings, attitudes, and describing places, events, colors, sensations. All these, and many other word images make it possible for us to experience more completely, to become more deeply involved in a subject, and to share experiences with others. Physical settings, lighting, music, and other factors can help, but the final job of "painting pictures in the mind" and sharing sensory images in the public speech has to come through carefully chosen, richly meaningful, fully appropriate words which have been adjusted to the speaker, the speech, the audience, and the occasion after careful analysis of all these factors by the speaker.

LOGOS

We often become frustrated with those who refuse to see the logic of something. We even accuse them of being too emotional and shout: "Don't be stupid." The terms *logic* and *reason* are associated with good in our society. Many people even believe that when something is logical it must be true. This is a basic fallacy. Take the following example:

> All Americans are rich.
> John is an American.
> John is rich.

That is a completely logical statement. The problem is not in its structure, which logic helps us to check, but in the basic premise. In other words, whether or not all Americans are rich does not depend on logic, but is something that will have to be determined by establishing certain standards of wealth and then testing those standards against the possessions of all Americans. A logical conclusion depends for its accuracy, or the truth contained in it, on evidence, not the structure of an argument.

The Relationship of Facts and Opinions

To accomplish his task the speaker relies upon two areas of support in addition to his own knowledge: *authoritative facts* and *opinions*. A more detailed schema looks like figure 16.

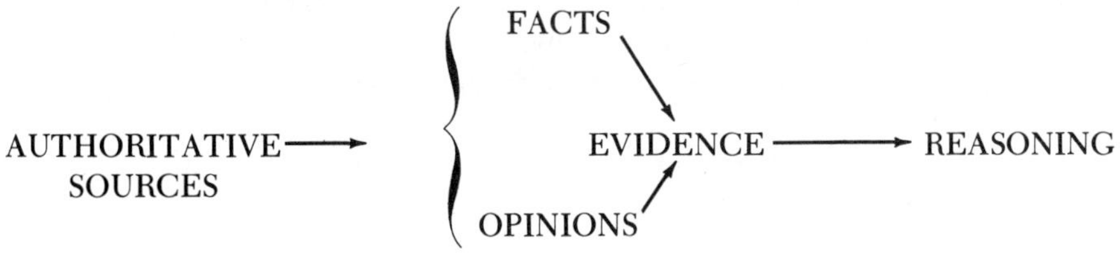

FIGURE 16

The way the facts and opinions from authoritative sources are combined depends on the ability and approach of the speaker. Once the combination has been accomplished we tend to think that we have evidence to back up a given case. A general officer may supply specific data about the Normandy invasion of World War II and proceed to give opinions about the role he played or should have played in that invasion. Thus, he provides strong evidence for a speech on that subject. From that information, his audience or another speaker might reason that the invasion was, for instance, carelessly planned, and that in future, instances of massive landings in an occupied country the lessons of World War II need to be considered. At the same time, this example reminds us of the fact that reasoning is a human process. While we have difficulty in seeing how anyone else may not accept our conclusions, the simple fact is that there are people who disagree. And they disagree on the basis of what to them are some very good facts and opinions because they have used the facts and opinions in a different way in their own reasoning or cognitive processes.

Reasoning

Human reasoning depends to a large extent on the use we make of language, our educational background, our experiences, the facts or opinions we use, and the way we arrange them. Thus, two equally intelligent, equally dedicated people may come up with opposing points of view.

The various levels of reasoning which human beings have identified or created should not be forgotten. Someone might present an overwhelming barrage of facts and opinions explaining why you should kill a certain ememy, but a higher, divine, or moral law may force you to reject the speaker's logic. In any case, all of us have been exposed to certain patterns of reasoning since childhood and we tend to look for these in public speeches or, even more importantly, we tend to organize any ideas with which we come in contact according to these patterns. There are specific methods which speakers have used consistently because they have been shown to make persuasion effective. In our culture we tend to reason from:

1. *Analogy:* reasoning which shows how something is similar to something else
2. *Cause:* reasoning which shows that something results from something else
3. *Example:* reasoning which indicates that certain things have taken place and, therefore, are likely to happen again
4. *Sign:* reasoning which leads from an observable to a nonobservable fact or prediction, such as drawing the conclusion that there will be much water in our streams next spring because there was a large snowfall this winter.
5. *Definition:* reasoning which puts a concept in a class or category, as is done in dictionaries.

The mere existence of arguments, facts, opinions, or any other available evidence does not guarantee acceptance of the evidence. Human behavior may be predictable to some extent, as in the case of pedestrians who usually stop for a red light. However, something can always go wrong, and there is always at least one person who will step into the line of traffic, regardless of the light. There are, indeed, many things which can interfere with the most carefully planned motivational message.

Two Logical Processes Used in Reasoning. Induction is the process used by a scientist who tests hundreds of substances, eliminating one after another until he finds an answer. It is the process used when we look at one black crow, at another, and at another, and at a hundred more, and from all *specific instances* we draw the *generalized conclusion* that all crows are black. As is true with all generalizations, especially when drawn hastily, if we run across even one *white* crow, the induction is no longer valid as it was stated.

Deduction is the second type of reasoning. Stated simply, it moves from a general premise to more specific ones. Deduction and induction work together in most reasoning processes, and we may find ourselves moving back and forth from one to the other. Deduction makes use of a method known as the *syllogism*. It is a logical device; a method of arranging ideas so we can check their relationship to one another. It is true of all logical arrangements that their format may be perfectly acceptable from a logical standpoint, but their components must be individually checked and detailed proof presented before we can evaluate their truthfulness or factualness.

A syllogism consists of three parts: *major premise, minor premise,* and *conclusion.* In public speaking one or more of these parts may be omitted, or supplied in the minds of listeners when a generally accepted truth is being discussed. This kind of syllogism, the rhetorical syllogism, is known as an *enthymeme.* We used one syllogism earlier.

All Americans are rich.
John is an American.
John is rich.

Cast in the form of an enthymeme it reads: John is a typical, rich American.

Problems in the Use of Reasoning. One of the biggest problems in logical reasoning results from the use of cause-to-effect or effect-to-cause arguments. This becomes particularly dangerous when we seek one specific cause for a certain effect, or one effect for a specific cause. For instance: "If we drop an atom-bomb on North Vietnam, China will attack us." Or using the effect-to-cause relationship: "Rebellion against authority results from poverty among American minority groups." Consider the following question: A man walks down the street. A flower pot falls out of a third story window and kills him. What caused his death? What killed him? Depending on the point of view, that is, whether the observer is a physician, member of a jury, a policeman, or a bystander, a variety of answers may be given, ranging from "hemorrhage," to "flower pot," to "his wife."

Another problem concerns the *black-and-white-reasoning* in which we often engage. For instance, if a speaker addresses members of a labor union, he will readily be identified as "antilabor" simply because he happens to be for the Taft-Hartley Act. Many audiences want their speakers to be either all for, or all against a subject. *Over-simplification* is a similar problem. "If we can just assure everyone an average income of $10,000 annually, all of our economic problems would cease," is an example of finding a simple solution to a much more complicated problem. *Misapplication* of facts also fits this area of difficulty. The statement: "More doctors smoke Brand-X cigarettes than any other kind," may be used as an endorsement for smoking when in reality a majority of physicians may be against smoking because it is a health hazard.

STRUCTURING AND OUTLINING
PERSUASIVE SPEECHES

The Appendix provides examples of an outline which makes it easier to develop a motivational structure. This type of arrangement is based on the five steps used in problem solving with which you are familiar from the chapter on small group communication.

    I. Define the problem
    II. Analyze the problem
    III. Suggest solutions
    IV. Evaluate solutions
    V. Put solutions into effect

These five points can also be incorporated logically into the outline form discussed earlier:

Introduction (define the problem)
Body (analyze the problem, suggest solutions, evaluate solutions)
Conclusions (put solutions into effect)

I. As the speaker defines the problem he is attempting to give a reason for his audience to listen to the speech. This material should cause listeners to become interested and to see some relationship between the speech and their interests. While the speaker may be certain that they should listen, he needs to convince the listeners to pay attention. There may be only one moment in a speech when the speaker has the attention of almost everyone in his audience, and that is during the first few words of his introduction. After that, many things such as the presence of other people, noise, heat, problems of daily living entering back into consciousness of listeners, etc., interfere with the oral communication process. Therefore, the first words or sentences must be especially well-prepared, perhaps even written out, although they may have to be changed at the last minute if some important factor for which the speaker could not plan makes it necessary. Remember the story of the physics professor reading an old lecture on the unlikelihood of nuclear fission the day the atom bomb was dropped.

II. If the speaker has succeeded in arousing the attention of the audience and defining the problem, he needs next to give his audience a reason for continuing to listen. As the speaker analyzes the subject or problem of his persuasive speech, he must involve the audience in it. Many speakers feel that the mere mention of a subject, or the fact they they themselves are interested in it also makes it of vital concern to the audience. Many things in the lives of the listeners are competing with the speaker and his subject; if they cannot see that it relates somehow to their vital interests, their desires, their needs, or wants, they will not continue to listen. This step thus serves to state and define the problem or challenge.

III. As the members of the audience develop a close relationship with the speaker and the subject, they will demand that he provide them with some answer to the problem he has set up for them. Nothing could be worse than leaving an audience in a state of frustration. The speaker must suggest ways and means in which the problem can be solved, or audience needs and interests can be met.

IV. As the speaker develops the next step it should become evident to his listeners that in evaluating the solutions, they and their needs are again very much on the speaker's mind. A general solution to which a listener feels no personal relationship will never get the job done. An audience which can walk away from a speech feeling that the speaker has addressed himself to every individual member, that he has done more than set up a straw man, that he has been doing battle with their personal "dragon," is truly persuaded.

V. The audience may agree with the speaker in principle or on a strictly theoretical basis, but only when he makes sure that they will put into effect solutions he has developed is the speech truly successful. At this point, many speakers falter or fail. A final blow for a cause must be struck before the speaker can be reasonably certain that the audience is with him all the way. The speaker should make sure he does not extend his concluding remarks too long. A definite ending is most effective: "As for me, give me Liberty or give me Death."

One of the most important things about a successful persuasive speech is that the speaker often can observe both immediate and long-range results. Only if he has presented members of his audience with the right informational and motivational material will they be prone to become involved and find, as time goes by, that they have good reasons to stay involved.

Supporting Material

Ideas in a persuasive speech need selling: It is not enough to state them simply and bluntly. Even the factor of timing is important. Not only is the speaker's own time limited, permitting him only a brief period out of the life of each listener, but the audience in turn has been influenced both by events in the past, and by events which are of importance at the very moment the speech is being given. A speech dealing with good hunting etiquette the day after the hunting season closes faces some very rough going. Attempts to persuade an audience to contribute large amounts of money the day after a similar campaign by some other charity closed calls for an outstanding effort by the speaker.

This does not mean that all difficult persuasive speeches are destined to fail. Some of the greatest speeches were given under the most adverse circumstances. One outstanding example is the "New South" speech by Henry W. Grady before the New England Society in New York after the Civil War. Grady, publisher of the Atlanta *Constitution,* was called on to address his northern audience after General Sherman had spoken and the audience had spontaneously risen to its feet to sing "Marching through Georgia." It is difficult to describe adequately the task facing Grady. But if you read his speech and find out how he related his own statements to previously expressed ideas and how he turned one disadvantage after another into an advantage, you will begin to understand how important great persuasive speaking can be. What is more, you can understand why his audience rose to its feet after Grady finished and gave him a rousing ovation.

Different people respond to different types of supporting material. This means that a speaker must use enough variety to reach at least every major group in the audience, whether they prefer statistics or a parable. This should not become a mere display of sparkling words and ideas, however. If an idea is clear and every reaction of the audience indicates it, the speaker does not need to add more ideas simply because he has some left over. On the other hand, he may find that one illustration was not enough, or that one set of statistics was not clear, and the listeners are uneasy about the speaker's statement. If he is well-prepared and has done more than merely memorize a manuscript, he can easily adjust and respond to that need by adding another type of supporting material, or by developing the same type still further.

Various types of support were mentioned in the preceding chapter. For motivational speaking, the following categories could be added or repeated:

1. *Quotations.* They help to indicate that a speaker is not merely expressing his own ideas, but that others agree with him, or partially support him. In addition, certain quotations from poetry or prose which tend to set or develop a mood can be very valuable.
2. *Extended Examples.* The development of a story or an illustration in such a way that the audience will experience it with the speaker can be a very important feature in any attempt at persuasion. Many television commercials use a visual form of this device in order to make us feel young, daring, or one of the crowd. Anecdotes or shorter incidents are also examples of this effective persuasive device, because they usually describe dramatic, humorous, emotional events in specific, precise, colorful detail.
3. *Personal Intention.* For a speaker who has strong ethical appeal because of his experience or background or because of his leadership position, this can be a powerful means of swaying his audience. Joshua, faced with a disheartened Jewish nation, spoke to them, encouraging them to make a vital choice. When he ended the speech by stating, "But as for me and my house, we will serve the Lord," the Israelites gained strength and determination from their leader's forceful declaration of his personal intentions.

Supporting material is intended to attract and to hold attention throughout a speech. It is a vehicle for making important ideas more easily understandable and more firmly accepted. As a result such persuasive details, forming a consistent pattern which does not confuse the audience with sudden switches in motivational appeals or widely divergent types of supporting material without transitions, need to be made consciously part of all segments of a speech. Supporting material tends to accomplish its vital tasks through change (even the most important idea becomes boring if it is repeated again and again in the same way), and its relationship to the audience. That which is important to us, that which is familiar or new to us, that which brings suspense, joy, or relaxation and fun into our lives, brings about our most ready response and steady interest.

If someone tells me that he will provide food to stop my hunger, I will listen to him. To avoid the impression that motivation is a neat, simple, one-way process, we should remember in the selection of supporting material that most human beings may at any given time have contrasting or conflicting motives. They may yearn for adventure, but they also yearn for relaxation and safety. Thus they will watch the white hunter traveling down the Lower Zambesi on television and share his adventures while they sit in their reclining vibrator chairs. If persuasion or the desired change is congruent with all the existing attitudes and motives of listeners, it probably will be effective.

BEGINNING AND ENDING THE SPEECH

Both the introduction and the conclusion of any formal speech should be kept short. Depending on the subject, the interests and background of an audience, and the specific occasion, there are specific ways of getting into and out of a speech, something which many speakers find problematic. Effective introductions will be discussed first.

1. *A statement of personal experience.* A speech dealing with safety procedures in underwater exploration will have more impact if the speaker begins it by giving an indication of his personal expertise: "Last year, while diving in the waters off the Florida Keys, I developed trouble with my regulator."

2. *A quotation.* The speaker's own concepts concerning the fight against cancer may be interesting, but they will lack the immediate impact of a summary report by the medical authorities of Johns Hopkins University, indicating that a major breakthrough can be expected in the next five years.

3. *A startling statistic.* A speech dealing with deaths due to automobile accidents could be introduced by indicating that more than 50,000 people were killed on America's roads during the last year. This simple number can be made more dramatic by comparing it to the loss of lives in wars Americans have fought, or indicating that deaths on our highways in effect wiped out a number of people comparable to the population of a specific neighboring town.

4. *Some unusual or humorously worded definition of the subject.* A speech dealing with the use of watchdogs for the protection of private property could begin: "Dogs are either man's best friend or man's worst enemy, depending on whether you are a home owner or a home burglar."

5. *A rhetorical question.* No answer is expected to such questions, but they may cause an audience to think. Telling listeners about the dangers of sunburns, a speaker may wish to start by asking: "How many of you would like to go out and get cancer—on purpose? "

For the conclusion, the following methods are effective:

1. A quotation summarizing the main points in the speech
2. A restatement of major points
3. An impressive picture or visual aid, such as a chart, leaving the audience with a clear image of the subject discussed
4. A statement of personal intention, as the one Joshua used
5. A final specific call for action.

ARRANGING APPEALS

There is always someone who informs us with a bland smile that he is "just being frank," or "not beating around the bush" as he behaves like the proverbial bull in the china shop. Surely there must be someone in this world who would not mind his doctor coming right out and saying "You are too fat." The physician's purpose of getting the patient to lose weight is admirable, and certainly he is having no problem with communicating his ideas. The words he chose are clear and easily understood, and little or no confusion should result from them. Whether or not he will ever treat the patient again or assist him in prolonging his life by losing some weight is questionable, however, because of the way he stated his point in approaching this sensitive subject.

The arrangement and order of appeals can have an important effect on the motivation of the audience.

1. If an audience is antagonistic to any part of the speech, the speaker should delay its discussion until he has had time to build up the interest of his audience and has provided basic information, or agreement on other points, making agreement on controversial ideas easier.
2. If the audience is sympathetic to a proposal or idea, the speaker can start out with it, making it as strong as possible by supporting it with adequate material afterwards.
3. If the members of an audience are disinterested, it may become necessary to leave the major point or idea for a while in order to discuss a subject of importance to them. After the speaker has gained their attention, he can relate the matters of interest to the idea he has to "sell."

In all public speaking efforts, existing research findings indicate that one-sided argumentation, or the presentation of only one side of an issue, does not result in as much long-range persuasion as does persuasion which also includes exceptions or contrary facts and arguments. Most persuasion represents a type of conflict resolution. A problem exists and both sender and receiver may want to solve it. If the solution is self-evident, or if there is only one way in which man can move, usually there is no need for persuasion. However, in most cases a variety of solutions are possible, and we need to apply our ability to reason (while not forgetting the powerful motivation of emotions) to the discovery of the best possible solution.

BODILY ACTIVITY

Enthusiasm, sincerity, and similar terms are difficult to define, but we know that audiences in order to be persuaded must feel that the speaker is personally involved in the speech or, more accurately, in his subject. One way in which we interpret such involvement is through observation of total bodily activity. Notice how children react to a Western on television! They are not merely content with observing, they literally "shoot back" at the actors, indicating their complete personal involvement.

Since we are trying to persuade an audience, more vigorous gestures are usually called for, while at times bodily activity may also express a controlled

but strong involvement. Any speaker who shies away from movement, gestures, and forceful delivery may have difficulty in convincing his audience that his subject is really worth their close scrutiny. Even the easiest going person would find it difficult to portray deeply felt emotion and personal involvement without some physical activity. Artificiality or carefully studied gestures must be avoided, but the speaker should be sufficiently free so that his feelings will find expression in bodily action. Only careful preparation of all other factors such as the sequence of ideas, varied support and audience analysis will allow him to become free and personally involved at the moment of delivery.

SUMMARY

Communication with large groups of people makes many of the concepts of interaction we have discussed earlier in this book very difficult. Instead of specific, personalized communication, the situation a public speaker faces is much more diffuse, indefinite, and often rather impersonal. He has to determine what the common denominators are. He must discover and use the common values held by a majority of the members of his audience.

Public speaking requires the development of structure, reasoning, establishment of relationships, and use of facts and opinions to which a sufficiently large number of listeners can relate in some fashion. In a free society repeated opportunities for addressing large audiences are provided and are sought by those who need to accomplish certain tasks by sheer number of involved listeners. Being part of a human society implies the concept of interaction, of relating to other people. We cannot be both part of society and insist at all times on doing our own thing. More than that, interaction implies that we exert some influence on others. A free society makes possible interaction based on persuasion rather than coercion. Persuasion in turn is based on motivation, which we achieve by providing listeners with rational and emotional appeals in an attempt to bring about a change in direction, degree, or amount of the receivers' actions, feelings, attitudes, or beliefs.

Carefully planning and developing a speech helps the speaker to know his subject matter more adequately, and probably will help him clarify his ideas in the public speaking situation. Because immediate understanding and response are a necessary part of this type of oral communication, such preparation is a prerequisite to effective oral communication with large groups.

There is no magic to persuasion. There is no proof that effective persuaders create new needs, create entirely new attitudes, or develop some foolproof method of making people do what they want them to do. Effective persuaders have an ability to sense and understand the needs, drives, motives, and attitudes of their listeners, and they have prepared themselves to use that knowledge in bringing about some change which is mutually beneficial to them and to their listeners. Good persuaders, at least by definition, are thus not really manipulators in the negative sense of that word, but they are responsible, ethical communicators interested in some concerted, beneficial interaction between all those who make up a speaking situation.

In reading this book I hope you have seen that it was written in an attempt to help you build concepts relating to speech communication. It was not intended as a collection of ideas which should be memorized and then repeated at certain appropriate moments, such as at midterm or final examinations. Since it is a book about communication, I hope it has been a stimulus for communicating with your classmates and your professors about human interaction—and for some meditative communication with yourself. Each chapter contains ideas which are related to the concepts in all the following chapters in an attempt to relate ideas to each other and let our study of communication grow in an organic fashion similar to all the aspects of that kind or type of interaction which we call speech communication.

EXERCISES

1. Write a 500-word paper, and present a five-minute summary speech dealing with the importance of order in the presentation of persuasive materials.

2. In a group discussion with four of your classmates, discuss for thirty minutes the ethics of persuasion. Consider carefully the arguments made by proponents and opponents of persuasive techniques, then open the discussion to participation by all of your classmates.

3. Develop a six-minute speech, including a careful outline, concerning a specific campus problem, in which you will attempt to move your audience to engage in some specific action. Consider carefully the values important to your audience.

4. Write a five-hundred word analysis dealing with the fact that most political speakers, especially in national campaigns, tend to address themselves to the most common factors or values held by all their listeners, often ignoring specific con-

cepts, questions or ideas. Is this a deceptive practice? Is it a necessary practice? What do you think a national, political candidate ought to accomplish in his public speeches?

5. Present a five-minute speech in class on the subject: "Major logical devices commonly used in Western culture." You may wish to start with major concepts in Aristotelian logic.

6. Select two speeches by each of the two leading presidential candidates during the last campaign, underline persuasive appeals, and write a 300-word paper evaluating them.

7. Develop a 300-word paper describing and evaluating a number of specific instances contributing to the ethos of a speaker which you have personally observed.

8. Select five newspaper editorials dealing with the same topic, underline all cause-to-effect and effect-to-cause arguments, and evaluate them.

9. From textbooks in any of your classes, select at least ten instances of inductive reasoning and be prepared to present them in a brief oral report, allowing for questions afterwards.

10. Give an eight-minute speech which heavily relies upon sensory appeals. You may use visual aids, color, sound, or anything else that will help to create an atmosphere conducive to your purpose. Develop a careful outline, including indications of the use of visual and audio materials.

11. Develop a six-minute speech, including a careful outline, which has as its purpose to inspire your audience as citizens of the United States.

BIBLIOGRAPHY

Bettinghaus, Erwin P. *Persuasive Communication*. New York: Holt, Rinehart, and Winston, 1968.

Brown, A. C. *Techniques of Persuasion*. Baltimore: Penguin Books, 1963.

Cronkhite, Gary. *Persuasion, Speech and Behavioral Change*. New York: Bobbs-Merrill, 1969.

Hovland, Carl L., Irving L. James, and Harold Kelley. *Communication and Persuasion*. New Haven: Yale University Press, 1953.

Minnick, Wayne C. *The Art of Persuasion*. Boston: Houghton Mifflin, 1969.

Packard, Vance. *The Hidden Persuaders*. New York: McKay, 1957.

OUTLINES

COMPLETE SENTENCE OUTLINE

Subject: Mental Illness
General End: To inform
Purpose: To inform the audience about the nature and effects of mental illness.

I. I will briefly summarize the early history of mental illness.

    A. Up until the 1700s people thought mental illness was caused by "demons" or "devils" possessing, or living in the body.

        1. Often skulls were opened by "trephining" to release demons.

        2. Religious ceremonies were used to drive them out.

    B. Early treatments for mental illness were sometimes cruel and ridiculous.

        1. Doctors used to jump up and down on patients to remove "mental obstructions."

        2. Hot irons were sometimes applied to patients' heads to bring them to their senses.

        3. Rotating devices were used to whirl the mentally ill around.

    C. Famous people often accomplished great tasks or gained a reputation in spite of their mental disorders.

        1. Beethoven and Schubert wrote some of their finest music while in deep depression.

        2. Mussolini had delusions of grandeur.

II. Today we recognize several main types of mental illness.

    A. Neurosis is a mild mental disorder that does not require institutionalization.

        1. Acrophobia is a fear of heights.

        2. Blaming others for our difficulties is another type of neurosis.

B. Character disorders are also called personality disorders.

1. Compulsive gambling is a character disorder.
2. Stuttering, tics, nail-biting, and enuresis, or bed-wetting, are also character disorders.

C. Psychosis is a severe personality disorder involving loss of contact with reality.

1. It is usually characterized by delusions and hallucinations.
2. Like other mental illnesses, it strikes members of all social classes.

D. Misconceptions about mental illness are widespread.

1. Mental illness is a sickness.
   a. It is not contagious.
   b. It is most often the result of one's environment.
2. Poor adjustment by others to mental illness can itself take unhealthy forms.
   a. Mental illness should not be a cause for shame.
   b. Most families have members who suffer from some mental illness.

III. The mentally ill can be helped.

A. We know much more about mental illness and its causes.

1. Many cases are curable.
2. Many others can be dramatically improved.

B. There is no need to fear ex-patients because of our ability to cure them.

1. Suspicion can be harmful to the person's happiness and self-confidence.
2. Society cannot afford to lose the talents of such people.

KEY WORD OUTLINE

To indicate the basic difference between a key-word outline, and the complete sentence outline, the speech on mental illness is used again.

Subject: Mental Illness
General End: To inform
Purpose: To inform the audience about the nature and effects of mental illness.

I. Early History

A. Caused by demons

1. Trephining
2. Religious ceremonies

B. Early treatments

1. Jumping on patients
2. Hot irons
3. Rotation

C. Famous People

1. Beethoven, Schubert
2. Mussolini

II. Today

A. Neurosis

1. Acrophobia
2. Blaming others

B. Character Disorders

    1. Compulsive gambling
    2. Stuttering, tics, nailbiting, enuresis

C. Psychosis

    1. Delusions, hallucinations
    2. Strikes all classes

D. Misconception still present

    1. A sickness
       a. Not contagious
       b. Environmental
    2. Poor adjustment by others
       a. Not a cause of shame
       b. Found in most families

III. Help possible

A. We know more

    1. Many curable
    2. Many can be improved

B. No suspicion of ex-patients

    1. Suspicion of ex-patients
    2. Can't afford to lose these people

TECHNICAL PLOT OUTLINE

After writing a complete sentence outline, in order to check the adequacy of arguments and variety of supporting materials, especially if persuasive and argumentative material permeates a speech, the *technical plot outline* can be used. This type of outline is similar to a lawyer's brief. Either in the right hand margin of the existing outline, or on a second piece of paper attached to the right side, the speaker might indicate for each of the major and minor points:

1. The intended purpose of the statement.
2. Identification of the types of material, such as "illustration," "statistic," "quote," etc.

Thus it can be checked if there is a logical sequence and a sufficiently large and varied number of supporting materials.

I. Quotation from College Bulletin.
"The preservation of our democratic way of life depends in part upon the ability of college graduates to enter effectively into the political process."

Using quotation and the factor of familiarity to stir attention.

II. Purpose Statement: Because "the pre-servation of our democratic way of life depends . . . upon the ability of college graduates to enter . . . into the political process. Therefore, I am here to urge you to take at least one political science course as an elective."

The college bulletin has a close connection with the audience's interests in academic work and will catch attention.

III. The need to study political science is
great.

Shows the audience that the subject is important.

A. Studying political science gives
us understanding of our own
political and governmental system.

Reason 1. Familiarity

B. Studying political science exposes
us to the contending ideologies of
government.

Reason 2. Opposing facts

C. Studying political science gives us
an insight into other fields of
study.

Reason 3. Variety

BODY

I. Studying political science serves three
functions.

A. Students will be made conscious of,
and helped to understand, our own
government.

Identification of areas to be
discussed. Shows that the proposed action is workable and
that it will benefit the audience.

1. Referring to the question, what is
meant by political process?

Question

a. That process by which our
government retains its smooth
running order.

Definition

(1) Two party-system is
one method.

Example

(2) Electoral College is
another.

Example

b. Political process is not to be
confused with the democratic
process.

Clarification

This is an example of the type of outline based on Dewey's five steps in the human thought process.

Subject: Senate Reapportionment
General End: To persuade
Purpose: To get the members of the class to write to their state representatives
and to the governor to demand fair reapportionment.

I. Residents of Los Angeles are not fairly represented in the state legislature.

A. One voter in three counties has the same representation as 428 voters in Los Angeles County.

1. Almost six million residents of Los Angeles County have only one representative.

2. Fourteen thousand residents in Inyo, Mono, and Alpine counties also have one representative.

B. Heavily populated areas are all underrepresented.

1. Four of the most populated counties of Southern California have 50% of the people, but only 10% of the representatives.

2. Fourteen large counties have 80% of the population but only one-third of the representatives.

C. Unequal representation is a disadvantage to the majority of the people.

      1. Less than 11% of the population control a majority of the state Senate.

        a. Majority vote is all that is needed to pass a bill.

        b. Laws can therefore be passed to benefit a minority of the people.

      2. In cases where a two-thirds vote is required, they can be defeated by the fourteen senators who are elected by 5% of the population.

        a. Ninety-five percent of the people could want a particular bill and still be defeated.

        b. A few people control the legislature.

II. Senate districts must be formed to give each voter equal representation.

    A. Urban areas are controlled by rural areas with different interests.

      1. Water projects for cities can be stopped by rural voters.

      2. Rural areas can get legislation in their interest at the expense of city dwellers.

    B. Each voter should have equal representation.

      1. The Supreme Court decision of "one man–one vote" must be carried out.

      2. Heavily populated areas must get more representation by redistricting.

    C. New reapportionment bills must meet two basic requirements.

      1. Districting should be accomplished strictly by population size without regard to county.

        a. Counties should be split into several districts if necessary.

        b. More than three counties should be joined to form a district.

      2. Senators must be elected by voters in each district.

        a. Representatives elected at large would have less contact with voters.

          (1) They would not know their needs.

          (2) They would not be under their control.

        b. Representatives would be subjected to pressure other than that of the direct voters.

III. In order to have a fair number of representatives, Los Angeles County must be divided into fifteen districts.

    A. Current bills give Los Angeles County only twelve seats.

      1. There are forty seats in the Senate.

      2. Los Angeles County has almost one-third of the population.

    B. Dividing Los Angeles County into fifteen districts would allow each person an equal vote.

    C. Counties are smaller in the north.

      1. The North has two-thirds of the senators.

      2. They control the State.

IV. You can see the importance of the reapportionment issue.

    A. Los Angeles County would have equal representation.

      1. The majority of the people would be represented fairly.

      2. Conflicting interests would be settled to benefit most of the people.

      3. An example is state gas taxes which would benefit people who have the greatest need for roads.

    B. Representatives would be close to voters.

      1. You would be better informed of legislation affecting you.

      2. Voters could get their interests heard.

V. You must write to your representatives and to the governor and demand fair reapportionment.

A. Stop control of the majority by a few people.

B. Make your vote equal to others.

C. Write now to affect the next legislative session.

OUTLINE OF A LONGER SPEECH

Subject: "Law Enforcement," A Vanishing Concept?
General End: To move to action
Purpose: To persuade the audience to assist in strengthening justice under the
law.

I. Our concept of protection under the law has suffered severely.
   A. Sometime ago a seven-year-old Canoga Park boy was kidnapped and brutally
      molested.
      1. The assailant was a known sex offender.
      2. The assailant should have been in a correctional institution.
   B. Mr. George Harris of Los Angeles was the victim of an attempted assault by
      a 19-year-old pervert.
      1. Mr. Harris signed a complaint for his attacker's arrest.
      2. The precinct captain told him not to expect too much.
         a. The assailant was a known pervert.
         b. This was the assailant's third or fourth arrest.
         c. Each time he was given a light sentence of 16 weeks to two months,
            or a nominal fine.
         d. He would soon be free to roam the streets again.
   C. Some years ago a young girl named Katherine Genovese was knifed to death
      in the streets of New York.
      1. She was attacked three different times in a thirty-minute period.
      2. Thirty-eight people witnessed the gruesome crime.
      3. Not one of them bothered to save her by simply calling the police.
      4. They just "didn't want to get involved."

II. The declining effectiveness of law enforcement in the last decade must be stopped
    and reversed.
    A. Crime is ever on the increase.
       1. The crime rate has increased five times faster than the population from
          1960–66.
       2. In 1963, 11 out of every 100 policemen were assaulted while in the line
          of duty.
       3. The arrests of juveniles and young people have increased three times as
          fast as their population from 1960–66.
       4. Rioting in the first eight months of 1964 exceeded that in the eight years
          between 1952 and 1960.
       5. Some questionable practices are being accepted in America today.
          a. Tax cheating
          b. Juvenile delinquency
          c. Sexual immorality
             (1) Many "call girl operations"
             (2) Influx of pornographic literature on the market today

       d. A rapidly rising divorce rate
          (1) In 1969, 300 out of every 1000 married people will be divorced.
          (2) During 1968 in California there were 52,266 divorces.

B. In recent years there has been an attempt to distort information about, harass, and discredit local police forces.

    1. Last Year, CBS-TV showed "The Biography of a Bookie Joint."
       a. Police officers were made to look like "grafting bums."
       b. An investigation later proved this to be basically untrue.
    2. The police chief in Birmingham, Alabama, had been doing a good job of maintaining order in a recent racial crisis.
       a. He let thousands of Negroes march.
       b. He let hundreds of white people protest as they wished.
       c. He had simply set up a line of police, protected by their dogs, to keep the two groups apart.
       d. Incidents didn't arise, so agitators "planned them."
          (1) One or more Negro instigators went over and deliberately kicked the police dogs.
          (2) Cameras just happened to be on the scene.
          (3) The result was a picture in the nationwide press.
             (a) It showed a policeman who was barely able to restrain his vicious dog.
             (b) The dog appeared to be straining to attack a Negro who wanted his civil rights.
    3. The establishment of police review boards discredits police activity.
       a. They are supposed to review cases of police brutality, and try to prevent them.
       b. Actually, they "scare" the officer into conforming with their policy.
          (1) Every action in dealing with vicious criminals is subject to review.
          (2) Officers may be given a loss of pay, suspension from the force, or even dismissal.
          (3) In most cases, the officer was only trying to protect himself while carrying out his duty.

C. What can be done about this serious problem?

    1. Laws must be passed.
       a. Stiffer penalties for certain crimes are needed.
       b. Tighter narcotics laws are needed.
       c. Tighter laws on probation and parole are needed.
    2. Information about the existing situation must be circulated.
       a. Encourage law enforcement.
       b. Encourage respect for the law.
       c. Encourage obedience of the law.
       d. Try to see that the real facts are always brought out.

D. Let us strengthen laws regarding criminals and our law enforcement.

    1. Our society will have a morally better atmosphere.
    2. The crime rate will decrease.
    3. The streets will be less dangerous.
    4. Our children will have a safer place to grow up.

E. The future of our country depends upon how well our laws are kept.

    1. Police Chief William H. Parker said, "As long as we expect to be the repository of human freedom, we must maintain a rule of law or we're going

to fall apart—and all human freedom will go with it." (Los Angeles, California)

    2. It is your responsibility—and mine—to see that justice under the law is firmly established.

III. Let us formulate our desires into action.

    A. Write your congressman and senators.

        1. Give them the facts of the problem.

        2. Ask them to sponsor the needed legislation.

    B. Oppose the establishment of police review boards.

        1. This was recently done in Los Angeles.

        2. Write your city councilman and tell him who you are.

OUTLINING THE PERSUASIVE SPEECH

This outline uses three divisions: Introduction, Body, Conclusion.

    Subject: Why you should own a Volkswagen
    General End: To move to action
    Specific purpose: To persuade members of the audience to buy a Volkswagen
    Probable audience attitude: Interested and favorable

I. Some of the fastest cars in the world are still following the Volkswagen.

    A. Quality in a car is much more important than speed, but it may be of some interest that VWs have a lot in common with cars that race.

        1. The VW has a private suspension system.

        2. The engine is in the rear.

        3. It has an aluminum-magnesium engine.

        4. Four-speed transmissions are standard.

    B. Most of the VW's features aren't included for the sake of speed but rather for performance. This causes . . .

        1. Easier driving

        2. Simple service

        3. Cheaper running

        4. Longer life

    C. The VW has a top speed of only 72 mph, but it's way ahead of many other cars.

II. What happens when you drive a VW?

    A. You start in the coldest weather.

        1. It has no radiator.

        2. It uses no water.

            a. There is no outlay for antifreeze.

            b. This eliminates potentially breakable parts.

    B. You drive a VW, it doesn't drive you.

        1. You have a personal control that you share almost exclusively with sports car owners.

        2. You use the four-speed stick-shift transmission which permits you to get the most work from your engine with less strain.

    C. You keep riding smoothly where most cars can't even operate.

       1. The engine is in the rear.

       2. It has a split axle.

       3. It has independent torsion-bar suspension.

    D. You save plenty of money.

       1. You get 32 miles to a gallon of gas.

       2. The motor needs 5 pints of oil.

       3. Longer tire life is usual.

       4. There are fewer parts to break down.

       5. Faster service is available everywhere.

         a. Mechanics don't have to relearn the car each year.

         b. Parts are the same on all cars.

         c. Service is simple.

         d. There are fewer parts to maintain.

       6. Lower insurance rates are part of your enjoyment of a VW.

    E. Place yourself with the other 9 million VW owners into a VW's comfortable bucket seats.

       1. You must have arrived at the conclusion by now that there is no quality car like the VW.

         a. It is a car of true craftsmanship.

         b. It is a car that has the highest resale value on the market.

         c. It is a car for which only a keen-eyed observer will be able to tell the year.

         d. It is a car that is not unique, but the idea behind it is.

       2. Own one

         a. Inexpensively

         b. Contentedly

III. If you are considering a new or used car, think Volkswagen.

    A. Go to your local VW dealer and test-drive one.

    B. See if it's not all I have said and *more*.

"PROBLEM SOLVING" FIVE-POINT OUTLINE

Title: "Something for Practically Nothing"
General Purpose: To move to action
Specific Purpose: To persuade the audience to have more inexpensive dates.

  I. Many of you would like to get something for practically nothing.

    A. Whether you are dating someone steadily or dating several people, you may be tired of doing the same old thing every weekend.

    B. Plan some new activities that have minimum cost and give a maximum in entertainment.

  II. There are two main reasons why more casual dates should be planned.

    A. The cost of dating is very high.

       1. Consider a date which consists of going to the show followed by a late snack.

        a. Cost at the minimum of $5 a week.

        b. That is $20 per month or $260 per year.

    2. There are, of course, those who date two or even three nights per week.

        a. Two dates per week would cost at least $40 per month or $520 per year.

        b. Three dates could cost $60 per month or $780 per year.

    3. You do not want to go to the show every weekend.

        a. So you must plan other activities that are even more expensive.

           (1) You go to places like Disneyland, boat shows, and car shows.

           (2) If you are sports-minded, you attend baseball, football, basketball, or hockey games or ice shows.

    4. Can you really afford this?

        a. Remember that none of those figures include gasoline for your car.

        b. These are minimum costs.

  B. A second reason involves your personal relationship with your date.

    1. How well can you get to know a person watching a movie?

        a. There is usually little or no conversation.

        b. The conversation is usually of a more formal type.

    2. You need to be in a more informal situation.

        a. Something that is stimulating and interesting to both.

        b. Where you can find out the person's interests and inner feelings.

III. A positive solution to your problem is readily available.

  A. If you are faced with this problem you can do one of three things.

    1. Cut out dating completely.

    2. Stay at home with your date and watch TV every weekend.

    3. Plan activities which cost less, yet are stimulating and fun.

  B. If you have chosen the third solution, maybe I can give you a few suggestions.

    1. Plan a drive to some scenic spot.

        a. Take a route that has interesting scenery.

        b. Take a picnic lunch to eat in a park or by the side of the road.

        c. Have a destination that has something of interest to both of you.

        d. Make sure you have enough time.

           (1) So that you can relax and enjoy yourselves.

           (2) So that you do not spend half of your time driving to the place and back.

    2. Look for opportunities to take tours of places that are of interest to you.

        a. At different times of the year, some places have free tours.

           (1) These occur usually when a business is trying to promote some product.

           (2) Someone who works for a certain company might arrange a tour for his friends.

        b. Some places are open to the public at all times.

           (1) Special exhibits are held in most communities.

           (2) Art shows are also held.

    3. Join in activities of your youth group at church.

        a. Plan beach parties.

        b. Have come-as-you-are breakfasts.

        c. Have a progressive dinner with a special theme.

        d. Plan sports activities, if you have the facilities.

    4. In those evenings when you would rather stay at home—discover games.

        a. There are many new games in the stores now.

           (1) Once you have paid the original cost, you can have many hours of fun.

             (2) You will actually save money in the long run.

          b. I would like to tell you about one such game.

             (1) The "Game of Life" which is something like "Monopoly."

             (2) It makes use of everyday events and can be played by two or more.

  C. You can use these activities to supplement your regular dates, thus cutting down on the cost.

IV. All of you have different interests; try to share these with someone else.

  A. You might be surprised to find that other people are interested in these things, too.

    1. It might be surfing, waterskiing, art exhibits, campaigning for your favorite candidate, church activities, or music.

    2. Look for someone to share these interests with you or tell your boyfriend or girlfriend about them; maybe they are interested, too.

  B. You will learn new things about your friends.

    1. Life consists of many facets besides festive occasions.

    2. As you learn more about your friends, you can better understand and appreciate them.

V. Begin today by doing several things.

  A. Decide on some activities which you believe would be interesting to you.

    1. Keep in mind the cost.

    2. Keep in mind the ease with which your ideas could be carried out.

  B. Ask your girlfriend or boyfriend whether he or she would be interested in doing this with you.

  C. Ask your girlfriend or boyfriend for suggestions about things that he or she would like to do.

  D. Try some of these activities this weekend and see how exciting and inexpensive they really are.

INDEX

DATE DUE

| NOV 10 1982 | |
| APR 2 5 1984 | |